LINCOLN CHRISTIAN UNIVERSITY

W9-BUT-118

# RAPE IS RAPE

# RAPE IS RAPE

**HOW DENIAL, DISTORTION, AND VICTIM BLAMING
ARE FUELING A HIDDEN ACQUAINTANCE RAPE CRISIS**

## JODY RAPHAEL, JD

Lawrence Hill Books

Chicago

Copyright © 2013 by Jo Ann Raphael
All rights reserved
First edition
Published by Lawrence Hill Books, an imprint of
Chicago Review Press, Incorporated
814 North Franklin Street
Chicago, Illinois 60610

ISBN 978-1-61374-479-6

Cover design: Debbie Berne Design
Interior design: PerfecType, Nashville, TN

Library of Congress Cataloging-in-Publication Data
Raphael, Jody.
   Rape is rape : how denial, distortion, and victim blaming are fueling a hidden
acquaintance rape crisis / Jody Raphael. — First edition.
      pages cm
   Includes bibliographical references and index.
   ISBN 978-1-61374-479-6 (pbk.)
1.  Acquaintance rape. 2.  Date rape. I. Title.

HV6558.R374 2013
364.15'32—dc23

                                                            2012045659

Printed in the United States of America
5  4  3  2  1

For TK Logan

// 37

127222

13.1099

All I maintain is that on this earth there are pestilences
and there are victims, and it's up to us, so far as possible,
not to join forces with the pestilences.

—Albert Camus, *The Plague*

# Contents

# Introduction

In the wake of rape allegations against WikiLeaks founder Julian Assange, feminist Naomi Wolf publicly denied that if a man holds down and tries to sexually penetrate a woman who previously agreed to sex but who changed her mind after he refused to wear a condom, he is a rapist. She also denied that penetrating a sleeping woman is rape. Wolf later went further, alleging that it is wrong to keep confidential the names of people who report that they've been raped. She reasoned that it encourages false claims and that women should grow up and be treated as "moral adults" who stand by their allegations. When the two Assange accusers' names were released, they received death threats and experienced other forms of humiliation, the very reason names are publicly withheld now.

In 2011, the US House of Representatives leadership introduced the bill H.R. 3, also known as the No Taxpayer Funding for Abortion Act, which disallowed federal funds for abortions for rapes that do not involve force. Although the provision, later excised from the legislation, was intended to further limit abortions in the United States, it perpetuated the idea that "real" rape always involves force and that acts of sexual penetration against drugged or unconscious individuals are not rapes.

Responding to the perceived problem of false rape claims, in 2010 the new governing coalition in the United Kingdom sought to extend anonymity in rape cases to defendants, a plan that was later abandoned after widespread protest. Later, the country's chief justice minister let it slip that he viewed acquaintance rape as less grave than "serious rape."

Defenders of Dominique Strauss-Kahn, the International Monetary Fund managing director and French presidential candidate who was charged with rape in 2011, launched scathing attacks on the veracity and credibility of the housekeeper who claimed the attack took place in his hotel room. They asserted that she was lying about the event, either on her own or as part of a political conspiracy by Strauss-Kahn's political enemies.

The controversies continued in 2012. In August, Republican representative Todd Akin of Missouri—then a US Senate candidate—explained his opposition to abortion, even in cases of rape, by stating that women's bodies blocked unwanted pregnancies when "legitimate rape" occurred. Thus any woman wanting an abortion due to rape was lying about being raped. Indiana state treasurer Richard Mourdock, who was running for an open Senate seat, minimized the horrors of rape by asserting his lack of support for an abortion exception in cases of rape: "Even when life begins in that horrible situation of rape, that is something that God intended to happen."

What is going on here? The more acquaintance rapes are reported—and the more acquaintance rape claims are taken seriously by prosecutors, judges, and juries—the more people clamor that women are falsely claiming they've been raped. And if the accuser is not lying, then she is responsible for the incident by drinking and being sexually promiscuous, her actions resulting in sexual penetration that, though unwanted, cannot be considered serious or harmful.

Ironically, the cacophony has gained in volume and vehemence just as rape researchers have conclusively demonstrated, through government-sponsored studies, that acquaintance rape remains a serious problem in the United States. The latest study from the Centers for Disease Control and Prevention (CDC) finds that 12.3 percent of American women over eighteen years of age, or more than fourteen million women, state they have been *forcibly* sexually penetrated within their lifetimes—620,000 of these within the last twelve months. Yet this information remains hidden to members of the public and the media.

At the same time, the number of rape cases in which charges are filed has actually declined. Research indicates that although the number of people who come forward to report rape has increased since 1975 in the United States, it has remained stable since the 1990s, despite claims that reports of rape have risen. However, the number of defendants charged with rape as a ratio of the number of rapes reported to police was cut in half between 1971 and 2006—this decrease contradicts allegations that out-of-control prosecutors are filing an increased number of rape cases. We know that, in well over 80 percent of these incidents, the accuser knows the accused. Is the decline in the number of rape charges filed the result of a growing public belief in false rape claims? Is it due to an increase in victim blaming, something for which our sexually liberated society has a special talent?

In the Assange and Strauss-Kahn matters, the attacks on the women who reported being raped were punitive, which encouraged others to voice their inappropriately vindictive opinions. The experience of Cassandra Hernandez in 2007 is a prime example of this type of backlash. A member of the US Air Force, the nineteen-year-old Hernandez reported that three of her fellow airmen gang-raped her at a party. Following a harsh interrogation, she decided not to testify against the men. In a letter to Texas governor Rick Perry, she noted that she chose not to pursue the case "under enormous stress and after consultation with the legal office." "The pressure of the judicial process was too much for me," she wrote.

After the collapse of the rape case, the air force decided to accuse Hernandez herself with underage drinking and "indecent acts," allegations leading to a court-martial that could have resulted in up to a year in prison and dismissal from the service. The new claim asserted that she performed an indecent act on one of the men while the other two watched. Then the air force offered immunity from the rape charges to the men if they testified against Hernandez. Some media commentators found it baffling that, in a case involving a female minor and three men, the air force decided the young woman was the guilty party. This categorization clearly blamed Hernandez for what had occurred. As Jessica Valenti noted in her book *The Purity Myth*, "She was charged with her own rape."

In fact, the current debate is just part of a long-running quarrel about the seriousness of acquaintance rape during an era in which people are sexually liberated. Opponents of feminism—and even certain groups of feminists—have denied that there is a high prevalence of acquaintance rape. Some feminists fear that the issue of acquaintance rape will interfere with the gains of women's sexual liberation—this concern causes them to minimize its frequency and consequences. For their part, conservatives find feminists' crusade against the rape epidemic to be an assault on men and the nuclear family. They view acquaintance rape as the inevitable consequence of women's sexual risk taking, and they blame girls and women for any harm that comes to them.

Acquaintance rape skeptics employ two basic strategies. First, they ridicule statistics about rape prevalence, claiming they are based on an overbroad definition of rape that is just "bad sex." Second, they aver that as many as 50 percent of rape claims are deliberately false. (For evidence of this trend, the deniers point to the 2006 Duke University lacrosse team case, in which DNA evidence contradicted a woman who alleged that several players raped her.)

Both approaches are intended to convince the media and the public to distrust the evidence-based claims of rape-victim advocates. It is obvious, too, that the battles between groups of feminists and between feminists and conservative women over a twenty-five-year period have deflected attention from the needed task of deterring acquaintance rape.

*Rape Is Rape* analyzes the tactics used by rape deniers and the agendas that fuel them. It considers the merits of their arguments to better understand why acquaintance rape has become such a bone of contention in the United States. It looks at what reputable social science has to say about the prevalence of acquaintance rape, and it questions why these data are not referenced in the ongoing debate. This book also explores the effects of the twenty-five-year argument on those who report that they've been raped and those who are accused of it.

In addition to evaluating rape deniers' assaults on acquaintance rape and unpacking false statistics about rape claims, *Rape Is Rape* also analyzes how and why deniers concentrate on one acquaintance rape scenario:

when alcohol obscures judgment and complicates social situations. Throughout the narrative, I present the moving accounts of acquaintance rape that several young women bravely shared with me. My hope is that readers come to understand that there are many acquaintance rape scenarios, not just one, and that our response to it must encompass all the varied situations in which women and girls are subjected to rape in social situations. Any reaction to rape today must be to their accounts—not to an idea of rape put forth by those somehow needing to minimize and deny rape.

# [ 1 ]

# Accusing Dominique Strauss-Kahn

On May 14, 2011, Nafissatou Diallo, a housekeeper at the Sofitel New York, a luxury Manhattan hotel, reported to security that she had been sexually assaulted by Dominique Strauss-Kahn, managing director of the International Monetary Fund and potential French presidential candidate. Her account, which she later gave to the New York Police Department, was simple and straightforward. Thinking the room was unoccupied, she entered the suite to perform her housekeeping duties, only to find Strauss-Kahn emerging naked from the bedroom. Diallo told investigators that, after closing the door to the suite, Strauss-Kahn pulled her into the bedroom, pushed her onto the bed, and attempted to forcibly insert his penis into her mouth, which caused his penis to make contact with her closed lips. Then, she said, he pushed her down a narrow hallway. He pulled up her uniform, partially rolled down her stockings, reached under her panties, and grabbed the outside of her vaginal area forcefully. He then physically compelled her to her knees, forcibly inserted his penis into her mouth, held her head, and ejaculated. This sexual act occurred at the end of the suite's interior hallway, near the suite's full bathroom. The housekeeper said that she spat his semen onto the suite's interior hallway carpet and continued to do so as she fled from the suite.

Her statements implied that the encounter lasted only a short period of time. Further investigation revealed that Diallo entered Strauss-Kahn's suite by keycard at 12:06 PM. Telephone records revealed that Strauss-Kahn called his daughter, with whom he later lunched, at 12:13 PM. Thus the encounter probably lasted only seven to nine minutes.

Police detectives tracked Strauss-Kahn to an Air France flight scheduled to depart from John F. Kennedy International Airport to Europe. They asked him to disembark, and he was taken into custody. The housekeeper later identified him in a police lineup. Preliminary results from DNA testing established that several stains on her dress contained Strauss-Kahn's semen and that his DNA was found on both the interior and exterior waistband of her panty hose and the waistband of her underwear. But the DNA evidence would not prove dispositive, because Strauss-Kahn admitted to a sexual act that he claimed was consensual. Medical personnel who examined the young woman noted no visible injuries but did find "redness" in the vaginal area, which could have been attributed to the incident but could also have been due to a host of other causes.

Strauss-Kahn appeared in court and was held without bail pending a grand jury investigation. On May 19, a Manhattan grand jury indicted Strauss-Kahn on seven criminal counts, two of which were first-degree criminal sexual acts. Eventually Strauss-Kahn posted bail—$1 million in cash and a $5 million bond. He was confined to twenty-four-hour home detention and made to wear an electronic monitoring ankle bracelet.

The story quickly became a media sensation. One French media analyst found that in the first ten days of the scandal it appeared on the front page of more than 150,000 newspapers around the world.

Subsequently, a young French reporter stepped forward to report that Strauss-Kahn had attempted to rape her during a 2002 interview but that her mother had dissuaded her from filing a criminal complaint. Now she had decided to contact the authorities.

# Riley

Riley is a relative of Richard, a colleague at my university. He heard me speaking about rape and approached me to tell me Riley's experiences. Then he asked if I would like to speak with her the next time she came to Chicago for the holidays. Knowing that many women are not comfortable talking about this subject, I jumped at the chance to hear her account and learn more about acquaintance rape.

Riley's scenario is one in which her date, Luke, exploited her extreme weaknesses (which is something rapists look for when marking their victims for attack, many people believe). Riley has cystic fibrosis, an inherited, fatal disease that causes mucus buildup in the lungs, trachea, and sinuses, blocking the airways and providing a fertile field for bacteria growth. The mucus also impairs the cilia critical to cleaning the airways; on average, individuals with cystic fibrosis lose 2 percent of their lung function each year, a development that drastically shortens their lifespan. Cystic fibrosis also drastically affects the digestive system; the body is unable to break down food on its own, which causes malabsorption and malnutrition. This state can lead to pancreatic insufficiency and diabetes. People also become deficient in vitamin D, which results in bone weakness.

When Riley met Luke, her health was increasingly precarious. Riley describes the course of treatment that began a few months before:

Due to coughing up blood and difficulty breathing, my
doctors started me on a strict, permanent regimen that I
am still on to this day. First, they started me on more oral
antibiotics to take daily. They also prescribed inhaled antibiotics, which I had to inhale twice daily for thirty minutes.
This was inhaled using a nebulizer, and after inhalation
I have to thoroughly clean the machine and parts to be
sure no bacteria or mold infected the parts that I breathed
through. I was also put on an airway-clearance vest for my
chest. It is literally a vest that I strap on to my chest, and
it pulsates and vibrates my chest to get me to cough up
mucus. I do that for twenty minutes twice daily as well,
in the morning and at night, like the inhaled antibiotics. I
was on many oral medications and an inhaler throughout
the day. I was also doing sinus rinses at the time to try to
clear up infection in my sinuses. I would have to squirt one
cup of saltwater up each nostril twice a day. And at night
I took a drink/mix medication for my digestion, because
cystic fibrosis clogs the digestive system and I can't digest
food on my own. I also had to exercise daily to try to get
myself to cough up more mucus and exercise my lungs as
much as possible to keep them as clear as possible.

The introduction to Luke came from Riley's mother, who was
employed by the university and met Luke on campus. Luke told her he
had just moved from California, and he complained about the lack of success he was having with dating—all the girls just wanted to drink and have
sex. Riley's mother thought Luke would be perfect for one of her three
daughters. It later turned out that everything Luke said was a lie; he might
have lived in California, but he moved from there when he was five years
old and had been in the college town for almost twenty years. Nor did his
family own a house on the California beach he was always talking about.

At age twenty, Riley, a junior at the university, had not had a great
many sexual partners, and she had just broken up with her first serious
boyfriend of two years. It could be said that Riley was a young lady on a
mission: given her health problems, she wasn't sure she would have the

opportunity to become a mother unless she met someone soon. So she was interested in dating seriously and not in having flings, hoping to meet a young man who was similarly inclined.

Riley took the initiative to e-mail Luke, and the two embarked on a lively e-mail exchange. Soon, the e-mails led to telephone calls. She revealed her disability and her upcoming foot surgery, which could have presented a medical risk due to her poor lung function.

> He knew that I needed to take medications; he knew that I was on breathing medicine; he knew that it affected me. He was going to take me to the surgery and take care of me afterwards. He was going to whisk me away to California to his beach house.

The first date began when Luke came over to Riley's dorm. Later that night, she consented to go to Luke's place to watch a movie, which she brought.

> I agreed to go to the house because trust was established. I had felt a chemistry, a fake chemistry obviously, and I think that was where Luke saw the vulnerability. But for me, I was going there because I felt trust and felt things were going well.

As the movie began, Luke started kissing Riley. She didn't mind kissing a boy on the first date, but that was going to be it, as far as she was concerned.

> I was attracted to him at first, but I was not interested in rushing, and I was not interested in doing anything on the first date. I remember thinking, I don't want to allow anything other than kissing to happen. If I date someone, I want it to be right and take it slow.
>
> But progressively things got worse. It was like a switch had gone off, and he started becoming very forceful. He forced oral sex on me, then forced me to perform oral sex on him. I was physically dominated; I was incapable of moving. And then he forced vaginal sex.

Although Riley was screaming and crying, saying, "No, no," Luke's roommate didn't seem to hear.

> I looked him in the eyes and told him, "No." I nonverbally communicated "no" by using my arms, legs, and whole body to try and push him away from me. All the while that he is forcing sex upon me, I was wondering, How does his roommate not hear me saying "no" or getting upset?
>
> I felt I couldn't breathe the whole time I was there. I was in shock. I had brought it up that I had cystic fibrosis. He knew about that before I went to his place. When he was forcing me to give him oral sex, he was straddled on my chest, putting compression on my chest. Literally, I couldn't get much air.

But Luke still hadn't ejaculated. Riley was confused by that. By the time he first penetrated Riley vaginally, she was totally fatigued.

> I couldn't struggle anymore physically. I was exhausted. I had to give up almost; I was so tired from the fighting. I don't know what he is going to do, but he is some animal, and he is not going to quit until he gets what he wants or something.
>
> In order to be able to survive, I need to leave this mentally. At the time I thought, I have tried physically to resist this. I'm exhausted. I need to quit resisting to survive. But that ended up not being the case, because that wasn't what he wanted. I didn't know that.

For when she stopped fighting back, Luke became flaccid and could not complete the sex act. This development was odd to Riley; it was also dispiriting, for she hoped to escape once he achieved orgasm. But the force was what excited Luke.

So Riley had to disassociate.

> Your mind leaves your body, has to go somewhere else to be able to survive. It was an instinct. I didn't know I was

doing it; it just started to happen. In order to be able to survive, I need to leave this mentally.

Screaming and crying, Riley got up. She began throwing on her clothes and said she had to go back to her dorm to get her medicine. Luke followed her as she went downstairs.

There was a couch right by the front door, and he shoved me over the couch and took my clothes off again and forced vaginal sex, and this time he ejaculated. During the intercourse, he told me he loved me, which was so demented to me.

While he was forcing himself on Riley, Luke continued what Riley calls his mind games, which were possibly calculated to cause confusion about his motives when Riley would later think back on the evening.

He kept saying, "This night has gone so well, and you are ruining it now. You're ruining our connection. We could have had such a good future, and you're ruining it. I really feel strongly for you, so sex should be the natural thing." He was saying things like, "In the winter time, I am going to take you to my place in California." And he said, "I'll take care of you. I'll be the boyfriend that you want me to be—however you want me to be, I'll be that for you." So demented.

After Luke's ejaculation, Riley saw that she could finally attempt an escape. Luke let her go, but he again tried to confuse her about what had just occurred.

He was sitting there; he looked tired and satisfied. "OK, go. I knew you would be mad at me—don't be mad at me. I knew you would leave me, but don't be mad at me." He was manipulating me not to go to the police.

It turned out to be a six-hour ordeal that seemed even longer—endless, in fact. Neither had ingested alcohol or drugs. Riley feared for her life the whole time.

I thought, I have to do something—this is very serious. I
felt like I couldn't breathe the whole time I was there.

It was torture. I would rather get shot than be tor-
tured like that. When you see the look in the person's eyes
when he is doing the act itself, it doesn't even feel like you
are human. The look: eye-on-the-prize type of a look. Not
looking at me. Objectifying. Almost like he is drooling.

Eventually Riley decided to prosecute Luke. But, years after the incident and the trial, she remains traumatized.

I have vivid nightmares all the time—nightmares of guys
trying to get me and hurt me, of Luke trying to hurt me
and my family, me running from danger, somebody shoot-
ing me. It was agony—trapped, a huge trapped feeling.
Now, when I'm at a place where I feel like I need to leave,
and let's say, for whatever reason, I get a trigger, and I
need to leave, and someone is talking and my heart races
and I get sweaty, I say, "I have to step out." If I get anywhere that I feel I can't leave when I want to, I start to get
very nervous and anxious, and the heart just starts racing.

Riley's health, which had never been good, deteriorated after the
incident. The restless nights caused exhaustion and pain, and her cystic
fibrosis symptoms became worse. This already vulnerable young person
had been broken.

Riley's cousin Richard described to me how "Riley works hard to
make meaning of her chronic illness. She will always have cystic fibrosis.
The length of her life will probably be diminished; the quality of her life
will as well. They are making strides all the time. She may get a lung trans-
plant, there are new medications, but she is looking at applying for disability. She wants to be a social worker and do good things in the world,
and she will, but she is not looking ahead to a lifetime of great opportunity because her health won't permit it. It's hard for her. She would like
to be a mom. She is not sure she ever will get a chance."

Richard thought Riley's vulnerability was probably obvious. "She
wants to make people happy," he said. "She is aware of this. This guy is

a nice guy—he is showing her attention. He says, 'Let's go back to my apartment and watch a movie,' and she says, 'Sure.' I don't mean to blame Riley, however. I don't even want to hint at the fact that Riley somehow invited this thing. He preyed on her because of her interest in finding that kind of connection with someone."

Today, Riley believes she is unable to fully function as a woman. Intimacy triggers paralyzing memories of that night. Luke destroyed her ability to connect with anyone else.

> There are elements in a relationship between a man and a woman that were taken away from me that night. It was robbed of me. I've struggled with this as I have found a counselor, and then I will have nightmares, and I will go out on a date, and I will get hysterical. I'm working so hard to become healthy and stable again. Why do I still have all these feelings? Why do I have to have all these triggers? I desire to be happy. I have a guy now, and I should be able to trust him. It just makes me angry at Luke, that he would do this to me. It makes you feel like there is one part of you that is ruined.
>
> You can't put it into words. You feel like this is not like what life should be. How are we as survivors supposed to look at sex as something special to be shared and not have some lingering fears and feelings and trauma inside of our hearts? That is the hardest thing. That act can be one of the greatest things in life—to celebrate love, to make children, to make a family. It is ingrained in women to have a family. In order to do that, you have to have sex. If you have been violated that much, and it has made an objectified power struggle, a torture thing, it makes it harder to get to that place where other people can get to, where sex is safe. He knew what he was doing. He knew exactly what he was doing.
>
> If you think about rape, it is the taking away of an ability to express love. It shatters the way that you connect to everyone. It involves where your core intimacy

lies and your love, and when that is involved, it shatters the way you connect to every human being.

Riley still suffers from the experience. She has nightmares and fears that she will be hurt again. If that ever happened, she says, "That would put me over the edge."

> I am trying to return to normalcy and have a healthy relationship and believe that men can be safe—and feel safe. I don't think I feel safe around men. Now I am trying to correct that. That is emotionally distressing. I am trying to be in a relationship that invites trust. You have your emotional and you have your physical connection. And that involves showing your physical affections. That can be very hard, and you can still be very vulnerable.

Richard explained, "She still feels isolated by the experience and damaged. Can she ever be whole again?"

Some years ago, in an article in the *Atlantic Monthly*, writer Wendy Kaminer criticized the women's liberation movement for making women believe they are victims: "In some feminist circles . . . it is heresy to suggest that being raped by your date may not be as traumatic or terrifying as being raped by a stranger who breaks into your bedroom in the middle of the night." And one academic has commented, "Comparing real rape to date rape is like comparing cancer to the common cold."

Could these commentators be unaware of the facts of date rape cases like Riley's? She finds this ignorance maddening:

> What are people not understanding when they ask about bad sex? I would say to someone who said that to me that a night of bad sex is two people consenting, who did not have a pleasurable and meaningful experience. Sex is one thing, rape is another. It is just like living and dying, living is one thing and dying is another, why would you put them in the same breath?

The rape inflicted humiliation upon Riley—which was surely Luke's desire. She doesn't understand why people dismiss the harms of acquaintance rape, why they are able to justify it. Riley explains:

I was embarrassed and humiliated. People can't understand it. This isn't normal; people shouldn't be able to understand why he did that. He pushed you down and came all over you like you were an animal. People shouldn't understand that. I think it is humiliating because you went through something that so few people understand.

Would this lack of comprehension prevent a jury from finding Luke guilty of rape?

# [2]

# The Distortion of Rape Statistics

## *Who's Doing It and Why*

How did we get to a place where young women like Riley are considered to be victims of "bad sex" but not rape?

It started with the discovery of the high prevalence of acquaintance rape in the 1980s. Researchers were sounding the alarm about their findings, but theirs was a claim that some just could not accept and did their best to discredit. What motivated this attack on acquaintance rape data? Why did they choose the methods they did to challenge the data?

The seeds of today's backlash against feminism can be found in Susan Brownmiller's 1975 book, *Against Our Will*, which argued that rape was "nothing more or less than a conscious process of intimidation by which *all men* keep *all women* in a state of fear." Brownmiller's purpose was to make the act of rape, like lynching, a political crime, more than just the act of taking sex for a person's own enjoyment. She saw rape as one potent tool, created by anatomical difference, in man's dominance of women. A featured selection of the Book-of-the-Month Club and named one of the ten outstanding books of the year by the *New York Times Book Review*, the bestselling work made Brownmiller a celebrity, ensuring widespread consideration of her views.

Brownmiller's analysis was met by skepticism from many who questioned her sweeping assertions about "all men" and "all women." This unfortunately led to the much-quoted statement that "All men are rapists," which actually came from novelist Marilyn French's 1977 *The Women's Room* and was uttered by a character in the work.

Some years later, Catharine MacKinnon, an influential feminist legal scholar, pointed out a blurry line between sexual intercourse and rape. Given the inequality between men and women, women's consent to sex, she said, is implicitly coerced: "Men in positions of power over women can thus secure sex that looks, even is, consensual without that sex ever being wanted, without it being freely chosen far less desired." In an instant, one can see just how unhelpful this observation—although accurate in some cases—would prove. MacKinnon appeared to be diluting rape by defining many consensual acts as sexual assault, giving rape deniers the opportunity to make the claim that rape-prevalence statistics are incorrect because they quantify the number of rapes based on this kind of expanded definition. Then, too, the formulation reduces the overall importance of rape. As psychologist Lynne Segal has written, "It is insulting to women who have been raped to imply all women have been raped; it diminishes rather than clarifies rape's hideous reality and prevalence."

Brownmiller and MacKinnon did not and do not represent all feminists, but antifeminists have been able to successfully take these comments and claim they represent the views of the entire movement. Then they improperly characterize it as anti-male. Much of the rape-denial campaign represents a backlash to this one form of anti-rape advocacy.

Not surprisingly, the MacKinnon formulation provoked ridicule in some quarters. Columnist Kathleen Parker lampooned MacKinnon for writing that rape and sex look an awful lot alike. In a 2008 book, Parker wrote, "No one's defending men who have literally forced women to have sex, but most people would argue that there's a world of difference between 'stop' after you've willingly climbed between the sheets with someone you found appealing five minutes earlier, and rape by a stranger at knife point."

Many conservative women sensibly point out that all men do not have the same innate propensity for violence against women. Although they do not deny that violence against women is a problem, they do not believe that patriarchy requires violence or the threat of violence to maintain itself. They also do not believe that the average man is, as alleged by certain feminists, a potential batterer or rapist.

Today, some antifeminist activists repeat the same quotes, but they mangle the original meaning of feminist theorists, demonstrating that they still thrill to the ideological battle. For example, college Republicans at Bowling Green State University staged an "antifeminist bake sale" in 2008. While selling treats for fifty cents, members of the club handed out sheets labeled "The Radical Feminist Agenda." They included quotations such as, "'All men are rapists, and that's all they are,' said Marilyn French."

Opponents of contemporary feminism base their objections on "family values." Some feminists, they argue, endanger the heterosexual family—the basic building block of society—by being anti-men and by alleging that most men have the potential to be dangerous to women. Thus conservative women like Christina Hoff Sommers object to feminists' attacks on men not because they like or feel sorry for them but because they view current feminism as having a "poisonous antipathy to men." They believe it encourages women-only societies that challenge their traditional view of the American family:

> The presumption that men are collectively engaged in keeping women down invites feminist bonding in a resentful community. When a Heilbrun or a Steinem advises us that men are not about to relinquish their hegemony, the implicit moral is that women must form self-protective enclaves. In such enclaves women can speak out safely and help one another to recover from the indignities they suffer under patriarchy. In such enclaves they can think of how to change or provide alternatives to the "androcentric" institutions that have prevailed in education and the workplace. The message is that women must be "gynocentric," that they must join with and be loyal only to women.

Indeed, if women were to forget men, might they have only one alternative? As Carrie L. Lukas of the Independent Women's Forum has written,

> Individual young women warned away from men may wonder what alternative they have. Some women's studies textbooks suggest an alternative. They challenge students to examine their sexual preferences and to explore the possibility that they're not hard-wired to prefer the opposite sex.

Sommers, too, cautions about the effects of this male-baiting on college students. She would like to see "gender-feminized" colleges like Wellesley print the following announcement on the first page of their bulletins:

> We will help your daughter discover the extent to which she has been in complicity with the patriarchy. We will encourage her to reconstruct herself through dialogue with us. She may become enraged and chronically offended. She will very likely reject the religious and moral codes you raised her with. She may well distance herself from family and friends. She may change her appearance, and even her sexual orientation.

Conservatives also believe antiviolence activists are trying to create more government regulation, because hundreds of thousands of victims mean more government programs. The conservative Independent Women's Forum asserts that feminist groups like the National Organization for Women exaggerate victimhood to support big-government policies and programs to implement them, arguing that there can be such a thing as a "limited government feminist" or a "red state feminist."

But more important, these domestic violence and anti-rape programs are viewed as fronts for promoting liberal ideology, with the money used to further an ideological war against men. According to *National Review* Washington editor Kate O'Beirne,

> Over the past ten years, hundreds of millions of dollars have fueled an ideological crusade against men and marriage in the name of helping victims of abuse. In design and operations [the Violence Against

Women Act] aims to batter men and proselytize women about the constant threat the men in their lives pose.

Domestic violence programs, say conservative groups, encourage women to leave their partners rather than to work through problems to reconcile differences. One conservative fact sheet on the Violence Against Women Act alleges that most cases of domestic abuse are minor and claims the act breaks up marriages: "But no-contact restraining orders and policies of women's shelters preclude persons from receiving couple's counseling or mediation."

## Attacking Mary Koss's Data

In their ideological war against feminism, conservative women have chosen to attack the accuracy of rape data. If rape-prevalence statistics are flawed, then a rape epidemic would not exist and one of the major platforms of feminism would fail. However, this challenge to researchers is seriously faulty.

One of the first researchers to establish a high prevalence of acquaintance rape among college women, Mary Koss, became the focus of attacks in the early 1990s. Because her research *appeared* to use an expanded definition of rape as articulated by Catherine MacKinnon, she proved to be an easy target. Remarkably the attacks on Koss continue to this day, although in the interim there have been numerous additional rape-prevalence studies with sound methodology largely confirming Koss's original findings.

It started twenty-five years ago. In a social-science survey published in 1987 and funded by the National Institute of Mental Health, Mary Koss found a 27.5 percent prevalence for rape and attempted rape for 3,862 women surveyed on college campuses. Although Koss made clear that the prevalence figure was the experience of college women since the age of fourteen and not just for rapes while on campus, this critical difference got lost in the shuffle. Koss's study did much to establish the existence of acquaintance rape: 84 percent of rapes in her sample involved a man known to the victim, and 57 percent were dates.

Now, Koss did not ask women whether they had been raped. Instead, she posed a series of questions, including whether the respondents had sexual intercourse when they didn't want to because a man threatened them or used some degree of physical force. Koss did inquire whether unwanted sexual intercourse was pursued through psychological coercion. Critics of the study incorrectly assumed that psychological coercion was included when the rape-prevalence rate was calculated, but it was not. Only penetrations through force or intoxication were combined.

Professor Neil Gilbert at the University of California, Berkeley, subsequently criticized the study, finding ambiguity in one of the questions: Have you had sexual intercourse when you didn't want to because a man gave you alcohol or drugs? Gilbert believed that with this question Koss had expanded the rape definition beyond forcible assault, although many state laws similarly defined rape. Thus, he thought, she inflated her prevalence figures. Gilbert wrote, "The definitions of sexual abuse and rape employed in the studies noted above extend the boundaries and transform the character of what is to be considered sexual assault."

Koss went back and recalculated the prevalence rate by removing the data relating to the question Gilbert criticized. She made the focus only on instances where unwanted penetration was attempted or obtained forcibly, and she found that a total of 20 percent of college women, or one in five, qualified as rape victims since their fourteenth birthday.

Interestingly, all the ensuing high-profile critiques of Koss's research rely totally on Gilbert's critique. As one commentator noted, "One of the striking things in this whole debate is that despite the amount of press that the date rape skeptics have received, the actual criticisms of the research methodology can be boiled down to a handful of quibbles originating from just one person: Berkeley Social Welfare Professor Neil Gilbert."

In an influential 1993 *New York Times Magazine* article, Princeton University student Katie Roiphe used Gilbert's analysis to attack Koss's rape-prevalence figures and popularize his attack. The next year, Christina Hoff Sommers repeated the criticisms in her book *Who Stole Feminism? How Women Have Betrayed Women*. She implied that *Ms.* magazine sponsored the study, and the Koss study was subjected to the same ridicule Gilbert and Roiphe had inflicted. Sommers also objected to a study by Dean Kilpatrick in 1992, which found a one-in-eight lifetime prevalence that, among other questions, asked women whether anyone had ever put fingers or objects in their vaginas or anuses against their will by using force or threat. For Sommers, unaccountably, having a finger forcibly jammed into a vagina or an anus just wasn't her idea of rape.

In a separate question in the Koss study, 73 percent of the women did not call the assault rape, even though they admitted being subjected to the forced intercourse. The statistic made Sommers again question the Koss study. Koss responded that this is "a deliberately twisted presentation of the data." She explained that the breakdown was as follows: one-quarter thought it was rape, one-quarter thought it was some kind of crime but did not realize it qualified as rape, one-quarter thought it was serious sexual abuse but did not know it was a crime, and one-quarter did not feel victimized by the experience. "Thus the great majority of rape victims conceptualized their experience in highly negative terms and felt victimized whether or not they realized that legal standards for rape had been met."

The script then became set in stone: the Koss study was flawed, using an overly broad definition of rape, and hence the feminist-invented rape crisis did not exist. However, in Koss's work, as we have seen, rape *was* defined as sex that is forced or obtained through threats of violence. She wrote, "Critics err in the assumption that these [broader] definitions undergird the empirical data base." In fact, in a 2011 article, Koss and colleagues criticized research instruments and definitions that included physical force but did not separately measure occurrences in which verbal threats, psychological coercion, alcohol, or drugs are used, demonstrating that researchers continue to focus on a conservative definition of rape accomplished by physical force.

But say it often enough and it becomes true. On the eve of the William Kennedy Smith rape prosecution in 1991, the *National Review* opined in an editorial that the definition of rape used in research was unacceptably broad:

It covers sex after being "overwhelmed by a man's continual arguments and pressure," sex after consuming alcohol, and unwanted
efforts by a man to go one step further than the woman, however
quickly such efforts were rebuffed and then withdrawn. . . . By lump-
ing together male-female relationships that do not follow feminist
protocols with genuinely assaultive rapes, these studies trivialize real
crimes against women committed by real felons.

The attacks on Koss's data and on her receiving publicity from *Ms.*
magazine continued into the twenty-first century, when a new generation
of writers and advocates began employing identical arguments to those
presented in the *National Review* article. In 2004, for example, FoxNews
.com commentator Wendy McElroy repeated an already-made characterization of Koss—that she had been "hand-picked" by Gloria Steinem to do
the research—and attempted to demolish the Koss study using Gilbert's
critique. Carrie L. Lukas recycled Sommers's twelve-year-old critique of
Koss at *National Review Online* in 2006, which was also printed on the
website of the Independent Women's Forum and in her 2006 book, *The
Politically Incorrect Guide to Women, Sex, and Feminism.* She questioned
prevalence data that Koss had already eliminated from her calculations
and then further discounted Koss's data because those surveyed did not
call it "rape":

> Correcting for the biases in the original survey yields a radically dif-
> ferent picture of the prevalence of rape in America. Subtract the
> women identified by the alcohol and drug question [*already done
> by Koss in her calculations*] and those who didn't think they had
> been raped, and total victims fall to between 3 and 5 percent of the
> women surveyed. This remains an alarmingly high number, but sig-
> nificantly less alarming than the one-in-four figure.

Heather Mac Donald, a fellow at the Manhattan Institute, employed
an identical attack on Koss in a 2008 piece in *City Journal,* which was
excerpted in the *Los Angeles Times.* Mac Donald committed the usual
error of confusing annual and lifetime prevalence of rape. Her statement,
which follows below, misrepresents the statistic by suggesting it is an

annual rate when it is lifetime. She then makes an unfair comparison to annual rates of other kinds of crimes, concluding that the rape crisis is nonexistent:

> If the one-in-four statistic is correct—it is sometimes modified to "one-in-five to one-in-four"—campus rape represents a crime wave of unprecedented proportions. No crime, much less one as serious as rape, has a victimization rate remotely approaching 20 or 25 percent, even over many years. The 2006 violent crime rate in Detroit, one of the most violent cities in America, was 2,400 murders, rapes, robberies, and aggravated assaults per 100,000 inhabitants—a rate of 2.4 percent.

The Mac Donald piece, originally printed in two media sources, had a robust life—it was reprinted in numerous blogs and quoted approvingly at other media outlets, including *National Review Online*. Mac Donald's critique of rape-prevalence statistics often appeared in national media outlets and college newspapers alike in 2008 and 2009. By this method, the analysis reached like-minded readers through a wide variety of portals but also others through Google searches. I say this not to contend that participants in the widespread reprinting of Mac Donald's article were formally organized (for which proof is lacking) but to point out that their linking to it enables them to reach a wider audience.

And in her 2008 book, *Save the Males: Why Men Matter, Why Women Should Care*, Pulitzer Prize–winning columnist Kathleen Parker reprised the Koss critique without reference to any rape-prevalence studies since 1987.

Pertinently, blogger Barry Deutsch asked, "Why don't they give up attacking Koss already?" Koss's findings have generally been replicated in recent, large, and more significant studies—why not attack the Centers for Disease Control? Deutsch noted:

> Criticizing the CDC, which is not a feminist organization, doesn't suit that purpose. The target must be feminist, like Koss. And to admit they were wrong about Koss would imply that they might be wrong about their caricature of feminists as a bunch of vicious

man-hating evil Feminazis—and to most anti-feminists, that's simply unthinkable.

Deutsch's conclusion, that "Koss's study . . . has led two parallel lives," is perceptive:

> In one life—a life lived in books funded by right-wing foundations, anti-feminist websites, and the like—Koss' work is an enduring symbol of feminist dishonesty and deception, and is considered a discredited joke, trotted out for rehashed debunkings every couple of years.
>
> In another life, however—a life lived among academic experts— Koss' work has been amazingly successful. Decades later, her work is respectfully cited in peer-reviewed studies—a few years ago I found that just two of Koss' articles had been cited over six hundred times.

Mainstream media currently providing space to Koss bashing have become key players in rape denial. Curiously, editors running these diatribes against Mary Koss do not stop to think why they never hear about rape-prevalence data published after 1987. Instead of publicizing recent research, the media give space to a fossilized dispute, probably because antifeminists play to the media's interest in featuring conflict and debate between conservatives and feminists and others who undermine them. But while the debate rages on, the prevalence of rape may actually be increasing (as we shall see in chapter 8).

What is important to note is that conservative women continue to interfere with antiviolence work by challenging data. Indeed, one can argue that their activities, facilitated by the Internet, have intensified in recent years. Author Jessica Valenti, founder of the blog *Feministing*, notes the trend in the escalation of the attack on feminism through rape denial. "I truly believe that the drift toward blaming feminism is the most telling shift in this national dialogue," writes Valenti in *The Purity Myth*. "Blaming feminism, blaming *women's equality*, for rape reveals the crux of the issue." Valenti struggles, unsuccessfully, to understand why some women would "try to disrupt feminist work that combats violence," which puts other women at risk. But journalist Leslie H. Gelb reminds us that "the reality is that neoconservatives will never be happy without promoting some form of ideological warfare."

Rarely do we hear what violence survivors have to say about the data debate. The dispute has irritated a woman who, as a child, spent four years in and out of domestic violence shelters with her mother. She challenged deniers to desist from criticizing other's research, writing, "Your criticisms seem mighty, mighty petty in light of the true horrors that go on every day. What in God's name are you doing to address these problems from your Ivory Tower?!"

But such are the passions that ideology sometimes proves more important than what happens to real people like Riley. Mary Koss has written that the phenomenon has nothing to do with the facts: "Their challenges reveal little regard for the scholarship on the subject and remind us that we are fighting ideological barriers that no set of numbers may be able to lower."

## Men Attacking Feminism

Through rape denial, some men, too, are currently waging war on feminism by challenging prevalence data as being based on expanded definitions. Male rape deniers, however, have ratcheted up the intensity and stridency of the attacks on feminism, describing the feminist view on rape prevalence as a gigantic lie about men, as in this quote from a major website about false rape claims:

> It is nothing more than a modern day "Chicken Little" fable, but instead of yelling "The sky is falling!" the hysterical mantra of these politically correct fear mongers is that "All men are potential rapists!" . . . It insults men, of course, because it unfairly suggests that the male gender is not just inherently but deeply and likely fatally flawed because it is populated by a staggering number of rapists.

In the writings of male rape deniers, anti-rape activists are described as "the rape industry," "the feminist elite," or a "cult." The blog *Angry Harry* consists of the vituperative thoughts of one extreme activist who is concerned with men's rights and is much quoted on other sites. Harry's target is feminism, and he is angry indeed. He claims, "Feminism is not about equality. It is about stirring up hatred towards men," and "There is nowhere on this Earth where the people can be happy if the men are not happy."

"Angry Harry" frequently turns to rape and asserts "the campus date rape campaigns of the early 1990s weren't motivated by a genuine concern for the well-being of women. They were part of an ongoing attempt to delegitimize heterosexuality to young, impressionable women by demonizing men as rapists." He believes rape-prevalence figures are inflated and are "used as some kind of justification to demonise men, to hurt them, to discriminate against them, to push them through outrageously unjust legal processes which have been corrupted through and through, and to make it possible for women to destroy their lives completely for no other reason than that they wish to." And like some women rape deniers, Angry Harry believes that rape-prevalence data rests on an inflated definition of rape. He alleges, for example, that "bogus research" counts "yes" answers to the following question as rape: "Have you been pressured into having sex when you are not in the mood?" Thus, he concludes, "The research into 'rape' is mostly politically corrected hocus pocus."

These male rape deniers admit that the anti-rape movement was overdue because those reporting rape had not been taken seriously and legal rules were rigged against them. But now they believe that the changes have gone too far and that feminists have undue influence, especially in academia. Their charge is that society is in thrall to feminist political correctness.

Thus, in 2006, Duke University president Richard H. Brodhead suspended the lacrosse team and fired the coach all because he was afraid of a vocal faculty group, representing about one-fifth of all the professors who were stridently alleging sexism and racism. Supposedly, President Brodhead was trying to avoid the fate of Lawrence Summers, who lost his job as Harvard's president due to his voicing politically incorrect views about the innate capacity of women to perform well in math and science.

In another example of political correctness involving rape, journalist Stuart Taylor Jr. wrote in the *Atlantic* of a case at the United States Naval Academy. After being accused of rape, the star quarterback, captain, and

MVP of the school's football team denied the report, claiming the encounter was consensual. Corroborating evidence either way was unavailable. Taylor alleged that the defendant was caught in the much-publicized campaign against rape and sexual harassment that the Naval Academy superintendent, vice admiral Rodney P. Rempt, was conducting: "Rempt's crackdown gives off an odor of sacrificing due process to appease feminists who have appropriately assailed the service academies' sometimes appalling trivialization of serious rape allegations."

> According to an affidavit sworn by prominent Naval Academy alumnus and football player Peter Optekar, he privately asked Rempt, then a dinner guest at Optekar's home four days after the rape acquittal, why he had subjected Owens to a general court-martial. Rempt's reported response was, "Pete, I had no other choice. If I did not take him to a GCM, we would have had every feminist organization and the ACLU after us."

Politically correct responses make poster children out of individual defendants, Taylor argued. He disapprovingly quoted a twenty-two-year-old African American student who told *Newsweek* that he wanted Duke students prosecuted even if innocent: "It would be justice for things that happened in the past."

Driven by their agendas against feminism, these particular males have succeeded in turning the anti-rape activist into a politically correct, self-righteous, sex-hating and man-hating fanatic who believes all men are potential rapists, a characterization that does not help women who report having been raped. One is reminded of Sister Aloysius in John Patrick Shanley's 2005 play *Doubt*. Set in a Catholic school in 1964, the drama features the school's principal, Sister Aloysius, who, despite a lack of evidence, comes to form a firm belief that a young and charismatic priest has sexually molested the school's only black male student. As one critic explained, "*Doubt* probes the dark side of conviction, the point where belief hardens into blind faith." Rape deniers have successfully characterized anti-rape activists as people with all the disturbing fanaticism and certitude of a Sister Aloysius.

One might ask, "Does it matter what is written on all these blogs? Who reads them, anyway?" Two points are important. With its capacity to link angry male bloggers with one another, the Internet enables like-minded people to interact, increasing their stridency. "People's tendency to become more extreme after speaking with like-minded others has become known as 'group polarization,' and it has been documented in dozens of other experiments," reports one investigator. Expert Cass R. Sunstein finds that the Internet is "serving, for many, as a breeding group for extremism, precisely because like-minded people are deliberating with greater ease and frequency with one another"—a phenomenon he calls "cyberpolarization"—and creating the perfect conditions for spreading misinformation.

Then, too, men's rights groups have become effective in society. For example, in 2008, they claimed to have blocked the passage of four federal domestic violence bills, and members of one men's coalition got themselves onto drafting committees for the 2011 reauthorization of the federal Violence Against Women Act. Their tactics always involve downplaying national abuse rates. Yes, Angry Harry may be one of the more extreme rape deniers on the Internet, and lately men's rights groups may have become far more polished and savvy about advancing their views. But at least one leader—Mark Rosenthal of Respecting Accuracy in Domestic Abuse Reporting (RADAR)—actually values bloggers like Angry Harry. He has commented, "In any movement, there is going to be a reasonable voice and people who are so hurt, who are so injured by the injustices, that they can't afford to step back and try to take their emotions under control. But no movement is going to get anywhere without extremists."

It would be easy to write off these individuals and groups as irrelevant crazies, but that would be a big mistake. Their ideas have a way of seeping into the consciousness of the public, as anyone who reads the rape-denying online responses to newspaper articles about rape has experienced. These rejoinders illustrate how many believe that rape claims are merely reflections of regret the morning after, like these: "I think it is most important to educate young women about what rape is—and what it is not. The feminists would have us all believe that if a woman feels bad about sex, or doesn't enjoy it, it is rape. This is not true, and doesn't justify ruining a man's life." Or, "It was a one-night stand and he left in the night and never spoke to her again. The feelings of 'he used me' turn into 'he took advantage of me' so therefore 'he raped me.'" "It is only in today's world that women call 'rape' when they are the ones who regret it in the morning . . . nothing more."

The idea that feminists have expanded and diluted the concept of rape has gained general widespread acceptance. To buttress their case and demonstrate that there is an unacceptably wide definition of the crime, rape deniers attack Mary Koss's groundbreaking 1987 prevalence research. Unfortunately, although the charges against Koss are false, the public has accepted the allegations as true, with deleterious effects on women who have suffered acquaintance rape.

# Tracy

first heard of Tracy through her attorney, who was representing her in a civil lawsuit. Unlike Riley, Tracy wasn't looking for a "superserious relationship." She had just broken up with her boyfriend of three years, and others were encouraging her to get out of her shell and meet new people. Tracy's account educated me about how young women today are aware of the fact that, in their social lives, they must take risks and how they believe they have learned how to successfully manage these perils.

However Tracy said that despite taking many precautions, she was still manipulated into a private space and violated. The episode left her physically harmed and deeply shamed. Initially Tracy blamed herself and didn't want anyone to know she had been attacked—she thought she had been "so stupid" and should have known better. Her account cautions us about labeling individual girls as "good" or "bad" or reckless. All acquaintance rapes may not be as violent, but Tracy's experience illustrates how it can result in serious physical and psychological injury that many often fail to acknowledge.

At the time, Tracy was a twenty-six-year-old graduate student at a prestigious private university. Her research had taken her to Europe and numerous times to the Middle East. Tracy was not sexually inexperienced, and she had been in many potentially dangerous situations during her field work. At Tracy's one and only trip to a dance club, she danced with an exceedingly attractive young man named Justin. He had a bald head and a strong upper body, and he said he lived near Tracy and was finishing college and working at the same time. An exchange of cell phone numbers ensued.

After two telephone calls, Tracy agreed to meet Justin for coffee.

> The coffee date is my safety date—I'm trying to figure out if this guy is a freak or not. Coffee is very safe. We talk, we flirt, the coffee shop closes, we walk around in the dark, talk about a lot of things.

They kissed and said good-bye between his car and where Tracy resided. Justin still didn't know where she lived, and that is how Tracy wanted it.

Several days later, he invited Tracy to go out for a drink after work. He would pick her up in his car, and they would have a real date. Tracy got dressed up in a black sweater set and sandals, just in case they ended up in a nice place. Still cautious, Tracy didn't give him her address and met him where they had parted after the coffee.

To Tracy's disappointment, Justin suggested going to his place and watching a movie. His roommates were home. Tracy was dressed up and wanted to go out, but she didn't want to make waves. After her breakup, all her friends were saying, "Go out and date. Get over it." After all, the girlfriend with whom she'd gone dancing had already been to the apartment with one of Justin's roommates whom she'd met at the club, and it had been fine. Tracy agreed to go.

After introducing her to his roommates in the kitchen, Justin gave her a tour of the townhouse, and they talked in his room for awhile. He then closed his door, turned off the lights, and put on a movie. No alcohol was imbibed, and no drugs were used. They were both sitting on the bed when the kissing started. Tracy had expected kissing, but in her mind that was going to be the limit. What she didn't expect was Justin's fierceness.

> I say, "You kiss very aggressively," knowing that in my world to say that would mean "Back off," but he doesn't.

He keeps trying to go up my skirt and trying to get up my shirt, and I wasn't really prepared for that on the second date. I keep pushing him away.

Then, suddenly, he was naked. He pushed Tracy's head down to give him a blow job. In an instant, Tracy decided to comply. She didn't think about trying to run. She had done it before, after all, under other circumstances. Like Riley, Tracy felt a survival instinct she didn't even know she had kick in.

> I remember just trying to appease him; I just didn't want to get hurt. He might have killed me. To survive, women have that instinct. Let's just solve this immediate problem. I didn't want to do this, but it will be easier—it will be OK.
>
> I'm thinking that if I do this, then I'm going to be able to leave. My brain doesn't think. I've been in some kind of dangerous situations before, but as far as I'm concerned, you don't have time to think about what's going to happen next, and you don't have time to pray. There is nothing. You just have what's there.

Unfortunately for Tracy, she couldn't make him ejaculate, although he didn't give her too many minutes to try. He began to forcibly remove Tracy's clothing; then there he was again with his tongue in her mouth.

> I didn't get that much air; he ripped out a piece of my tongue. That really hurt. It was bleeding. He just forcibly suctioned and bit a little bit of my tongue, and because of that I wasn't getting much air. It was hard for me to communicate because of that.

Again, Tracy decided to stop crying, fighting, and wrestling. She wanted to leave, and she wanted to leave alive.

> I say, Fine, I'll just let him do this. But it is starting to dawn on me that this isn't about sex; it's not about my body.

Like Riley, Tracy quickly learned that

> the rapist gets off on the fact that you are fighting back.
> You can't disrupt the narrative by fighting back. I think
> it was more about his just having the power. You know,
> there is nothing that is going to stop him from killing me.
> I wanted him just to climax soon.

Tracy said she then felt him forcibly entering her anus.

> It hurt so bad. I felt like everything was ripped. I do start
> screaming, and he pulls out. The constant tearing pain has
> stopped. He says, "You have to stop being so loud." I made
> it very clear that I didn't want him in me. There is nothing
> I can do to get out of this situation. I am just there. At the
> time I was thinking, This doesn't happen to girls like me.
> I'm supposed to be smart. I'm supposed to be older.
>
> He came back. Every time I tried to get away, he
> pulled me down and got in again—he gripped me. The
> more I struggled, the more it hurt, and it really hurt. He
> finishes, finally, and gets off.

Tracy got dressed and tried to make small talk. She just wanted to
make Justin happy at this point because she wanted to get home safely.
And it worked; she did.

"My blood was all over the place," Tracy remembers. For days she
couldn't sit because of the pain. Now Tracy knows she was walking
around in shock.

> I just wasn't functioning. I didn't know what to do. I was
> completely out of it—out of it enough so I couldn't explain
> why I couldn't sit down. I just wasn't functioning. I didn't
> know what to do. I was just sitting there and I was com-
> pletely out of it.

The attack continues to affect Tracy. Even now, several years later,
she doesn't like going out after dark and can only go to school during
the day, even though she has moved out of the neighborhood. She is

uncomfortable with anyone being behind her. Interactions with people are difficult because Tracy has lost the ability to trust anyone, even herself. Tracy doesn't want anyone to know what happened to her.

> Because it is an issue of stupidity and sluttiness. You were raped because you didn't take precautions so it wouldn't happen. I would have said that I was to blame for this beforehand as well. Smart women don't get themselves in these situations. . . . Smart women don't go to parties and get drunk so they black out. I didn't want to be judged. If I had been attacked by a stranger, this would have been so much easier.

People, Tracy believes, are always going to blame the woman for the attack.

> The problem is, though, once you are stuck as a victim, you get classified as a whore; there is no way around that. Because I went to someone's apartment, because I sat down on the bed.

Now, several years later, Tracy still believes she has been splintered.

> Rape victims still feel that once raped, they are broken Ming vases. I very much feel like I'm not as good as the next girl because this has happened. I know this is not true, but it is still there. It is still the same today. I don't know where it comes from—society or internal—but it is still there.

New relationships are difficult for Tracy because not only does she now have difficulty trusting men, but the men also have a hard time with Tracy. They are worried, Tracy says, about doing something she doesn't want. This is how rape takes something from women and why some have said that rapists, even though they may disappear from their victims' lives, have bound the women to them in exclusive possession.

So these are the elements of women's responses to rape in this modern age: Tracy is not sexually inexperienced and is prepared to give in to save her life and make a speedy escape. But her date is only interested in forced sex, making her strategy of nonresistance ineffective; Justin can only "get off" when she fights back.

Later, as we shall see, when Tracy reports the rape to the police, she will find them blaming her for going to Justin's apartment and appearing indifferent to the violence she suffered.

# [ 3 ]

# The Feminist Attack

*Acquaintance Rape as the Price for Women's Sexual Freedom*

As acquaintance rape statistics became available in the early nineties, some feminists reacted adversely, viewing the issue of acquaintance rape as a threat to women's sexual liberation. They argued that acquaintance rape was not a problem but an acceptable risk of sexual freedom. For these feminists, talking about rape was pernicious. In her 2006 book, *The Female Thing*, feminist author and cultural critic Laura Kipnis wrote:

> But the paradox now to be grappled with is that upping women's awareness and anger about rape has also had the unintended—and probably not so beneficial—by-product effect of reinforcing conventional feminine fear and vulnerability, which also impedes women's lives, wending its way into every corner of female emotional existence, including the propensity for emotional injury by men.

If rape is seen as an inevitable result of women's sexual liberation, girls and women like Tracy will blame themselves for their own bad judgment if they are harmed. This characterization of rape as an unfortunate by-product of a greater social good minimizes the effects of acquaintance rape on girls and women and encourages the criminal-justice system to take it less seriously. Some feminists continue to respond to acquaintance rape this way—evidence of this trend is the demonization of the two Swedish women who accused WikiLeaks founder Julian Assange in 2010 of having raped them.

Even some pioneer advocates of women's sexual liberation downplayed rape. One of the most influential proponents of unmarried women's sexual freedom was *Cosmopolitan* editor Helen Gurley Brown. Her biographer, Jennifer Scanlon, documented how considerations of sexual violence and dangers from unprotected sex only rarely made it into the magazine. Brown's publishing an article that reassured women that their catching HIV was for the most part unlikely reflected

> her longstanding and sometimes problematic refusal to present female sexuality as anything other than positive and self-fulfilling. It highlights her very real fear that women's sexual freedom would prove, without continued vigilance, little more than a fleeting reality. Brown interpreted the media blitz on the risks of HIV infection not as an attempt to assist women but rather in the context of a more general societal backlash against sex. She considered the attention to AIDS specifically as symptomatic of a renewed attack on women's sexual freedom.

> "We spent such a long time getting sexual equality for women," she lamented, "and just when we're beginning to enjoy ourselves, somebody's got to come along and say sex kills."

Camille Paglia is another noted activist and author who has urged women and girls to express themselves sexually, to "accept the adventure of sex, accept the danger!"

> My sixties attitude is, yes, go for it, take the risk, take the challenge— if you get raped, if you get beat up in a dark alley in a street, it's okay. That was part of the risk of freedom, that's part of what we've demanded as women. Go with it. Pick yourself up, dust yourself off, and go on. We cannot regulate male sexuality. The uncontrollable

aspect of male sexuality is part of what makes sex interesting. And yes, it can lead to rape in some situations.

In Katie Roiphe's influential 1993 *New York Times Magazine* article, she argued that college rape-prevalence statistics were erroneous because what she considers just "bad sex" was being equated with rape. Rape, she wrote, had become a word to define everything unpleasant and disturbing about relations between the sexes. Feminists were promoting a utopian vision of sex "without struggle, sex without power, sex without persuasion, sex without pursuit." She went on:

> People have asked me if I have ever been date-raped. And thinking back on complicated nights, on too many glasses of wine, on strange and familiar beds, I would have to say yes. With such a sweeping definition of rape, I wonder how many people there are, male or female, who haven't been date-raped at one point or another. People pressure and manipulate and cajole each other into all sorts of things all the time.

Everyone, she said, feels the weight of emotional coercion at one time or another, but characterizing these occurrences as full-blown assaults will have detrimental consequences for women's sexual liberation. Roiphe's message was clear: the movement against rape fosters a model of sexual behavior based on the idea that men are out to get some and women really don't want any. She wanted a new paradigm in which women and girls can actively pursue sex. For Roiphe, young women like Riley are attaching a "quasi-religious value" to what is just a physical act. Inconveniently, rape appears to disrupt this new model.

Roiphe reserved rape for cases involving force or threat of physical violence. She would not quibble with labeling Riley's or Tracy's cases as rape, but she implicitly assumed that the majority of acquaintance cases are not like Riley's or Tracy's, a categorization that research does not support.

Most acquaintance rape cases, Roiphe asserted, are sexual encounters that would not have occurred absent alcohol or drugs. For Roiphe, young girls who drink need to take responsibility and live with the consequences:

"If we assume that women are not all helpless and naive, then they should be held responsible for their own choice to drink or take drugs," a statement that attributes blame, by the choice of the word "responsible," to the young woman and not the young man.

But Roiphe went further than just apportioning blame; she chose to attack those who decide to speak out and report rape, questioning their accounts. Coming from a young feminist, her accusation was damaging: "In the heat of the moment, in the confessional rush of relating graphic details to a supportive crowd, the truth may be stretched, battered, or utterly abandoned. It's impossible to tell how many of these stories are authentic, faithful accounts of what actually happened. They all sound tinny, staged."

Roiphe had a second line of argument. She declined to place the bulk of acquaintance rape cases within the category of rape. She wrote, "If a woman's 'judgment is impaired' and she has sex, it isn't necessarily always the man's fault and it isn't necessarily always a rape." This assertion conflated several scenarios. If, in a social situation, a young man deliberately plies a young woman so full of alcohol that she is unable to consent to sex, reasonable minds could attribute fault to the man. If, in a social situation, a man comes upon an intoxicated woman and takes advantage of her due to her inability to protest, reasonable people could likewise assign blame to the man. Only one scenario remains: if both parties are intoxicated and incapable of rational judgment, should the man be held responsible for ultimately unwanted sexual contact? Here reasonable minds can differ; in fact, some states have lesser penalties for cases involving intoxication as opposed to force.

But Roiphe declined to call any case of sex involving intoxication (without physical force) "rape." That choice led her to attack acquaintance rape statistics as being based on an expanded and illegitimate definition of rape. Detailing Neil Gilbert's allegations, which were based on the question about alcohol or drugs, Roiphe's attack resulted in rape-prevalence data being called into question for some time to come.

As Gilbert delves further into the numbers, he does not necessarily disprove the one-in-four statistic, but he does clarify what it means—the so-called rape epidemic on campuses is more a way of interpreting, a way of seeing, then a physical phenomenon. It is more about a change in sexual politics than a change in sexual behavior. Whether or not one in four college women has been raped, then, is a matter of opinion, not a matter of mathematical fact.

This statement, as we have seen, is slightly erroneous. Koss had two figures, 27.5 percent and 20 percent—never 25 percent. But harmful is the suggestion that all acquaintance rape statistics are open to question because of dubious definitions, because the public is led to consider rape-prevalence data fraudulent.

Although Roiphe has herself moved on to other topics, a new generation of feminists continues today with a similar theme. These younger feminists accuse older feminists and rape-victim advocates of perpetuating a culture that encourages women and girls to view themselves as victims. Indeed, it is true that young women today, like Tracy, are resistant to the theme of victimhood. As academic Linda Martin Alcoff has noted, "In our highly individualistic, competitive society, to be a victim is actually to be vilified as weak, as not strong enough to have avoided the victimization, as not hardy enough to swallow one's victimization in silence."

A well-publicized instance of young feminists' minimizing the effects of rape occurred on a 2008 episode of *Thinking and Drinking*, a live TV interview program hosted by Lizz Winstead. There, Winstead asked Maureen "Moe" Tkacik and Tracie Egan, bloggers on the website *Jezebel* (which is said to reach almost a million US readers every month), whether they felt the need to caution young readers against the dangers of going home with strangers.

Tkacik: What's going to happen?
Winstead: You could get raped.
Tkacik: That's happening too, but you live through that.
Winstead: Sometimes you don't.
Tkacik: That's true if they have weapons.

Later, some older feminists publicly responded to their younger, hipper counterparts who minimize rape. After viewing the program with

Moe and Tracie on the Internet, Linda Hirshman, for example, attacked them on *Salon*. Decrying the chaotic, "anything goes" attitudes of Moe and Tracie, she condemned the lack of politics at *Jezebel*:

> Doing what feels good to you is the only standard that is allowed. The problem is that no one really wants to admit that some things feel bad, because that admission would threaten the whole system of unlimited individual action. . . . As Jezebel stories reflect, women begin to numb themselves so that everything feels OK—so that nothing, not even rape, is predictably bad enough to call the police.

Columnist Katha Pollitt joined the debate on Hirshman's side, pointing out that the world is not going to change just because a lot of young women feel sexually free—they still lack women-friendly policies, decent work-family support structures, and solid political clout.

An extreme and somewhat cruel example of the battle between feminists occurred in 2010 over a disagreement about trigger warnings, which are often posted on Internet sites to warn about material that could set off painful memories for certain readers. On the blog *True/Slant*, Susannah Breslin mocked feminism, trigger warnings, and women who report having been raped:

> These days, feminism isn't a movement at all, really, but a collection of blogs obsessed with the pop culture it claims to be victimized by, a forum for women who promote themselves as victims of a patriarchy that no longer exists, a pretend movement that contains within itself no forward movement at all, only a fetal-like desire to curl up on itself, muttering Women's Studies jargon, and handing out trigger warnings like party favors at a girl's only slumber party.

At one of the sites using trigger warnings, *Feministing*, one feminist blogger condemned Breslin's indifference to other women's suffering, noting that it is now "so uncool and passé to care about rape victims." Indeed, it is a fact that some of today's young, sexually liberal women equate concern about rape with an antiquated and moribund feminism, with rape victims the losers and rapists the winners.

Laura Kipnis also took up the cudgels and joined the feminist rape deniers. She too disbelieves current rape statistics in an analysis that seriously misinterprets current rape-prevalence data. First, she made the claim that rape has declined every year since 1992. For this assertion, she used those cases reported to the police, but we know that only low percentages of those who admit to researchers they've been raped report the crime to authorities (see chapter 8). Then she made the dramatic statement that more men than women in the United States are raped every year—but the men she referenced were men in prison. To reach this conclusion, Kipnis compared *estimates* of male prison rape from human rights organizations with female rape cases reported to the police.

The real story, however, is rather different. In the first-ever survey of prisoners—both women and men—in 2007, the US Department of Justice found 47,200 actual occurrences of rape at the hands of other prisoners or staff within the last twelve months. And in its 2008–2009 survey of prison rape, the Department of Justice found that female prisoners were more than twice as likely as male prisoners to report sexual victimization. Compare this number to the Federal Bureau of Investigation's figure—90,427 rape cases reported to the police in 2007—or the 248,300 victims of rape and attempted rape reported by the Department of Justice's annual National Crime Victimization Survey in 2007, the vast majority of which involved women.

In seeking to establish the value of sexual liberation and casual sex for women, Kipnis's agenda was no different from Roiphe's thirteen years earlier. Kipnis viewed worries about rape as disguised attacks on casual sex and new definitions of femininity. Seemingly oblivious to the existence of predatory rapists, Kipnis persisted in characterizing men as merely "emotionally disappointing, watching porn, or having midlife crises, or being needy, pants-dropping, self-destructive presidential clowns."

The subject is perplexing, Kipnis admitted, because sexual violation and sexual pleasure share the same venue: "Who wouldn't get confused, politically and otherwise?" Unfortunately, labeling the issue as bewildering encourages the idea that rape is difficult to define and measure, a concept playing into the hands of acquaintance rapists.

In Sweden in late 2010, reactions to rape accusations against WikiLeaks founder Julian Assange revealed that, for some, the progressive agenda trumped concern about violence against women. Noted political activists and even feminists defended Assange by organizing public attacks on the women who made the accusations. The episode illustrated the trend of minimizing acquaintance rape charges by focusing on the women's actions and motives.

The charges were as follows: One woman asserted that Assange used violence, forcibly holding her arms and spreading her legs while lying on top of her, his body weight preventing her from moving or shifting so he could penetrate her without a condom, which did not succeed. Another woman said that Assange sexually penetrated her—also without a condom—while she was asleep. UK authorities approved his extradition to Sweden on the rape charges; Assange lodged an immediate appeal, but the extradition was upheld.

Admittedly, the circumstances of the cases are more complex than they first appear. The first woman was agreeable to sex but not to *unprotected* sex, which she says Assange then forcibly tried to arrange. Before falling asleep, the second woman may have had consensual sex with Assange, but he had reason to know of her strong desire for condom use and allegedly penetrated her a second time without a condom while she was asleep.

Assange and his attorneys did not deny that sexual intercourse with the two women occurred. Of their complaints about force and sexual penetration while asleep, Assange said only, "I may be a chauvinist pig of some sort but I am not a rapist, and only a distorted version of sexual politics could attempt to turn me into one. They each had sex with me willingly and were happy to hang out with me afterwards."

In arguments against extradition to Sweden, his attorneys agreed that their client's behavior was "disrespectful" and "disturbing" and that he "pushed the boundaries of what [the women] felt comfortable with," all statements attempting to minimize the harm of the encounters.

The Assange case confuses the public about acquaintance rape. Both women were not averse to having sexual intercourse with him, but they did not want to have unprotected sex, giving the idea that acquaintance

rape involves simply miscommunication between sexually liberated partners. The fact that in one case the woman claimed Assange used force got
lost in the shuffle. The case also perpetuates the idea that acquaintance
rape involves scenarios in which individuals might reasonably differ about
the degrees of both consent and harm, minimizing for the public the
extent of the damage suffered not just by women such as the Assange
accusers but also by young women like Riley and Tracy.

Activists defended Assange by attacking the women's motives, asserting they were part of a political conspiracy to do him in. After naming
one of the accusers, Alexander Cockburn charged that she had ties to
US-funded anti-Castro and anticommunist groups and that the CIA was
probably "at work fomenting these Swedish accusations."

In a posting on the *Huffington Post*, protofeminist Naomi Wolf also
minimized the charges, claiming they were no more than allegations of
consensual sex with two women who were "upset that he began dating
[the] second woman while still being in a relationship with the first."
Belittling the accusations, Wolf alleged "global manhunts to arrest and
prosecute men who behave like narcissistic jerks to women they are dating," again publicly trivializing acquaintance rape complaints.

Later Wolf called for removing anonymity of women who report
having been raped, arguing that secrecy harms them by perpetrating the
shame of rape. But clearly her motivation is to protect the reputation of
Julian Assange:

> If one makes a serious criminal accusation, one must be treated as
> a moral adult. The importance of this is particularly clear in the
> Assange case, where public opinion matters far more than usual.
> Here, geopolitical state pressure, as well as the pressure of public
> attitudes about Assange, weigh unusually heavily. Can judicial deci-
> sion-making be impartial when the accused is exposed to the glare of
> media scrutiny and attack by the U.S. government, while his accusers
> remain hidden?

Feminist columnist Katha Pollitt reacted with dismay, noting that the
progressives who defended Julian Assange seemed unable to hold two

ideas at once: (1) WikiLeaks is a good thing, revealing information citizens need to know, but (2) its founder may have committed sex crimes according to Swedish law. The damage, however, was done. Assange's accusers were branded as frivolous, vindictive, or politically motivated, charges often made against those who report acquaintance rape.

Another particularly vicious example of how ideology trumps concerns for victims of violence occurred after the rape suffered by CBS News's chief foreign correspondent Lara Logan at the hands of mob members in Cairo during the February 2011 uprising. Journalist Nir Rosen made clear he had no sympathy for Logan, whom he characterized as a cheerleader for the US invasion of Iraq. Apparently disbelieving the rape, he dubbed it an attention-getting stunt calculated to make Logan a martyr so she could compete with CNN's Anderson Cooper, who had been assaulted in Cairo.

Subsequently Rosen expressed regret, asserting that joking with friends had gotten out of line. That rape is seen as fit material for humor demonstrates the extent to which the effects of rape have been trivialized. His employer, New York University, quickly terminated his fellowship.

A controversy on the American University campus in 2010 illustrated how some progressives continue to believe that individuals who pursue sexually liberated lifestyles must accept the risk of rape, an attitude that understandably affects judges and juries as well. Alex Knepper, an openly gay sophomore, wrote in his column in the campus newspaper, "Let's get this straight: any woman who heads to an EI party as an anonymous onlooker, drinks five cups of the jungle juice, and walks back to a boy's room with him is indicating that she wants sex, OK? . . . Don't jump into the sexual arena if you can't handle the practice!"

Protestors, numbering in the several hundreds, wrote into the newspaper. They argued that the column promoted the culture of victim blaming and crossed a line into excusing rape. If these thoughts represent the views of male students on campus—that a student is entitled to have sex with a female who is inebriated whether she wants it or not—then, one student wrote, "attitudes like his are a serious threat to my safety and those of my peers."

It seems clear that Knepper has well captured the current zeitgeist, and despite the protests, his views are those with which many young men and women would agree. For Knepper and others, the excitement of sexual empowerment and sexual exploration do inherently involve some risk taking. Tracy, for one, carefully sought to eliminate the danger while at the same time trying to open herself up to different experiences and a new relationship. That she was subsequently anally penetrated against her will is for her a matter of shame and regret.

Since then, she has thought a great deal about her behavior, especially her attempt to stay alive by trying to speed up her attacker's climaxing. To her relief, she eventually determined that she did exercise some power during the assault, which was very important to her.

> I did some serious thinking about this. Because it came down to an issue of whether you can control what happens to you. The issue of choice, the issue of power. It really felt good to own up to the fact—not good, but it felt really important to stand up to the fact that I made some choices. One of my really good friends said, "You made a bargain and you got out of there alive. This is the most important part." She said, "You chose that bargain. You chose it on your terms." In that sense, knowing that I wasn't completely passive was really important.

The harshness of this victim blaming has wide-ranging effects. Tracy agrees that girls want freedom and experience, but they "are judged adversely when things go wrong." She remembers thinking that this was not about alcohol: "I wish it had been, because it might not have hurt so bad." Tracy movingly describes the severity of the blame and its effects on her:

> People made judgments about me. I didn't want to be judged, but people did judge me. I wouldn't want to tell most people. What was she doing going to his house? If I had been attacked by a stranger, this would have been so much more valid. I would not have felt this way, not at all.

# [ 4 ]

# The Conservative Attack

*Acquaintance Rape as the Result of Women's Promiscuity*

S urely some of the somewhat extreme instances of feminist rape denial represent a response to the current purity movement. Some conservative women decry a proclaimed "rape epidemic" as a myth because they view most rapes as caused by women's and girls' promiscuity. Christina Hoff Sommers declared, "There isn't this date-rape epidemic that has been described on campuses. It's wildly exaggerated. There are problems but it's mainly problems with drinking and then ridiculous and sometimes dangerous behavior with binge drinking and so forth."

If feminists define the right to be promiscuous as a cornerstone of female equality, then there will be risks, Heather Mac Donald recently averred: "The booze-filled hookup culture of one-night or sometimes just partial one-night stands" is the cause of rape. "Putting on a tight tank top doesn't of course lead to what bureaucrats call rape," she continues. "But taking off that tank top does increase the risk of sexual intercourse that will be later regretted, especially when the tank-topper has been mainlining rum and Cokes all evening." Mac Donald concluded:

Some students are going one step further: organizing in favor of sexual restraint. Such newly created campus groups as the Love and Fidelity Network and the True Love Revolution advocate an alternative to the rampant regret sex of the hookup scene: wait until marriage. Their message would do more to return a modicum of manners to campus male-and-female behavior than endless harangues about the rape culture ever could.

In a piece in the *Wall Street Journal* in 2006, journalist Naomi Schaefer Riley argued for what she too called common sense. Three-quarters of college rapes, she claimed, happen when the victims are so intoxicated they are unable to refuse. "And these are just the ones who admitted it." The culprit is contemporary feminism and women who follow its tenets and try to behave like men. Columnist Kathleen Parker blamed the "ho culture" that encourages women to dress in revealing ways, in which even babies are adorned in "porn star" T-shirts and other sexualized clothing. But Parker extended the discussion to rape, writing in 2008, "Once women sexually objectify themselves, it becomes harder to insist that others not."

Conservatives continue to denigrate rape prevalence and minimize the effects of acquaintance rape on college campuses along these lines. An article in the *Weekly Standard* in 2010 criticized Jaclyn Friedman's statement in the *Washington Post* that 150,000 young women a year are victims of rape: "Friedman derived that extraordinarily high figure by counting drunken sexual encounters between students as rape."

For these individuals, promiscuous girls and women cannot be rape victims. Jessica Valenti put it best:

Under the purity myth, the only women who can truly be raped are those who are chaste—and given how limiting the purity myth is, and how few women actually fit into its tight mold, the consequence is that *most* women are seen as incapable of being raped. . . . A woman who has had sex? Well, she's done it before, hasn't she? Not rapeable. . . . Had a few too many beers? Take some responsibility for yourself! . . . Pure women aren't out at bars or on the street; they're not in public life—they're home, where women should be.

Astonishingly, Dan Rottenberg, founding editor of the *Broad Street Review*, blamed reporter Lara Logan for her own gang rape during the Egyptian uprising in 2011. He had seen an earlier photograph of Logan at a social event wearing a dress that revealed her cleavage. The male animal, he wrote, craves the drama of sexually conquering a woman, a proclivity that it is difficult to change: "Earth to liberated women: When you display legs, thighs or cleavage, some liberated men will see it as a sign that you feel good about yourself and your sexuality. But most men will see it as a sign you want to get laid." Then Rottenberg chastised women reporters, saying, "If you want to be taken seriously as a journalist, don't pose for pictures that emphasize your cleavage."

These arguments are nothing more than restatements of the opinions about chastity that conservative women have made. But extending them to a gang rape in an Egyptian square, executed by an unruly mob of men who had never seen a picture of Lara Logan in evening dress, who did not sexually assault her in the square because they wanted sex, puts into focus the lack of understanding of rape. As one commentator has written, "They sexually assaulted her because *they were trying to hurt her.*"

A chronicler of casual hookup culture, Laura Sessions Stepp, has created a new term, "gray rape," to describe cases in which she says alcohol on both sides and mixed signals result in unwanted sex. In these situations, she explained in a *Cosmopolitan* article, it is unclear whether a rape has occurred: the girls and women knew their attackers; they believed they contributed to the assault because of their own behavior (that is, each had been drinking and went up to the fellow's room); and when the sexual intercourse commenced, they protested, but in the end they froze and disassociated through the assault. None of the women and girls wanted the sex, and all continue to suffer from the effects of the attacks, some more seriously than others.

Devising a new category, a less serious classification, for a large number of nonconsensual sexual encounters feeds into the effort to deny the prevalence of "real rape," persuading girls and women that the episode was their fault. But why not call it rape and use it as another argument against hooking up? Stepp herself betrayed an ambiguity in her writings.

At times, she seemed to understand that the young women have been raped and that intoxicated individuals cannot, under the law, consent; at other moments, she talked about the young men's alcohol abuse and their confusion "when things end up in bed."

In the end, Stepp resolved her own uncertainty by condemning hookup culture and providing tips for girls on how to avoid the gray area, which takes the focus off the young men. However, "gray rape" plays into the hands of conservative rape deniers who believe that many young women are reckless and should be blamed for what happens to them.

Wendy Shalit, a noted young advocate for girls' modesty, does not challenge rape-prevalence statistics and understands the attack on Mary Koss to be manipulative and not fact based:

> Presumably, conservatives should have something to say to men who cannot have sexual intercourse with their dates without physically restraining them. Attacking feminists for expanding the definition of rape seems a distraction from the harder but clearly more necessary task of socializing our males.

Yet Shalit does blame sexual liberation for rape and domestic violence, and she urges girls and women to return to modesty forthwith:

> In pursuit of a unisexual society in which we deny that men are physically stronger than women, drunks (and sober opportunists) with total disregard for women will simply have more chances to prey on them. All our unisexual society has achieved is precisely this greater opportunity for women to be taken advantage of. . . . Specifically, though they are physically stronger and may be capable of forcing a woman to have sexual intercourse, they should not because this is not how it's done in civilized society.

But, because Shalit does not believe it is possible to change men, women and girls must be the ones to pursue modesty:

> Unfortunately, if a man does not behave like a gentleman and treat women with respect, there is very little a woman can say to change his behavior. . . . Girls, on the other hand, even when they do not

have the best role models, can learn to let a boy go if he wants more than they are willing to give.

Ongoing arguments about the hook-up culture and "gray rape" reveal confusion and disagreements within feminism. Some feminists believe that Laura Sessions Stepp is trying to quash female sexual liberation by exaggerating the dangers of casual sex. Others caution that the hook-up culture should not be defended or its existence minimized just because it was being attacked by conservatives with an agenda: women's liberation can be used as a means to sexually exploit women. As one young woman wrote on an online discussion:

> There is an expectation on college campuses that women are and should be sexually available. . . . The meaning of a sexually liberated woman has been changed to mean a woman who is always willing and available for sex. . . . Patriarchy has taken women's sexual liberation and turned it on its head for the benefit of men. Women feeling compelled to have sex with men in order to be cool is not sexual liberation.

This virulent debate strands many young women, who lack the ability to integrate tenets of sexual liberation with concerns about unwanted sex. Is it any wonder, though, that confusion reigns in the media and the public, preventing strong responses to acquaintance rapists? Much ink has been spilled over these ideological charges and countercharges in recent years, with battles against feminism and between groups of feminists proving a giant distraction from the task of preventing rape. With this murky backdrop of sexual liberation, predators are free to operate on vulnerable victims.

In their book, *The Flipside of Feminism*, conservative activists Suzanne Venker and Phyllis Schlafly forgot the perpetrators altogether when they blamed acquaintance rape on women's liberation for encouraging women to become sexually available. Of today's women, they wrote, "They fight to protect themselves from their own mistakes, but then they fight for the freedom to make these mistakes. They want free sex, but they also want the ability to punish the man when they change their mind."

Men will always take advantage of what is available, Venker and Schlafly claimed. "Inebriated women who end up having sex without meaning to can cry date rape, and the guy could end up in prison!" they wrote. Their sole focus on inebriated casual sex has the unfortunate effect of reducing all acquaintance rape to just one scenario and, even within that situation, blaming the person harmed for taking the risk.

UK justice secretary Kenneth Clarke demonstrated the widespread acceptance of Venker and Schlafly's position when he commented on newly proposed sentencing policies in a television interview in May 2011. The country's senior legal politician believed there to be a strong distinction between "serious rapes" and "date rape" and that no one guilty of "serious rape" would be released as quickly as those guilty of "date rape." The ensuing firestorm required Clarke to return to the television studio to state that he regarded "all rape as a serious crime." But the secretary's off-the-cuff comments undoubtedly represented his true beliefs and those of many in society. As one commentator noted during calls for the minister's dismissal, "Clarke's comments highlight the fact that rape is regarded as a different kind of crime to other assaults," a position unhelpful to those injured by acquaintance rape.

But the important thing to remember is this: both feminist rape deniers and conservative purity advocates place the blame on the women for what happened to them. This idea has powerful repercussions for holding rapists accountable in our culture. Two wildly different philosophies have converged into a detrimental theme of victim blaming, well captured by professor Carine Mardorossian:

> Responsibility is still laid on the victim. Years of educating the public about these issues seem to have resulted only in the expectation that women should now know better than to let themselves get raped . . . only gendered crimes generate the kind of victim-blaming responses rape and domestic violence produce. Whereas forgetting to set the antiburglary alarm or getting robbed despite the "neighborhood watch" does not exculpate the thieves, getting raped always elicits an investigation into the ways in which a victim might ultimately have been responsible for what happens. Bad judgment becomes cause.

## Too Many Victims?

Another backlash against feminists comes from a group of writers some have dubbed "victim culturalists." These critics describe a new society of victims, individuals who refuse to be held accountable for their own behavior by blaming others for their problems. Allegedly, fake victims drive out compassion for real victims in society. We've all seen examples of false victimization—the substandard employee, for example, who wants to claim racism, sexism, or ageism when his or her employer takes disciplinary action. But including rape in the analysis gives the impression that those who report they've been raped are evading responsibility or exaggerating the harms of their experiences, which in the end contributes to the indifference to acquaintance rape.

In his book *A Nation of Victims*, Charles J. Sykes extended the victim analysis to rape. The crime is serious and horrific, he explained, but false claims drive out compassion for the real rape victims. And the false victims are those who have expanded the concept of rape to include minor issues such as sexual harassment. Sykes wrote, "Far more important to its champions is the effort to redefine what constitutes sexual assault and to expand the zone of sexual oppression to cover the entire range of nuance, complexity, tentativeness, and confusion that surrounds the relations between men and women."

To support this statement, Sykes turned to Mary Koss's research, misstating its methodology along the lines already discussed. He concluded that her rape-prevalence research was based on an overly broad definition of rape, an idea alleged so often that it has entered the mainstream and has falsely shaped the public's understanding of acquaintance rape. Rape experts find this attitude pernicious, noting that deniers' "almost categorical dismissal of rape and battering victims as hypersensitive or exaggerating is particularly chilling."

Psychologist Sharon Lamb saw it slightly differently. She reminded us that the problem is that young women like Riley and Tracy blame *themselves* too much, letting perpetrators off the hook. Lamb presented a more commonsense balancing act that more nearly reflects reality. By exaggerating their blamelessness, we deny those reporting rape a sense of responsibility and agency, she explained. However, apportioning some blame need not absolve the perpetrator:

> Self-reflection will often lead to some self-blame. And for victims of violence in which the coercion was not so utterly total as to reduce them to mere objects, a proportion of blame could be theirs. When we rush out to stop the victim-blaming it is not useful or accurate to blame everyone *but* the victim; in so doing we thwart the very impulse of change, self-assertion, and courage that underlies recovery. But we also must remember that when we apportion some blame to the victim, this cannot diminish our holding perpetrators accountable in a realistic and full way.

## The Role of the Media in Victim Blaming

Many members of the media appear to embrace victim blaming for acquaintance rape. From the beginning in the 1990s, the media had difficulty in accepting the concept of acquaintance rape. For example, while covering a campus demonstration protesting the handling of a date rape case, ABC news correspondent John Stossel actually grabbed the microphone and asked the protestors to define rape: "To me it's a man holding a woman at gunpoint or knifepoint," he said. "There seems to be a new way of looking at it."

Not much progress appears to have been made on this front since that time. Student newspaper columnist Alex Knepper made clear that, in his mind, rape only occurs when a stranger "thrusts sex into a non-sexual situation." It appeared that many in the media and the public agreed with him.

In 2009 a reader asked advice columnist Amy Dickinson, whose column appears in over two hundred newspapers and four hundred National Public Radio stations, whether she had been raped. The reader, a young woman, was drunk at a frat party but didn't want sex, and she had said so before going to the fellow's room. She wrote Dickinson, "I guess my question is, if I wasn't kicking and fighting him off, is it still rape? I feel like calling it that is a bit extreme, but I haven't felt the same since it happened. Am I a victim?"

Dickinson's response?

Were you a victim? Yes.

First, you were a victim of your own awful judgment. Getting drunk at a frat house is a hazardous choice for anyone to make because of the risk (some might say a likelihood) that *you will engage in* [italics added] unwise or unwanted sexual contact.

You don't say whether the guy was also drunk. If so, his judgment was also impaired.

Dickinson's reluctance to assign any blame to the young man who took advantage of a drunken young lady—who said ahead of time that she wasn't interested in sex—was deeply troubling but not surprising after the many years of rape deniers' blaming victims. And although the young woman said she was overpowered against her will, Amy's use of the phrase "will engage in unwanted sexual contact" obscured the true nature of what occurred.

After a minifirestorm of protest, Dickinson did attempt to apologize in a later column ("I certainly didn't intend to offend or blame her for what happened"). But she reiterated her view that the young woman should "take responsibility for the only thing she could control—her own choices and actions," again attributing fault to the young woman.

From this sequence, it is evident that Dickinson understood the entire episode to be a misunderstanding fueled by alcohol consumption and nothing else. And it is also clear that large percentages of the public agree, believing that women who drink to intoxication have generally made themselves sexually available. This belief makes rape convictions in these circumstances difficult to obtain. In 2010, one-third of persons surveyed online in the United Kingdom blamed victims who had dressed provocatively or had gone back to the attacker's house for a drink for their own injuries.

And in March 2011, a *New York Times* reporter wrote of eighteen young men charged with gang raping an eleven-year-old in Cleveland, Texas. In the short item, he saw fit to cite unnamed residents who said the young woman dressed older than her age, "wearing makeup and fashions more appropriate to a woman in her 20s," and hanging out with teen boys at a playground. The article also quoted a community member who blamed the girl's mother for negligence and neglect while decrying the tragedy that the boys "have to live with this the rest of their lives." No person was found to express the opinion that it was a disgrace that eighteen community members might have seen fit to take advantage of the eleven-year-old girl in this way.

The result was an article that seemed to imply the eleven-year-old was at fault for the incident. A nationwide petition drive to the newspaper garnered forty thousand signatures in a few days. Several days later, the paper's public editor, Arthur Brisbane, posted a piece online in which he admitted the story pilloried the girl. He said the *Times* journalist expressed concerns about the ruined lives of the young men but did not acknowledge the girl's distress. Brisbane's apology criticized the paper for a lack of journalistic balance. A community's concern for the men's lives and the girl's wayward behavior was the only sentiment in the original article, but the public editor did not believe that the comments reflected the only attitude to be found in the community.

Several harrowing observations can be drawn from this episode. That members of the community would blame an eleven-year-old child for her own rape shows the extent to which victim blaming has become accepted in our culture. It is also likely that the reporter subconsciously agreed with these attitudes. Nor were they the only individuals holding these views. In the wake of the tragic episode, a Florida legislator, representative Kathleen Passidomo, decided that school dress-code legislation was needed in her state.

"And her parents let her attend school like that," said Passidomo. "And I think it's incumbent upon us to create some areas where students can be safe in school and show up in proper attire so what happened in Texas doesn't happen to our students."

As pointed out by numerous comments on the *New York Times* website, the issue was not a matter of journalistic balance. Can there ever be an excuse for gang rape? Would we expect a newspaper to present balanced commentary about whether a woman should have been murdered or robbed?

The *New York Times* article was not atypical for coverage of gang rapes. In the most heinous gang rape scenarios, media reports often stress the young women's drinking. In an analysis of coverage of ten major rape cases between 1980 and 1996, researchers were disappointed to find that, in five cases involving even gang rapes, reporters were fixated on the young women's actions. Researchers noted, "It would appear that victim behavior, such as drinking, is still such a forceful consideration that even the presence of multiple offenders cannot override it in terms of attributing cause, motivation, precipitation and the like to victims in rape offenses."

Recently, there has been evidence that these attitudes are affecting public policy and police practices in the United States.

## Redefining Abortion Exemptions

For years, antiabortion activists have been fighting exemptions for rape and incest victims because they believe these exemptions facilitate more abortions. Their tactics borrow from the classic rape-denial playbook.

First, they try to establish a category of "legitimate rape" or "assault rape." All the other nonforcible occurrences aren't really rape and the individuals are not really victims, so we shouldn't worry if they have to deal with an unwanted pregnancy. This approach perpetuates the notion that a great many rapes are no such thing at all. We saw this strategy in H.R. 3, introduced in the US House of Representatives early in 2011 by 173 sponsors. It would have limited taxpayer funding for abortions as a result of pregnancies caused by rapes, but only forcible rapes would qualify.

Next, antiabortion activists argue that exemptions are unnecessary in forcible-rape situations because pregnancy does not occur; hidden defenses kick in to prevent pregnancies in these scenarios. As a result, one can conclude that those claiming pregnancy in forcible-rape situations are lying about rape.

The rape-denial strategies of antiabortion advocates were brought home in August 2012 when representative Todd Akin, running for one of Missouri's US Senate seats, famously commented, "If it's a legitimate rape, the female body has ways to try to shut that whole thing down."

(Horrifyingly, Akin's contention may have relied on evidence from a Nazi experiment. In it women were told they were headed to the gas chambers but were allowed to live, and an obstetrician determined that they failed to ovulate.) The American Congress of Obstetricians and Gynecologists responded to this erroneous biological science, stating that a woman who is raped has no control over ovulation, fertilization, or implantation of a fertilized egg. President Obama also responded by saying, "The views expressed were offensive. Rape is rape."

Although the number of pregnancies resulting from rape is unknown, each year in the United States 10,000 to 15,000 abortions occur among women whose pregnancies were the result of reported rape. Minimizing the harms of most rapes and putting forth erroneous science or statistics create a false reality in which there is only one conclusion: women who claim pregnancy as a result of rape are lying about rape, and women will exploit bans on abortion by falsely claiming rape.

## Using Negligence as a Defense

One dialogue in law reviews has centered around the concept of contributory negligence as a defense to criminal charges. Rutgers School of Law–Newark professor Vera Bergelson has argued that a perpetrator's liability should be evaluated in the context of victim-perpetrator interaction. She concluded there are situations in which the conduct of the individual reporting the crime should mitigate the accused's criminal liability. For Bergelson, these situations occur when the crime victim has waived his or her rights voluntarily (by consent or assumption of risk) or lost them involuntarily (by attacking or threatening some legally recognized rights of others).

Applying Bergelson's new theory is not easy. She would, for example, allow victim fault to be considered when the individual claiming victimization has willingly participated in a dangerous endeavor, such as Russian roulette. But she would distinguish that type of case from situations in which the injured party merely does not take sufficient precautions against crime and falls prey to wrongdoing—for example, taking a late-night jog in the park. Bergelson put the crime of rape into this latter category and thus excluded it from her proposal.

Although Bergelson went to extreme lengths to craft a legal theory that did not simply enshrine the community's moral perceptions of responsibility—"A rape victim is not, and should not be responsible for rape even if the community believes otherwise"—the idea of contributory negligence in criminal law puts us down a path ploughed by rape deniers. And that is just what is being advocated in a 2010 book by defense attorney Vanessa Place, who tries to make a case for contributory negligence in rape law in the United States:

> Voluntarily engaging in inherently dangerous activity could preclude criminal liability for foreseeable harms. If you're a woman and desire to go to a bar and get drunk and then opt to sample the fresh bit you've just met, he ought not to be liable for rape. This is a delicate proposition, and we could carefully circumscribe the limits of the risk assumed: he should not be liable for your rape unless you withdraw your consent and he does not comply.

Thus, for Place, the burden in such a scenario is on the woman to show she has actively withdrawn presumed consent, not to actively consent. Furthermore, Place does not buy the presumption that an intoxicated person cannot agree to sex: "Absent any real evidence that a woman would not have consented had she not been intoxicated, a man should not be held to have committed the acts with the requisite intent—a knowing lack of consent." Again, Place's theory would squarely incorporate aspects of victim blaming into the criminal law of rape.

## Attitudes in the Criminal-Justice System

Evidence is also emerging that some law-enforcement officials have embraced these attitudes. During a recent Take Back the Night march on a college campus, for example, police on the scene responded to the chant "Sexual assault has to go" with "Then maybe you shouldn't drink!" shouted through a bullhorn. And in January 2011, a police officer told students at Toronto's York University that if women want to avoid rape, they shouldn't dress like "sluts."

Amazingly, one judge even went public with a statement demonstrating the extent to which some individuals have accepted the notion that inebriated females are fair prey. One Baltimore County jurist gave probation rather than jail time to a man found guilty of raping a drunken woman; she was a friend of the man and had voluntarily laid down on his bed, fully clothed, to sleep off a drinking binge. The jurist commented that the sight of a supine female in an alcohol-induced coma was "the dream of a lot of males, quite honestly."

A highly educated juror told of a case in which a woman met two men in a bar and then agreed to go with them to another drinking establishment. Instead, they took her to their apartment and sexually penetrated her. The men asserted consent and were acquitted, even though the complainant told the jury she was a lesbian and was unlikely to want to have sex with men. One juror explained their reasoning: because she got in the car, the woman was agreeing to anything that happened thereafter.

Research from the United Kingdom by Betsy Stanko and colleagues demonstrates the difficulties of prosecuting rape cases due to the vulnerabilities of complainants. The study reviewed 697 allegations of rape recorded by the Metropolitan Police in London during April and May 2005, tracking the outcomes of the cases over time. Researchers labeled complainants as vulnerable if they were younger than eighteen years of age at the time of the attack, had a mental health issue noted in the police record, were currently or previously intimate with the offender, or had consumed alcohol or drugs just prior to the attack. Of the cases reviewed, 87 percent had at least one of these vulnerabilities. Individuals with multiple vulnerabilities were less likely to see their allegations result in a conviction for rape, with those with mental health issues the most disadvantaged in the process.

These findings were troubling for the researchers, because "rapists may very well be targeting that vulnerability in their conscious actions." In other words, they may choose their victims based on how likely they are to get away with the rape. It thus becomes important for law enforcement, and the public, to resolve not to blame those reporting rape. Instead, they must develop strategies to hold accountable those who attack these vulnerable women.

If researchers are correct—that rapists seek out vulnerable victims like Riley—then the voluntarily intoxicated woman is one who can be raped. As former prosecutor Teresa Scalzo has reported,

> The unfortunate reality of rape cases is that the flaws that make the victim a target for the offender also make the victim less credible in a jury's eyes. For example, a victim who goes to a bar and drinks to the point of vomiting and unconsciousness will be an easy target for a predator. This victim may be viewed with skepticism or dislike by a jury that assumes that she put herself in danger with her behavior.

Professor David Lisak, who has studied men who rape, believes that sexual predators prey on inebriated young women. These rape cases are ones that prosecutors often decline to charge, with the result that the criminal-justice system may essentially be giving a free pass to sexual predators. Lisak noted, "It is quite well-known among college administrators that first-year students, freshman women, are particularly at risk for rape. The predators on campus know that women who are new to campus, they are younger, they're less experienced. They will probably take more risks because they want to be accepted. So for all these reasons, the predators will look particularly for those women."

One real-life case, the rape charge against high school student Adrian Missbrenner, demonstrates the effects of victim blaming in the age of women's sexual liberation. Novelist Scott Turow wrote a novella, *Limitations*, loosely based on the facts of the case, but Turow's version has an outcome in which the young men are held to account. *Limitations* is, unfortunately, just fiction. The actual case had a starkly different ending, sparking a short-lived media outcry.

A teenage party in Missbrenner's home in an affluent Chicago suburb was the site of the real event in 2002. During the celebration, one party-goer videotaped three young men as they sexually penetrated an inebriated sixteen-year-old girl. After gulping two or three slugs of vodka, the young woman said she threw up, and she remembered nothing after that. When she awoke the next afternoon, she was nude from the waist down and found sexual slurs such as "slut" scribbled in black marker across her thigh and chest.

Only the jury and the attorneys viewed the tape of the incident. Reportedly, the young woman is clearly inebriated when the three men enter her. By the last portion of the tape, the girl appears to be unconscious. It is then that the three, along with two others, write the sexual slurs, spit on her body, and put a condom across her face and a cigarette in her vagina.

Prosecutors charged four teens in the incident. Two were acquitted; a third fled to Eastern Europe; and a fourth, the videographer, pled guilty to child-pornography charges and served a short stint in a prison boot camp. In acquitting Adrian Missbrenner in March 2006, jury members commented that the defense attorneys convinced them that the girl was not comatose and might have consented when Missbrenner entered her. One juror commented, "Clearly, we knew what those young men did was wrong. Clearly, they took advantage of her. But there was reasonable doubt."

Prosecutors thought differently. The state pointed out that the teen videographer can be heard on tape asking Missbrenner to lift the girl's legs; when he does so, she does not speak or move. And the prosecutor pointed out the statement, "Good drugs are really paying off," which occurs at the point in the tape when her leg is held up to display its lifelessness. Unfortunately, the young woman did not report the crime early enough so that drugs could be detected in her system.

What garnered all the headlines, though, was the judge's order threatening to jail the young woman for contempt of court—she refused to view the videotape so she could be questioned about it by defense counsel on cross-examination. Since she remembered absolutely nothing, the young woman did not want to be assaulted anew by the tape of the event. Arguing that their client would be severely harmed if she watched the tape, the prosecution viewed the move as an attempt on the part of the defense to humiliate and embarrass her. The judge gave the young woman, then twenty years old, a chance to reconsider her stance overnight.

An uproar ensued; even then–Illinois governor Rod Blagojevich got into the act. By the next morning, as anti-rape and civil rights activists converged on the courthouse, the judge had reconsidered and withdrawn his order. But the insensitivity of the judge left many commentators stunned.

After the not-guilty verdict, Adrian Missbrenner crowed to the *Chicago Sun-Times*, "I suffered more than the girl. Being portrayed on television as brutal gang rapists, as child pornographers—I mean, it was unbelievable." *Chicago Tribune* columnist Eric Zorn's take on the case probably reflected the majority opinion. Clearly, he wrote, the teen boys, themselves impaired by alcohol, took advantage of a young woman who was "herself too impaired to give meaningful consent to what happened to her. And while, if I'm right, I don't think such an act should go unpunished, I also don't think society is well served by sentencing the young man to 20 years in prison and effectively ruining his life."

Acquittals in gang rape cases fail to make sense. An experienced prosecutor will point out to the jury that a rape conviction can be obviated only by the presence of affirmative consent; in other words, a complainant who may have put herself in harm's way does not excuse a defendant who has taken advantage of her. Do judges and juries really believe that young teens consent to have sex with an entire sports team or even part of one? Or are they really saying that if a young woman drinks to excess, then she gets what is coming to her or has contributed to an attack against her due to her own negligence?

Consider the case of college student Beckett Brennan, interviewed on CBS's *60 Minutes* on April 17, 2011. At a party during which she drank six shots of vodka, Brennan accepted a ride with two college basketball players back to the student dorm complex at the University of the Pacific. Once they arrived, Brennan said, the two young men led her upstairs into an empty bedroom and raped her. Then a third player came into the room, pushed her into a closet, and raped her again.

After a conversation with a Stockton police detective, Brennan decided not to press charges, but she did bring the matter to the school's disciplinary panel. Two of the players asserted the sex was consensual, and one of the players claimed he wasn't even present. All three of the young men received punishments, but the penalties differed. The school expelled the player who asserted he was not there and suspended for one year the one who put forward the consensual defense. A third, who claimed the young woman had been flirting with him at the party, was suspended for just a semester.

Brennan said she failed to understand how the three could have received differing penalties. Obviously the panel members believed consensual sex occurred with at least one of the players, and in another case they accepted that the basketball player thought it was consensual. But why would a disciplinary panel think it believable for a young woman to have consensual sex with two young men in the space of a few minutes? Surely they did not. Yet Brennan's heavy drinking and alleged flirting made it difficult for the panel to believe the young men were guilty. This attitude was echoed in the Missbrenner case; it is one that enables acquaintance rape to continue unabated.

In an interview in January 2012, CBS reporter Lara Logan explained how her gang rape at the hands of Egyptian demonstrators has caused posttraumatic stress disorder. The article in the *New York Daily News* described in graphic detail the brutal and sustained sexual assaults she said she received. That one individual filed the following comment is simply unbelievable but demonstrates the extent to which blaming the victim has become a reflexive action:

> She did nothing to protect herself because she's trying to be a high-powered media feminazi elitist like the Diane Sawyer's and Katie Couric's of the mainstream media. CBS didn't do anything to protect her either so I really don't feel sorry for her whatsoever. If she wasn't such an elitist, she would have refused to report on the situation. She shouldn't have even been there, period.

In his book *The Better Angels of Our Nature*, psychologist Steven Pinker reminded us that victim blaming serves a broad purpose in our culture, one that was historically based and that we seem loath to relinquish. Men, he said, have had an interest in protecting their property interests in exclusive possession of women. If it is always considered her fault, then the woman can never explain away consensual sex as rape. This provides her with incentives to stay out of risky situations and to resist a rapist.

DePaul University College of Law professor Deborah Tuerkheimer believes that the ideas of police, prosecutors, judges, and jurors lag behind current social norms. Sex outside a monogamous relationship, sex with perceived frequency, sex on the part of teenagers, and sex that is initiated by the woman are, she says, deemed deviant, creating a presumption of "unrapeability." Those women who transgress these sexual boundaries "are suspected of proclivities toward perpetual consent. . . . By placing off-limits consensual sexual conduct of a disfavored kind, rape law subordinates sexual agency to a judgment about what women ought, and ought not to do."

Tuerkheimer asserts that these attitudes about women's sexual agency are outmoded. Yet there are vocal women writers, not without influence, who challenge the acceptability of new social norms for women, who insist that women and girls exercising these new freedoms must assume the risks. And as there are groups of feminists who also believe that the risks are on the women's side, it is not a simple task for criminal law to catch up.

◆

It was October 2009. Riley was in the hospital, where she spent fifteen days trying to get her lungs cleared out. She received antibiotics intravenously, physical therapy four times a day, and nutritional and vitamin therapies. Riley said her health had deteriorated since the episode with Luke; her lungs and sinuses will always be affected because eradicating the bacteria will never be a possibility. But the infection had progressed to the point that she simply was no longer able to function. Unfortunately, while in the hospital, Riley experienced several seizures for the first time, undoubtedly caused by the disease. This new development necessitated further testing and ultimately seizure medication, which was added to a growing list of daily prescriptions.

While there, Riley read this book in draft form—unfortunate tim-
ing, because October was the month when Luke sexually penetrated her
against her will. The combination of her perusal of the manuscript and
the anniversary caused Riley to experience traumatizing flashbacks.

"It was really difficult to get through reading it," she said. Riley had
some strong reactions to the rape deniers in the book, and to this chapter
in particular.

Like others who have reported their rapes, Riley said she was torn
apart by the victim blaming.

> After something like that happens, you start second-
> guessing. What if I had just done that? It is so hard on
> your insides to think like that. Did he really force his head
> against my genitals, or did I let him force his way down
> there? Or I should've kicked him or ran—anything than
> what I did. These are typical reactions, because we are in
> a state that is so unknown to our body that we try to make
> up for it by trying to make it go away or make excuses for
> what happened. It instills some form of shame or guilt that
> we did not do or say enough, therefore it's our fault. For
> instance, after I was raped, I doubted myself for going to
> the rapist's house. I didn't give myself credit that the rea-
> son I went was because I had actually known and trusted
> him prior to the assault, and that it wasn't my fault for
> going there; it was his fault for deceiving me. But when
> you are scared of what others might see or say, that plays
> a role in how you relate to what happened.

Riley realized that Luke was trying to instill thoughts of self-blame
that would prevent her from going to the police.

> He knew what he was doing. Why else would he say, "Don't
> be mad at me"? He knew exactly what he was doing. The
> next day, he tried calling me over and over again. I didn't
> answer my phone, and he left me a message: "I knew you
> wouldn't answer your phone. Have fun going to the bars
> and getting on all the guys." Again, trying to make me feel

like I'm the one who is the easy girl. Those things made me want to go to the police more, because it made me realize he is not right. He really needs help.

Riley is very clear now about victim blaming.

What I would tell women facing the silence, the assault, the fight, is that it is never your fault. It doesn't matter how short your skirt is, how much you flirted, how much cleavage you show, where you chose to go and whom you chose to be with, what you said or didn't say, or how you responded. Keep telling yourself it's not our fault.

But knowing there are people out there like that, rape deniers, I have a sense of the hostility. I've heard of it in this town, people coming forward and then backing down and saying it didn't happen. It is really frustrating; it is really hard. I was really lucky to be around educated, supportive people. Or I guess I was lucky to have only told the people I thought would handle it and make the best decisions. No one for a second ever doubted.

After reading this chapter, Riley made a simple but telling observation about both feminist and nonfeminist rape deniers. "They are all talking about sex and promiscuity," she said. But, she observed, "Rape is not about sex at all."

This isn't just bad sex. . . . How could anyone think that? It isn't even sex. Sex is consensual and rape is not. This isn't sex. Is it sex for the rapist? I don't think rapists know sex as sex. This is using sex as a weapon. Sex is absolutely a weapon.

# Danielle and Shae

Because many acquaintance rapes involve alcohol, do Riley's and Tracy's experiences adequately represent today's world of acquaintance rape? Surely such rapes aren't always so violent? Several readers of a draft of this book wondered if these young women's accounts weren't too sensational.

I think it is fair to say that predatory rapists use only as much force as necessary and undoubtedly prey on vulnerable people who can be easily subjugated and whose accounts are unlikely to be believed. Riley's and Tracy's experiences may represent only one kind of acquaintance rape scenario, but it is one that is rarely mentioned—even though research demonstrates that among college women, more have been affected by forcible rape than alcohol-facilitated rape (see chapter 8).

So what about cases involving alcohol? I wanted to interview an individual who did not want to engage in sexual intercourse but due to inebriation was unable to make her wishes known. Danielle and Shae told me of their experiences, a brave thing to do because of the degree of shame they felt about putting themselves in situations in which they could easily be taken advantage of. I was struck, however, by how their vulnerabilities enabled others to take advantage of them. And what Danielle and Shae had to say raised a serious issue: If we judge a rape case based on the actions of the complainant, then we condone attacks on defenseless individuals. Is this a result with which we are comfortable?

Danielle, from a small town in the Midwest, was a nineteen-year-old sophomore at a large state university thousands of miles from her home. Raised in the Catholic faith, Danielle did not intend to have sex with the high school sweetheart she planned to marry—or anyone else—until she walked down the church aisle.

But while she was at college, Danielle experienced low self-esteem and desperately wanted to fit in.

> If people said "Let's go party" at two o'clock in the morning when I had to be at work at seven in the morning, I was there, because I didn't want to seem to be a party pooper or anything else like that. So I started drinking. I had a ton of friends and everyone loved me, but I don't know if they loved me because I was fun to go drink with or whether I was fun in general. Because that is what we did in college.

She and her roommate met two older men, one of whom, Tom, Danielle had already kissed. But she told him she was still a virgin and planned to remain so. What she didn't understand at the time was the challenge this information presented to Tom. Danielle had been at about ten parties with Tom and his friend Dick. Dick had recently told Danielle she was "uptight" when she was sober and that she was only fun when she was drunk.

So before the party that night in their suite, wearing a jean skirt, a scoop-neck T-shirt, and flip-flops, Danielle drank some tequila shots with her roommate. At the get-together, Danielle said, the men organized a card game that she now believes was rigged against her. Each time, the loser had to drink a slug of vodka. As the perpetual loser, the slight-framed Danielle consumed about ten drinks of vodka. She remembered staggering to her bedroom, shutting the door, and lying down on her bed without taking off her clothes.

> The next thing I know, it's morning and the only thing I am wearing is my bra. My shirt was on the floor, the skirt

was under the bed, and my underwear was not on me. I was in a little bit of pain in my vaginal area. I didn't understand. I wasn't bleeding or anything. I was sore. I felt both dirty and sticky.

When she put her clothes on and went into the living room, Dick was there and asked, "Did you have fun last night?" He said, "Tom was in there and you were having fun." Danielle started crying, because she realized that something had obviously happened to her. She had a bruise between her legs: "I could have been violated by several people."

She called Tom. His first response was to say, "We had fun last night, we had fun, you were great." Danielle told him that she didn't remember anything, and she reminded him that she had wanted to save herself for marriage and that he knew that. Tom stuck with his story of consensual sex a little while longer. Then he apologized, saying he didn't mean to hurt her.

Danielle's roommate was unsympathetic, because she did not want trouble with her own boyfriend, who was there that night. "Get over it" was her advice. What was the big deal? But Danielle remained upset.

A week later, she had dinner with Dick's sister, who told Danielle that Tom and Dick were joking about how they had taken advantage of a girl while she was drunk.

> She said Tom was laughing, that the girl had passed out and he had sex with her anyway. At that point, I just lost it, and I started crying, and she says, "Was it you?" At that point, I realized that I wasn't present for it. I was passed out. That made me feel a little better. It still made me feel awful that someone could come into my room and have done something like that to me.

For two years, Danielle blamed herself.

> I thought, If I hadn't drunk so much, if I hadn't worn a skirt, if I hadn't been there, it wouldn't have happened to me. I became a recluse. I stopped drinking, I didn't go out. All my friends that I hung out with, they said, "What happened

to you?" Because all they wanted to do was drink, and I wasn't willing to do that, so they stopped calling me.

Danielle fell into a depression.

> Shortly after it happened, there was a switch in my personality, almost immediately. I used to be carefree, I used not to be afraid of anything. I wasn't afraid of heights, I wasn't afraid of dark hallways, I wasn't afraid of anything. After that, I was scared to go outside in the dark. I came home from work at eleven o'clock at night, I ran as fast as I could up the stairs to my apartment. I couldn't go on the balcony in my apartment house because I was scared that I would fall off. I couldn't drive over a bridge because I thought I would fall off. I still don't like to be in the dark. I don't like it when people come up behind me.

To remind herself not to let anything happen to her again, Danielle constantly wore the outfit she had on that night. Once she worked up the courage to tell her mother about it a year and a half later, her mother got her to a therapist. There Danielle learned she was punishing herself by wearing the clothes. Advised to confront Tom by writing him a letter and then burning it, Danielle composed a ten-page letter, which she then incinerated along with the clothing.

Danielle is now happily married, with a young son, but even today, more than six years later, she fears being by herself in the dark. She still has problems with people coming up behind her. "I still feel like I should get into my car as fast as possible because someone is going to come and hurt me."

> They stole my life. Even though I don't remember it. I used to have dreams and I imagined what happened. In the dreams I would be participating, and in some I was lying there and he was doing it and slapping my face and laughing. The dreams were always different.

Her roommate, not wanting any trouble with her own boyfriend, who had been in on the plot, kept saying, "At least you don't remember it."

My response to her at the time was, "He took me from me." I really feel like I changed a lot. My life changed completely. I question everything now and I'm scared of things.

And when Danielle told her fiancé over the telephone what happened, he was unable to handle it.

He was so disgusted by what I had to tell him, and he got off the phone with me really quickly. It was a lot for him to handle when I told him. He said, "Well, then you're not a virgin anymore." This was the point at which I realized that he was not the person I need around me. It was then that I realized that he was not going to be in my life. At the time, it was hurtful.

A year later, Danielle's roommate contacted her. She told Danielle she was now in a relationship with a man who had told her he was raped in the military.

She said, "I thought it was his fault. But then I realized it wasn't his fault. I hurt you, and I destroyed our friendship because I didn't believe you. I was just interested in my boyfriend."

I forgave her. I said, "Thank you, and all this time I had bad feelings towards you because you didn't believe me, and you didn't care, and you told me it was my fault." She thought I had had sex and I didn't want to remember it, and I was calling it rape. It was my fault because I caused tension in her relationship with her boyfriend. People don't want to believe the way life is. They don't want to believe it.

Danielle's account illustrates a premeditated attack on a vulnerable and naive young woman and the vengeful robbery of something that was valuable to her. Ask yourself, What kind of person aspires to have sex with a comatose young woman? And how do you label someone who deliberately gets a girl drunk in order to do so?

Riley knows what to call him.

> You have to have something wrong with you to think that
> she is lying there and not responding, and I am doing this
> to her. I think it is the same violation, manipulation, to get
> what you want.

The episode also demonstrates the lifelong effects of the attack, even when it is one Danielle can't remember.

> The feelings are still with me every day. It's amazing how
> one event that you don't even remember changes your
> life forever.

If Danielle resembles Riley in her preference for a serious relationship, then Shae more nearly resembles Tracy in her self-confidence and experience. But Shae too had a shock coming.

Shae was vulnerable in the sense that she was new to the small Southern town. After two years of methamphetamine addiction, she got clean and moved far from home to live with her grandparents and rebuild her life. She desperately needed and wanted a set of new friends, people who were not on drugs.

Over a period of weeks, Shae got to know some young men she had met at the local country-club swimming pool. Because one actually worked in antidrug enforcement, she figured they were not drug users. After being invited to a party at the house of one of the men, Shae decided to go. After all, it was her twenty-first birthday. Dressed in pants and a short-sleeved shirt, she drove out to the house in the country.

> I went to that party, and I drank one half of a drink, and the
> next thing I remember I woke up in a bed. I was deathly
> ill, like never before. I'd had hangovers before, but noth-
> ing like that. I was throwing up all afternoon.

Shae's pants were off, and her rear end hurt badly. She knew someone had entered it. Whoever it was had stolen the rings off her fingers and taken all the money from her wallet. The rings had both monetary and sentimental value.

Because she vomited continuously for three hours once she got home, Shae was certain the drink was doctored. And Shae thought it quite possible that more than one person was involved in the anal penetration. She blamed herself for putting herself in that situation.

> Not knowing these people, I shouldn't have been there.
> I was [living] with my grandparents, so part of the allure
> was that I could go there and party. I obviously can't do
> that at my grandpa's house. It was an escape.

Shae said she was ashamed and also afraid to come forward to report the rape. It was a small town, and she feared reprisal from some of the people in that crowd. After experiencing the depths of hell on methamphetamine, ironically she had an even more horrific experience once she got clean.

> That made me feel crazy, and kind of doubting myself. I
> had always been able to take care of myself.

And like a lot of young women today, Shae doesn't want to consider herself a victim, even though she knows she was.

> It made me feel violated. I don't want to let it ruin my life
> and I don't want to be a victim either. I know a lot of girls
> claim they were raped. Now that it has happened to me, I
> believe them more. There seems to be a consensus among
> people that women lie about it. Some people think they
> do it to get attention.

On that day five years ago, Shae learned something about evil in the world, and it has changed her.

> I'm still single. I have feelings like I am not good enough.
> Why is that? I really don't know. I don't know what makes
> me not good enough, but I feel that way.

Like Tracy, who felt like a broken vase, Shae has feelings of inferiority vis-à-vis men. She shies away from getting involved. Although admitting that the women in her family "have never really had good luck with men," Shae, like Riley, does want to be in a committed relationship.

> I want to be involved. I have to work this through. I know
> men are attracted to me. I'm not attracted back to them.
> That is starting to worry me a little bit.

Shae's life has been torn asunder by an event of which she has no memory. One can only imagine what it is like when someone who has been raped remembers the details of the ordeal. Danielle and Shae, like Riley and Tracy, now have an awareness of their own vulnerability, which makes it difficult for them to proceed through life. Their world has been split open; knowledge of the dangers makes it difficult for them to trust people. The incidents effectively detached them from others.

Both Danielle's and Shae's experiences illustrate the many ways that women reporting rape are mistrusted. For reasons of her own, Danielle's roommate chose not to believe her. Until her own assault, Shae admitted, she thought many young women were lying about rape.

# [ 5 ]

# Is There a Rape "Epidemic"?

Despite attempts to discredit or distort the data, the fact is there can be no possibility of disagreement about rape prevalence in the United States. Assertions to the contrary are either uninformed or deliberately calculated to shake public confidence in social-science research and rape researchers in particular. So what do recent, methodologically sound research studies tell us about the prevalence of rape in America?

Rape-prevalence researchers can ask about a broad range of sexual abuse, including unwanted touching or alcohol-facilitated rape, as well as attempted rapes. They also can inquire about rape during the last twelve months or within the subject's lifetime. Lifetime prevalence captures childhood rape, often overlooked by rape deniers. By now, however, most researchers have learned to use consistent definitions and ask about rape, attempted rape, and other kinds of non–physically forced or threatened penetrations through the use of drugs, alcohol, or psychological coercion, *and report them separately.* Finally, most of the surveys ask about specific behaviors and occurrences, but they do not rely on the respondents to label them as rape.

To ascertain a lifetime rape prevalence across all recent studies, I will use a conservative definition of rape about which there can be no argument. Looking at rape as any forcible penetration (vaginal, anal, or oral penetration) within one's lifetime provides a definition that is narrow and makes a good starting point. This does not suggest that there are not other legal definitions of rape, including statutory rape, that vary from state to state or other kinds of sexual assault measured by research studies, including rapes of alcohol-impaired individuals when force is not necessary. But this most-conservative description of rape provides a uniform definition that matches most of the public's perception.

Two studies undertaken by Dean Kilpatrick and colleagues at the Medical University of South Carolina, one published in 1992 and the other in 2007, provide important rape-prevalence data. Because of the similar methodology employed, Kilpatrick is able to determine whether lifetime rape prevalence has increased or decreased over a period of seventeen years. In the first study, Kilpatrick interviewed 4,008 US women eighteen years of age and older over the telephone using random-digit-dial methodology. Prevalence of lifetime experience of rape, conservatively defined as forcible penetration, was 13 percent (12.1 million women), with 0.7 percent of the women (683,000 women) experiencing a forcible rape within the last year of the study. Only 16 percent stated they had notified law-enforcement officials.

In the 2007 survey, which involved 3,001 women older than eighteen years of age sampled from US households using random-digit-dial methodology, 16.1 percent of the women reported a lifetime experience of forcible rape. This percentage equals *approximately 18 million women* (in the year prior to the survey, nationally 0.74 percent, or 829,000 women, would have been raped) for a 27.3 percent growth rate during this time. Eighteen percent said they had reported the incident to the police.

Some believe that many individuals prefer not to reveal their victimization (especially over the telephone); thus all this research may represent an undercount. Furthermore, many people who are at high risk of rape do not have or cannot be reached by telephone, including homeless men and women and those in jails, prisons, drug treatment facilities, or mental health institutions.

In 2010, the CDC, with support from the US Department of Justice and Department of Defense, launched the National Intimate Partner and Sexual Violence Survey. The organization administered the survey from January through December 2010. A whopping 16,507 interviews were conducted over the telephone in fifty states and the District of Columbia. When asked about completed forcible penetration within their lifetime, 12.3 percent of the women responded in the affirmative, translating into 14,617,000 women. One percent, or about 1,581,000 men, also responded positively. Of these, 620,000 women (0.5 percent) said they experienced a forcible rape within the last twelve months. And the large majority of females who reported having been raped knew the perpetrators; only 14 percent of women said the rape was committed by someone who was a stranger to them. Again, these prevalence data are likely to represent an undercount, because the survey did not include individuals under the age of eighteen, nor did it include those who are homeless or in hospitals, nursing homes, jails, prisons, or residential treatment programs.

Unfortunately, however, in its press release—and hence in newspaper articles in major publications where the release was cited—the CDC chose to highlight a different finding. In addition to asking about forcible penetration, surveyors inquired about rapes when the individual was drunk, drugged, or passed out and thus unable to consent. These findings were broken out separately from the forcible-rape statistics. But when amalgamated, the prevalence was 18.3 percent, which, curiously, in its press release, the CDC rounded up to 20 percent.

The CDC's combining the figures resurrected the usual arguments about alcohol-related rape and a definition of rape that appeared to be expanded, although in truth it closely resembles many state laws' definitions of rape. Christina Hoff Sommers was there, in the *Washington Post*, to challenge the study and demand its recall on these grounds. Totally overlooking the startling fourteen and a half million women who said they had suffered forcible rape in their lifetimes, Sommers questioned labeling inebriated sex as rape and in the process called the entire report into question. At the same time, she made the common mistake of confusing annual and lifetime rates, comparing the *lifetime* rate with 84,767 rapes reported to law enforcement authorities in 2010 and 188,380 rapes in the National Crime Victimization Survey for that year.

Sommers labeled this major study as another example of "careless advocacy research." Instead, it is a lesson in careless and confusing written presentation of solid research results playing into the hands of rape deniers.

Two other studies, one from 1995 to 1996 and another survey administered between 2001 and 2003, found lifetime rates of 14.8 percent and 10.6 percent respectively. Taken together, these five major studies find lifetime prevalence of completed forcible penetration in a range between 10.6 percent and 16 percent of American women.

| Table 1. Forcible penetration of women, lifetime | | |
|---|---|---|
| Kilpatrick (1992) | 13% | 12.1 million women |
| Tjaden and Thoennes (1995–1996) | 14.8% | 17.7 million women |
| Basile (2001–2003) | 10.6% | 11.7 million women |
| Kilpatrick (2007) | 16.1% | 18 million women |
| CDC (2010) | 12.3% | 14.6 million women |

| Table 2. Forcible penetration of women, within last 12 months | | |
|---|---|---|
| Kilpatrick (1992) | 0.7% | 683,000 women |
| Tjaden and Thoennes (1995–1996) | 0.3% | 302,091 women |
| Kilpatrick (2007) | 0.74% | 829,000 women |
| CDC (2010) | 0.5% | 620,000 women |

Although four important, methodologically sound rape-prevalence studies had been completed before the Centers for Disease Control's 2010 effort, news stories made no mention of them. In fact, a spokesperson for the CDC even stated, "I don't think we've really known that it was this prevalent in the population." This lack of awareness of rape-prevalence studies is amazing and troubling. Researchers and the federal government, which sponsors a great deal of the research, likely share much of the blame. Members of the media do, too; they have had a decided lack of curiosity about existing rape-prevalence research, which has helped the cause of rape deniers.

## Rape on College Campuses

Interpreting campus-rape research, which is most often the focus of media and public attention, requires caution because of the different time frames used. Researchers often seek to ascertain lifetime rape prevalence among students, measuring (1) rape prior to college attendance as well as that during college up to the time of the survey, (2) rape occurrences within the current or last school year, or (3) both. It is important to remember that researchers survey a sample of college women who were enrolled at the time, regardless of what year they are in; freshmen, however, may be more vulnerable and more prone to attacks from rapists than college students in other years. For this reason, taking the annual rate and multiplying by four or five does not produce a reliable figure for rape over the course of college careers. Only longitudinal research following the same cohort of students during the four- or five-year college-attendance period can determine a prevalence figure during a student's college years.

One CNN story reported that one in five college women will be raped or experience an attempted rape before graduation, and the *Chronicle of Higher Education* stated "studies estimate that as many as one in four college women is a victim of rape or attempted rape." These frequently cited figures may be traced to this highly speculative computation that multiplies established annual rates by four or five. They may also derive from Mary Koss's 20 percent figure, but that was a *lifetime* prevalence rate from age fourteen, not a campus-rape rate.

In interviews with two thousand college women selected from a representative national list of women attending four-year colleges and universities in 2006, Dean Kilpatrick and colleagues found a lifetime forcible-rape rate of 8.7 percent and an annual rate of 3.23 percent. Only about 12 percent of the college women had reported the rape to police authorities. Before that, in 2000, Bonnie Fisher and her colleagues assembled a larger sample—4,446 enrolled in two- and four-year colleges and universities. Almost 3 percent said they experienced a rape or attempted rape since the school year began (an average of seven months). Researchers then estimated that 5 percent would be victims of completed or attempted forcible sexual penetration over a one-year period while attending college. A startlingly small number—5 percent—had told law enforcement authorities about the rape.

In 2007, a college study interviewing 5,466 college women found that 3.4 percent said they had been subjected to forcible rape since entering college. Research involving younger participants has discovered even higher percentages; the Centers for Disease Control's 2009 Youth Risk Behavior Surveillance study, involving 16,460 questionnaires completed in 158 schools in grades nine through twelve, concluded that 10.5 percent of females and 4.5 percent of male students had ever been sexually penetrated against their will.

## Alcohol-Facilitated Rape

Many rape deniers believe that the majority of acquaintance rape cases involve alcohol use by either or both parties. Kilpatrick's latest research does not entirely corroborate this assertion. His study asked about unwanted sexual penetration occurring when the victim was drugged, drunk, or passed out. He inquired about it in two different situations: when the woman voluntarily used the drugs and alcohol, and when her acquaintance gave her the drugs without her permission or deliberately tried to get her drunk. These findings were kept separate from those of forcible rape.

Not surprisingly, women in the college group were more often involved in alcohol- and drug-related lifetime rape compared to the general population sample, and voluntary (rather than deliberately induced) intoxication was significantly more common in the college cohort. More lifetime forcible rape than alcohol- or drug-facilitated rape occurred in the general population sample (14.6 percent compared to 6.4 percent).

Important, however, is the following: in the college sample, forcible rape occurred more frequently than drug- or alcohol-facilitated rape; 6.4 percent were ever affected by alcohol-facilitated rape, while 8.7 percent were forcibly raped in their lifetimes. The CDC's study also asked about instances when a woman was penetrated while under the influence of alcohol or drugs and unable to give consent. As in Kilpatrick's study, these data were removed from forcible penetration and reported separately. Eight percent, or 9,524,000 women in their lifetime, reported affirmatively, and 0.7 percent, or 781,000, said they experienced this type of sexual penetration within the last twelve months.

## The Rapists

Research confirms that most rapes are performed by individuals known to the victims. In Kilpatrick's general population sample in 2006, corroborated by the CDC study, only 11 percent of the rapes were at the hands of strangers; 14 percent were boyfriends, 10 percent husbands and ex-husbands, 12 percent friends, 11 percent stepfathers, and 18 percent other relatives. An important study ten years earlier found that only 16.7 percent of all women and girls who reported rape to researchers were raped by a stranger; 24 percent of the assailants were spouses, cohabiting partners, or ex-spouses; 4.3 percent a current or former cohabiting partner; and 21.5 percent a current or former date, boyfriend, or girlfriend.

The relatively high prevalence rate for spousal or marital rape is largely unrecognized in discussions of acquaintance rape. Just how marital rape affects children is an issue that has also received inadequate attention. One study, for example, found that 5 percent of the women in the sample said their partners had forced their children to participate in the rape, and 18 percent reported their children had witnessed an incident of marital rape at least once.

Two research studies lead to interesting speculation that some men may be repeat predators who employ specific strategies to prey on victims. Lisak and Miller surveyed almost two thousand students at a mid-sized urban commuter university between 1991 and 1998, asking them whether they had ever tried or succeeded in having sexual intercourse with someone against his or her will. Although the results certainly are an undercount (many may not be willing to admit rape to researchers), 4 percent of the sample, or 120 young men, self-identified. Of these, 63.3 percent (76 individuals) reported committing repeat rapes, for a total of 483 rapes, an average of six each. Only forty-four young men had committed just one rape. How is it, the researchers ask, that these men have escaped prosecution?

The answers may lie, in part, in their choice of victim and in their relative abnegation of gratuitous violence. By attacking women within their social networks—so-called acquaintances—and by refraining from the kind of violence likely to produce physical injuries, these young men create "cases" that women are least likely to report and that prosecutors are less likely to prosecute.

Stephanie McWhorter and colleagues obtained similar results in longitudinal research with 1,146 men processed into the navy in 1996–1997. Thirteen percent said they had perpetrated at least one rape between their fourteenth birthday and the end of their first year of military service. Twenty-nine percent were involved in only one incident, while 71 percent perpetrated two or more, with an average of over six. Of the 865 total lifetime rapes reported, repeat predators committed 95 percent of them. As in Lisak and Miller's study, respondents reported using substances (83 percent) more frequently than force, and 92 percent knew their victims. Interestingly, most reported using only one method, suggesting that they specialized in both techniques and targets.

## The National Crime Victimization Survey

One commonly cited source of information on rape prevalence is the National Crime Victimization Survey (NCVS), which is conducted annually via telephone by the US Census Bureau for the Department of Justice. In 2007, it had a national sample of 41,500 households. Surveyors ask all persons in the household twelve years of age and older (thus not capturing sexual attacks on younger children) about crimes they have experienced during the preceding six months and whether they reported them to a law-enforcement agency. Once a sample household is selected, it remains part of the survey for three years, and household members are interviewed a total of seven times at six-month intervals. New sample members are rotated in, and because respondents report more victimizations during the first-time surveys (they tend to recall events as taking place more recently than when they actually occurred), researchers do not include the first-time interview in the yearly crime estimates.

Since the NCVS began gathering annual data in 1972, determining long-term US rape trends should be possible. However, the NCVS did not specifically ask about the crime of rape prior to 1993, so that earlier rape estimates were based only on those participants who volunteered the information. The 1993 redesigned survey added this question: "Incidents involving forced or unwanted sexual acts are often difficult to talk about. Have you been forced or coerced to engage in unwanted sexual activity by someone you didn't know before? A casual acquaintance? Some one you know well?" After the introduction of this question, NCVS analyst Michael Rand wrote, rape-prevalence rates more than doubled, causing him to caution that data collected after the redesign were not comparable to that collected prior to 1992.

Rape researchers, however, have consistently attacked the current NCVS methodology because it does not query participants about behaviorally specific occurrences. One researcher undertook studies with two different samples of college women, one employing the revised NCVS methodology and the other using a detailed series of twelve behaviorally specific sexual victimization questions. Prevalence estimates were ten times higher when the twelve-question scale was employed, leading many researchers to agree that NCVS methodology dramatically underestimates the number of rapes. Examining trends even within this limited NCVS methodology could be helpful but in the end is not, because the low number of cases reported to researchers affects the usefulness of the data.

For 2009, for example, the Bureau of Justice Statistics found a 38.7 percent decrease in rape prevalence over 2008, and in 2010 it reported an increase of almost 50 percent. However, the Bureau cautions that rapes always represent a small number of cases reported; for 2008, fifty-six cases were disclosed to researchers, with thirty-six in 2009 and fifty-seven in 2010. As a result, small absolute changes can result in large year-to-year percentage change estimates. Because of the small number of cases reported to the survey, the Bureau urges caution in making too much of these year-to-year fluctuations.

Changes made in 2006 and 2007 may also have affected rape-prevalence rates, making recent comparisons problematic. In 2006, the sample was adjusted to account for shifts in population and locations of households, and in 2007 budget cuts necessitated a 14 percent reduction in sample size. To offset the smaller sample, in July 2007, interviews with first-time households were included in the production of survey estimates, producing a small increase in rape prevalence. For these reasons, although overall violent crime has decreased about 4 percent a year between 2001 and 2009, changes in rape occurrence cannot be measured with any confidence using the NCVS data.

In his book *The Better Angels of Our Nature*, Harvard psychologist Steven Pinker put forth the idea that over time violence of all kinds has decreased on earth. When addressing the issue of rape, he declared that it has declined by more than 80 percent. For this proposition, he relied on NCVS data, unaware of the fact that the small number of cases reported each year to NCVS surveyors makes fluctuations and trends impossible to statistically measure with any confidence.

## Confusion About the Uniform Crime Reports

To demonstrate low and declining rape prevalence, rape deniers often rely on the Uniform Crime Reports (UCR), which the Federal Bureau of Investigation (FBI) issues annually, but these data capture only those crimes reported to the nation's police departments. Research demonstrates that most crime victims in the United States do *not* inform police. According to the National Crime Victimization Survey, only 49 percent of all violent victimizations and 37 percent of all property crimes experienced by the sample in 2011 were reported to law enforcement. As for rape, in 2011 only 27 percent of interviewees who had been raped had told police about their attacks. Other research studies have found even lower reporting rates—between 5 and 20 percent—for rapes in their samples.

Consistent reasons for failure to inform police of rape surface in research studies. The majority of those who do not report being raped say they do not want family or others to know about the incident, they lack proof, or they fear reprisal from the assailant. Other explanations advanced include fear of bad treatment from the police, ignorance about how to report, and "not [being] sure [it] was serious enough."

Several other issues affect the utility of UCR data. The UCR uses a definition of forcible rape that excludes certain forms of assault. These include assaults involving anal penetration and penetration with a finger or foreign object, of children under the age of twelve, against males, by blood relatives, and of minors, among others. For this reason, crimes meeting the definition of forcible rape in the UCR may represent only a minority of the rape reports that law-enforcement agencies typically receive. In January 2012, the FBI announced revisions to the definition of forcible rape to include vaginal or anal penetration of a person with any body part or object without that person's consent and included male victims for the first time.

Furthermore, an investigation by the *Philadelphia Inquirer* in 2000 found that in an effort to build an impressive arrest record for rape, the police department hid difficult cases and did not report on them. In another inquiry in 2004, the *St. Louis Post-Dispatch* found its police department similarly failing to record rape complaints, which were maintained on paper, not the computer, and were later shredded. Another practice was to downgrade the crime of rape to a lesser battery. To make matters even more complicated, the FBI allows police departments to remove reports that are "unfounded" (false or baseless), meaning that the numbers reported are not even the sum total of cases coming into police departments.

Between 2000 and 2007, the FBI reported that rape cases known to the police fluctuated between 90,000 and a high of 95,000 with no discernable pattern. Beginning in 2008, the number declined slightly, with, however, a larger decrease between 2009 and 2011. But as these are declines in rapes reported to the police, and represent only some of the rape cases coming to the attention of police departments, the decrease cannot really be considered to be a reduction in rape prevalence.

The Wikipedia entry on rape statistics discusses rape prevalence in the United States; using only NCVS data, it fails to mention a single rape-prevalence study mentioned in this chapter. The invisibility of these methodologically sound and consistent research reports remains baffling. And although no specific examples are provided, the article goes on to perpetuate the idea that rape statistics are unreliable:

> Inconsistent definitions of rape, over reporting, under reporting, and false reporting create controversial statistical disparities, and lead to accusations that many rape statistics are unreliable or misleading. According to *USA Today* reporter Kevin Johnson "no other major category of crime—not murder, assault or robbery—has generated a more serious challenge of the credibility of national crime statistics" than rape.

Using similar and unambiguous definitions of forcible rape, recent research *has*, contrary to Wikipedia assertions, produced consistent lifetime rape-prevalence figures within a range of 11 to 16 percent, amounting to 18 million US women at the upper range. But whether this is a rape "epidemic" is open to argument.

## A Rape "Epidemic"?

Certainly, rape deniers are reacting to exaggerated claims from some anti-rape activists who have ratcheted up rape prevalence, either from ignorance or in their eagerness to underscore their position that rape is serious and worthy of more attention. Inflating rape statistics has played into the hands of rape deniers. What one frequently finds is the erroneous claim that one in three or one in four women will be rape victims in their lifetime, when, as we have seen, the prevalence figure is no more than 16 percent, or one in six.

A second common mistake in citing rape-prevalence research is confusion about lifetime rates. Thus, on college campuses, the assertion is all too often made that one in four or one in five will be raped *during their time in college*. In her graduation speech in 2009, the class valedictorian at the University of California, Berkeley, stated, "Even here, this university, one in three women will be sexually assaulted by someone else at this university." One poster seen on the campus of Northern Kentucky University in 2008 mangled statistics even further by declaring, THINK OF THREE OF YOUR BEST FRIENDS. ONE OF THEM WILL BE RAPED *THIS YEAR* [italics added].

Feminists appearing on television or radio often cite erroneous statistics. One prominent feminist attorney repeated the one-in-three statistic on the *Donohue* program in 2003. A feminist website in 2008 stated that one in three women who join the US military will be sexually assaulted or raped by men in the military, a wild overstatement. This statistic was then approvingly quoted in one organization's Memorial Day e-newsletter, which reached 9,500 people. In testimony before a House panel, a congresswoman declared, "We have an epidemic here."

Indeed, use of the term "epidemic" is frequent in materials from rape-crisis providers. And a former president of the American Medical Association has said, "Sexual assault is a 'silent-violent epidemic' growing at an alarming rate and traumatizing the women and children of our nation."

Although use of the term "epidemic" properly emphasizes the fact that rape is a public health issue in the United States, the medical comparison sounds an alarm that the statistics may not warrant. An "epidemic" indicates the *rapid* spread of an infection to a large number of individuals in a *short* period of time. Repetition of the term "epidemic" unnecessarily opens rape advocates to charges of exaggeration and duplicity. One can readily agree with Christina Hoff Sommers, who said in a 2009 lecture, "The plight of women is not improved by sexual politics and exaggeration—no matter how well intentioned. Misrepresentation almost always clouds the true causes of suffering and provides obstacles to genuine ways of preventing it. Truth is on the side of compassion."

It was easy for the *False Rape Society* blog (which later became *Community of the Wrongly Accused*) to spoof the wildly erroneous allegations made by one college campus anti-rape program that one in four women on campus (or roughly 3,000 female students) would be rape victims during their four years at the school. The blog concluded, "To put the degree of exaggeration into perspective, the claim made by CARE is the arithmetric equivalent of claiming that 900,000 people died in the terrorist attacks of Sept. 11 and the moral equivalent of using that statistic as a bludgeon to justify the global war on terror."

Now and then, a report surfaces indicating that statistics *have* been inflated for funding purposes. In 2009, for example, the University of California, Davis, revealed that for at least three years almost 200 percent more rapes on campus than actually occurred were reported to the federal government. The duplicity was discovered while the former director of the campus violence-prevention program was on medical leave. A federal grant application had also greatly exaggerated the number of rapes.

Rape-crisis providers and campus sexual-assault programs may repeat erroneous figures out of ignorance. Or does the failure of many groups to properly cite recent data reflect the fact that they have rejected them because the figures are lower than what they might like? Anti-rape advocates should realize that 18 million women raped in their lifetimes is not a small number.

Science journalist Michael Specter has written, "We must learn to accept data that has [*sic*] been properly judged and verified—no matter what it says, or how much we might have wished that it pointed in another direction." This statement could apply to rape deniers as well as rape-crisis advocates. Aptly, writer Barbara Ehrenreich asked in her book *Bright-Sided*, "How can we expect to improve our situation without addressing the actual circumstances we find ourselves in?"

Facts about rape prevalence confirm what we know to be the truth: most women's experiences when socializing with men are positive, which explains the shock experienced by young women like Riley and Tracy when they are not.

# Megan

Megan was a student at the university at which I work. One day, she revealed to me a traumatizing incident that occurred when she was a freshman at a small and prestigious liberal arts college. As horrific as it was, for Megan the aftermath was much worse: she found her experience greeted with indifference. Later, she felt that she was not believed, and eventually she was punished by the college and members of the student body.

In her second month at the college, the five-feet-four-inch-tall Megan found herself with few friends and regretted her social awkwardness, which made meeting people difficult.

> I chose the college, ironically enough, because I thought that it being a very small college it would have a really nice sense of community and we would all get to know each other. I had some utopian ideal in my head. I had previously met one of my few friends at a party. I am not really a party person. I am kind of socially awkward to be perfectly honest. I decided that I should get out and try to meet people more, so I went to another party that this friend had invited me to. When I got there, he was not there. I kind of was standing around, extremely awkward. I didn't drink at the time, so that was also awkward

97

because everybody else was. It was very loud, and I felt very stupid being there. I wasn't meeting anybody, everybody was drinking, and it was too loud to even talk.

Megan described what came next: a basketball player with a very strong athletic build approached her.

He asked whether I was a freshman, where I was from, small talk. I was so happy to have somebody just give me an excuse to act like I was a semisocial being. And he said, "It is really loud in here. I have a bunch of friends upstairs. Do you want to go up and just hang out?" I said sure, because I totally didn't want to be at that party. I had no intention of hooking up with this guy at all; I just wanted to get out of the party and meet some people.

Megan went with him to the third floor of the building. Her escort said he had to go to the bathroom. Megan was peeking into a lounge on the floor when, she said, he came up behind her and pulled her into one of the restroom's stalls.

Pinning her down, with her head wedged two inches from the toilet seat, he first forced her to suck his penis. Then he pulled her pants down and penetrated her vaginally. Megan resisted and made it clear that she wanted to escape.

"Do you feel these arms? Do you think you are going to get away?" was his response. There could be no confusion about her lack of consent. "In fact," said Megan when I interviewed her, "this wasn't about sex. I wasn't thinking of this as sex."

Megan now understands why, in her words, colleges are such breeding grounds for predatory rapists. As a newly arrived freshman, she had few friends, and her neediness and vulnerability were probably obvious. She distinctly remembers the basketball player asking her if she was a freshman.

Eventually Megan found her way to the building in which she lived. She was in shock. Later she would be diagnosed with posttraumatic stress disorder and have trouble sleeping. The self-blame began.

It made me play the "what if" game. What if I hadn't gone
to the party? What if I hadn't gone upstairs with him? What
if I wasn't so socially awkward? What if I wasn't so stupid
and naive? None of these things would have happened.

Megan said she later started to play the "I wish" game. At times she
actually wanted to be assaulted again, just so she would have another
opportunity to "get it right"—to fight back more vigorously, to "act more
like a real victim is supposed to act."

I wish I were a stronger person, I wish I were a different
person. That he had just killed me. Then I wouldn't have
to feel anymore. Then people would believe me.

Although she didn't know it then, Megan's punishment was just
beginning.

# [6]

# The Truth About False Rape Claims

Authorities were investigating a reported rape of a student on the University of California, San Diego, campus, explained the local newspaper. Sixteen days before, the coed said she was pushed to the ground by an Asian male, who stood five feet nine to six feet one, and sexually penetrated. But the responses on the newspaper's blog were interesting.

"An Asian? That tall? Took *two* weeks to report? Very suspicious. Very suspicious. My BS meter just pegged. Based on this news item, her story is a stunning economy with the truth. Another lacrosse team scam in the making?"

"It's time to stop believing women outright, without iron clad, copper bottom evidence. Women reports rape because man dumped her."

By late afternoon, a user named FalseRapeArchivist had logged on, declaring that every serious research study has found a 50 percent rate of false rape reports. He referred readers to his website, falserapesociety .com (later named *Community of the Wrongly Accused*), where readers could find example after example of rape charges withdrawn or dropped, as well as links to every article ever written about the problem of false rape claims from the point of view of the wrongly accused.

The presence of FalseRapeArchivist on the San Diego newspaper's site demonstrated the degree of organization of rape deniers; presumably Google Alerts allow rape deniers like FalseRapeArchivist to easily follow up by inserting their claims on news blogs throughout the country.

These particular rape deniers claim that 50 percent of rape claims are false. For this proposition, they cite a 1994 research report by Purdue University professor Eugene J. Kanin, and they make no reference to *seven* newer studies with better methodology that show false rape reports to be in the range of 2–8 percent. This false-rape-claims campaign has been successful in persuading the media that a new social problem exists: lying about rape.

After the 2006 Duke lacrosse case, the campaign gained strength, no doubt encouraging college authorities, police, prosecutors, judges, and juries to look upon acquaintance rape claims with suspicion. In 2011, rape charges against celebrities like Dominique Strauss-Kahn resulted in unprecedented attacks against the women who reported being raped by him.

As with rape-prevalence studies, rape deniers seek to sow confusion about false-rape-claims research, alleging that disagreement about the prevalence of false rape claims exists. In a letter to the editor challenging an article I had written on this subject, Christina Hoff Sommers wrote, "Reasonable and well-intentioned scholars, criminologists, and journalists can and do disagree on rates and incidence of false accusations." Despite this assertion, findings from recent false claims research strongly support the conclusion that there are in fact no grounds for legitimate disagreement about the prevalence of false claims.

## Assertions of False-Rape-Claims Activists

In discussing false-rape-claims research, it is important to be clear about definitions. A false report is one in which, based on thorough investigation, it can be demonstrated that the rape did not occur. For example, a woman claims to have been raped at a certain location, and the evidence conclusively proves she was in another city at the time.

A rape report cannot be considered to be false if the person describing the crime is unable to provide corroboration that it happened or if investigators decide, based on their judgment of the evidence, that it did not occur. According to the FBI's Uniform Crime Reports Handbook, this is an inconclusive or unsubstantiated report, not a false one.

So far, this definition sounds clear cut. If rape deniers are saying that over half of rape reports are inconclusive or difficult to substantiate, that would be one thing. But they are not. They are declaring that in half the cases, the individuals are lying outright to police.

False-rape-claims activists, like rape-prevalence deniers, mention only one researcher. At first blush, Eugene J. Kanin's 1994 research report, on which rape deniers rely, is intriguing, because the police department whose records he reviewed prevented a report from being labeled false unless the complainant admitted that no rape had occurred—that is, the victim had to recant. However, in this jurisdiction, the investigation of all rape complaints always involved a serious offer to polygraph the complainants and suspects. This practice has now been widely rejected by law enforcement because of its adverse impact on those who report they've been raped. Many of them will recant when faced with apparent skepticism from the investigator and the intimidating prospect of having to take a polygraph examination.

Kanin himself cautioned about the validity of the recantations: "Rape recantations could be the result of the complainants' desire to avoid a 'second assault' at the hands of the police." Based on concerns about the applicability of his sample, he explained the need for further research. With the polygraphing, he wrote, this could be a small police agency that "seriously pursues to closure all rape complaints," obtaining a high number of recantations and continuing with the rest.

In a sample of 109 rape reports made over nine years in this Midwestern jurisdiction, Kanin found that the police determined that 41 percent were false. Professor David Lisak, however, reminds us that Kanin undertook no independent research in the police files. He merely accepted and repeated the police officers' characterization of the cases, preventing his study from being classified as social-science research:

Nor does Kanin describe any effort made, systematic or otherwise, to obtain independent information about the cases. All of his data are furnished to him by the police officers. Thus, Kanin's "Method" section simply reiterates the opinions of the police officers who concluded that the cases in question were false allegations. . . . This violates a cardinal rule of science, a rule designed to ensure that observations are not simply the reflection of the bias of the observer.

And in a one-paragraph addendum, Kanin reported on his review of the police records of two large Midwestern universities. In a small sample of sixty-four cases over a three-year period, he found a 50 percent rate of false forcible-rape complaints. Polygraphing was not an issue here, but no complaint was marked false without a recantation. Again, it does not appear that Kanin undertook any independent research. He relied solely upon the police categorization of the rapes, which was not necessarily based on evidence or investigation.

The Duke lacrosse rape case renewed interest in the false-rape-claims issue. As is now well known, in March 2006 members of the Duke University lacrosse team held an off-campus party during which alcohol was served and two strippers performed. One of the entertainers, a low-income African American woman, reported that three of the players raped her during the party. Although two different DNA tests found no positive matches with lacrosse team players, they did reveal the DNA of four unidentified men on the rectal swabs and undergarments taken from the young woman. Still, the prosecutor proceeded to charge members of the team and even withheld the evidence of the DNA from defense lawyers. Later, the accuser modified some of her account. All charges were ultimately dismissed, with the unusual statement that the accused young men were innocent. For his actions in the case, the prosecutor was disbarred.

A veritable cottage industry of false-rape-claims books, articles, and blogs ensued. For these advocates, citing Kanin's research, which confirmed their contentions, was the end point; apparently no further search was made for more recent false-claims information. One such false claims activist is journalist Stuart Taylor, who in numerous columns and articles waged a war against the actions of the Duke case prosecutor. In 2007, he and coauthor KC Johnson turned these articles into a book on the case. After presenting the facts of the Duke episode in several hundred pages, the authors concluded that the case is emblematic of what is going on in the world of rape prosecutions: "But the changes have gone too far, driven by radical feminists' wild exaggerations of the extent of male sexual predation and female victimization and their empirically untenable view that women never (or hardly ever) lie about rape."

To prove their assertion, the authors cited several pages of proof, purporting to demonstrate that false rape claims are in the neighborhood of 50 percent. The weakness of the evidence proffered for this assertion went unnoticed in reviews in major publications.

Although the authors quoted from a few prosecutors around the country, their 50 percent contention rested on three major sources. First was a statement from former Manhattan sex-crimes prosecutor Linda Fairstein in a 2003 *Cosmopolitan* magazine article, in which she purportedly wrote that of four thousand reports of rape each year in Manhattan, about half simply did not happen. A perusal of that article finds no such quote. Ms. Fairstein herself referred me to the KC Johnson website that confesses to the error; the authors had taken the reference from someone else's website without consulting the original piece.

Eugene J. Kanin's article from 1994 was the second source. Finally, the authors cited a Department of Defense report, which found that over 70 percent of those enrollees surveyed thought that fraudulent rape complaints were perceived as a problem at the three service academies. Participants, however, were not asked their own opinion in the matter but whether they thought that their classmates considered false reporting to be an issue. Obviously, in no way does this study present data about the true extent of false reporting at the academies.

From his vantage point at Brooklyn College in New York City, KC Johnson continues to maintain his blog, publishing information about the case as well as developments in local government and at Duke University. It is all part of his campaign against false rape claims.

A number of false-rape-claims sites on the Internet convey nearly identical messages, including the sites of RADAR (Respecting Accuracy in Domestic Abuse Reporting), the Community of the Wrongly Accused (formerly the False Rape Society), the Center for Military Readiness, and Glenn Sacks. All of these sites link to one another. The blog of the Community of the Wrongly Accused provides daily updates about recanted and dismissed rape cases throughout the world. Relying on Eugene J. Kanin, these websites firmly espouse as fact that the majority (more than 50 percent) of rape claims are false. They also argue that, with these false charges, women destroy the lives and reputations of innocent men while facing no repercussions themselves.

Two sacred texts are featured at these websites. One is by freelancer Cathy Young, who often speaks on false rape claims under the aegis of the Federalist Society. Wendy McElroy's 2006 piece is also cited approvingly, although she admits that Kanin's study seems unbelievable: "I would need to see more studies with different populations before accepting the figure of 50 percent; to me, the figure seems high." That does not, however, prevent her from concluding, "False accusations are not rare. They are common."

The statements on these websites represent a worldview that is diametrically opposite to that of rape-victim advocates. The latter often believe the problem is that no one believes or gives credibility to women and girls making rape accusations, but false-rape-claims activists assert that the presumption in society is disbelief of the men: "In today's politically correct world, men accused of rape often face a de facto presumption of guilt that is hard to dispel no matter how strong the evidence of innocence." And another wrote, "When it comes to rape, one gender is incapable of telling a lie while the other is incapable of telling anything *but* lies."

Inflammatory reader responses at these blogs demonstrate a deep distrust of women: "The problem here gentlemen, is that you cannot reason with an animal. Women are animals in a constant state of survival. Animals are selfish, and as such become destructive to others around them." "I also agree with Steve 'women are animals' but I would go 1 step further, they are lying scheming devils with out 1 shred of moral decency, and have no capacity for love or compassion . . . they only ever do things out of self interest, especially in the area of sex which makes [*sic*] ALL WOMAN are whores as well . . . men need to wake up."

Perhaps the most strident false claims advocate is blogger Angry Harry, who believes that "women are encouraged daily by the media to make allegations of abuse." The purpose of their false claims, he has written, is to demonize men, "to hurt them, to discriminate against them, to push them through outrageously unjust legal processes which have been corrupted through and through, and to make it possible for women to destroy their lives completely for no other reason than they wish to."

Harry has his own statistics on false rape claims. Some 5 percent of women have borderline personality disorder or something close to it, he asserted, features of which allegedly include the habitual making of false accusations. "And given that some 1 *million* women in the UK and 5 *million* women in the USA have this condition," Harry wrote, "the various allegations of 'abuse' that are made every year—sex assault, domestic violence etc.—are undoubtedly *mostly* the result of these women attempting to portray themselves as victim." Next, Harry added all the women suffering from PMS every month—"I imagine that these sorts of things account for most of the rape allegations that are made"—concluding that the vast majority of rape allegations are false and most of the real rapes go unreported.

It is foolish to suggest that no woman has ever lied about a rape claim, but to make assertions such as these puts Angry Harry in the crank category. But as journalist Charles P. Pierce has written, "Anything can be true if someone says it loudly enough."

In her book *The Word of a Woman: Police, Rape and Belief*, researcher Jan Jordan identified the curious paradox: "When women accuse men of wrongdoing, they are doubted; when they retract, they are believed. If they allege abuse, their word is suspect; if they retract an abuse allegation, their word suddenly becomes credible. One is prompted to ask: Why is women's word to be trusted only when it excuses and absolves men of responsibility for their violence against women?"

Although people on these websites seem to be talking only to those with like views and may seem hardly worth mentioning, they can in fact be influential to more mainstream thinking because so much research today is done on the Internet. In August 2009, for example, the first two items that popped up when "false rape claims" was typed in a search field were Wendy McElroy's article on the Fox News website and another from falserape.net, both alleging the falseness of the majority of rape reports. Because few organizations have websites dedicated to the topic, those seeking information can have difficulty finding reliable data via the Internet.

Startling is the lack of response by rape-victim advocates, who are admittedly overworked, to the false-rape-claims campaign. Their silence may be due to the difficult posture in which they found themselves when the Duke lacrosse case played out, as the media forced advocates into taking uncomfortable or indefensible positions.

Rape-victim advocates, for example, were no match for commentators like Fox News's Bill O'Reilly. Appearing on his program in April 2006, the director of a state coalition against sexual assault explained that it was her role "to support a woman or any victim that comes forward to say that they were sexually assaulted."

"Even if they weren't?" queried O'Reilly.

Rather than pursuing her thought that it was her function to support rape victims, she replied, "Well, Bill, I can't say that I've come across one that wasn't. And I've been doing this for eleven years."

O'Reilly was then able to run rings around the advocate, claiming she was undercutting the presumption of innocence in the US Constitution. Her statement was repeated all over the Internet and interpreted as a declaration that no women make false rape reports.

The cause of the problem was the media's interest in pursuing only one story line, which was severely lacking in nuance. They pitted the defenders of the lacrosse team against feminists who would support the accuser. Gail Dines, an antipornography academic and activist, had a more complex message that she said she was unable to deliver on CNN's *Paula Zahn Now*, where she was asked to talk about the Duke case.

"I was set up on the show to be an example of the problem," said Dines. "White liberal elites who have taken political correctness too far. I was not brought in as a researcher or activist but as an example of how feminists 'rush to judgment' in order to further their man-hating propaganda."

Cable networks often employed former assistant district attorney Wendy Murphy to make arguments for the guilt of the lacrosse team members on air. Later, she agreed that she had been extreme but believed it was necessary to provide balance to counteract the other side. However, one of her comments was endlessly repeated over the Internet: "I never, ever met a false rape claim, by the way. My own statistics speak to the truth."

In the main, however, rape-victim advocates have clung to the proposition that only 2 percent of rape claims have proven false. This statement rests on no firm research foundation. The oft-quoted figure may stem from a mention by Susan Brownmiller in 1975. She wrote that when New York City instituted a new sex-crime-analysis unit, the number of false charges reportedly dropped to 2 percent. Yet, although it does not appear to rest on firm research, those trying to counteract the 50 percent claim have repeated it as gospel for a number of years.

Shedding some light on the matter are some recent methodologically sound research reports that have gone largely unnoticed. Remember first that whether any social-science research can produce a reliable estimate of false reports—which are cases in which the accuser is lying about rape—is problematic. The existence of solid evidence to prove a lie is often unavailable. In addition, there are numerous instances in which police and prosecutors discount the veracity of the reports, rendering false report data inaccurate when new facts later emerge. In one case, for example, sex-crimes investigators could not believe a woman's report that a stranger gained entry to her apartment through a seven-inch gap in the security bars of her window. They concluded that she was lying. Because the man continued raping women in the city, eventually his DNA was found, and it matched what was discovered on the woman.

Seven methodologically rigorous research studies on false rape claims exist, with estimates for the percentage of false reports converging around 2 to 8 percent. Although no study can be definitive, their data liberate us from the endless battle between the proponents of 2 percent and the advocates of 50 percent.

The Making a Difference (MAD) Project, a multistate study of eight communities conducted between 2005 and 2006 and published in 2008, has been one of the few research studies undertaken in the United States to evaluate the percentage of false rape reports made to law enforcement. In the project, officials collected data on all rape reports during a period of eighteen to twenty-four months. All participating agencies were trained to apply consistent definitions for a false report, and a random sample of cases was checked for accuracy of data entry. Of the 2,059 cases in the study, forty (7 percent) were classified as false.

Researchers studied all 116 rape cases that Toronto's police department investigated in 1970. They concluded that seven cases (6 percent) involved false reports, with an additional five reports from relatives or friends determined to be false. The United Kingdom's Home Office–sponsored researchers undertook a similar analysis of all 348 rape cases reported to police in England and Wales during the first three months of 1985. They reviewed case files, reports from forensic examiners, and the statements of women who reported being raped as well as the statements of suspects. A little more than 8 percent were determined to be false rape claims.

In 1996, the Home Office sponsored a similar study. Here, researchers examined 483 rape case files but supplemented the information with a number of interviews with the accusers and law-enforcement officers. The final determination of falseness was left to the police, however, and the estimate was 10.9 percent.

An even larger research project commissioned by the Home Office analyzed 2,643 rape cases reported to police over a fifteen-year period, publishing its findings in 2005. Of these, the police had classified 8 percent as false. Researchers collected additional information for each one, including reports from forensic examiners, data from interviews with those reporting rape, and content analyses of the statements made by reporters and witnesses. Then they evaluated each case to determine whether there was a "clear and credible admission by the complainant" or "strong evidential grounds" for a false claim. After this investigation, the percentage of false claims dropped to 2.5 percent. In 2000 and 2003, Australian researchers examined 812 rape cases in Victoria with sufficient information to make a determination, and they found that only 2.1 percent could be classified as false reports.

Finally, researchers reviewed case summaries of every rape reported to the police department of a major university in the northeastern United States from 1998 to 2007. In scrutinizing the 136 cases, the label "false report" was applied if the investigation had yielded evidence that the reported rape had in fact not occurred. But in some cases, researchers had insufficient knowledge to assign a category. Eight cases, or 5.9 percent, were coded as false reports, while 13.9 percent contained insufficient information to be classified. Interestingly, the police department had labeled as false all eight cases, even though half of these categorizations were based on complainants' recantations. We know, however, that many recant as a result of threats from the accused or distress under the investigation. As researcher Liz Kelly noted, "A culture of suspicion remains, accentuated by a tendency to conflate false allegations with retractions and withdrawals, as if in all such cases no sexual assault occurred."

In addition to citing a 2 percent false-claims rate, rape-victim advocates commonly assert that the false-claims rate for forcible rape is comparable to other crimes. Does this assertion hold up?

FBI data are useful in this regard. Law-enforcement agencies inform the FBI of the number of rapes, among other crimes, reported to their departments each month. In addition, they provide the number of cases that are "unfounded." A case is "unfounded" if it is determined, after investigation, to be "false" or "baseless," giving the impression that the "unfounded" category involves more than false or fabricated cases. It could cover a situation in which the complainant clearly has not fabricated an account but the facts do not indicate that a rape as defined by the law has occurred. The FBI does make it clear that the refusal of the accuser to cooperate with prosecution or the failure to make an arrest does not "unfound" a legitimate offense. One can readily believe, however, that inconsistencies in the application of this definition are widespread; for example, at trainings, it is not uncommon for law-enforcement participants to say they "unfound" cases if they do not believe the woman making the claim or are unable to prove the claim conclusively. However, these scenarios are not part of the definition of "false" or "baseless." At any rate, it would be interesting to see just how many "unfounded" rape cases are reported yearly to the FBI.

Unpublished FBI data about unfounded crime reports provided to the federal agency on an annual basis reveal declining unfounded rape rates. In 1996, 7.4 percent of rape cases were reported as unfounded, but by 2008 the number had decreased to 5.8 percent, comparable to the 2001 rate. Since the unfounded category undoubtedly includes more than just false cases, one could confidently say that the number of false claims is below 5.7 percent; that it has not, according to police departments, been increasing over time; and that it has, in fact, decreased from a high of 8.6 percent in 1990.

The unfounded rate for rape *is* higher than all other crimes. Compare the 2008 unfounded-rape rate of 5.8 percent with that of motor vehicle theft, 2.7 percent, or burglary, 1.5 percent, or robbery at 1.0 percent. Thus the frequently made statement that the rate of false rape claims is no different from other crimes is demonstrably false. However, the data do indicate that, from 1996 to 2008, false rape claims have not been an increasing problem.

Rape deniers, however, have consistently misstated and thereby exaggerated the FBI unfounded rate for rape. Cathy Young, in a July 2011 article about the Dominique Strauss-Kahn case, claimed that, according to the FBI, approximately 9 percent of rape reports are dismissed as unfounded. And defense attorney Roy Black, in a similar opinion piece on the case, put the FBI unfounded-rape rate at 8 percent. In addition, between 2010 and 2011, Wikipedia users edited and added some of the new studies—as well as Professor Lisak's critique of Eugene J. Kanin—to the site's "False Accusation of Rape" entry. As recorded by the entry's "Talk" page, the article's author, a rape denier, then removed some of the new material. These actions caused the new research, non-Kanin material to be unavailable to Wikipedia readers. The hullaballoo stands as a mini-version of the whole controversy.

Despite these issues, new false-claims research demonstrates remarkable consistency, as noted by researcher Kimberly A. Lonsway:

> Because the studies . . . meet generally accepted standards for social science research, they instill confidence in the credibility of their estimates—which range from 2–8 percent, depending on which specific studies are included. In fact, the diversity of methods means that the convergence of findings is especially noteworthy. At this point, there is simply no way to claim that "the statistics are all over the map." The statistics are actually now in a very small corner of the map.

Rape is probably the only offense in which a suspect can successfully defend himself by claiming that the victim consented to the crime, which causes the police to intensely scrutinize the believability of the injured party's description of events. But there is no foolproof method for determining whether in fact a rape occurred. The best we can do is to rely on the ability of police officers and detectives to investigate cases with unbiased hearts and minds. If police officers consider that as many as 50 percent of rape claims are false, these beliefs may well compromise their investigations.

Rape researcher Jan Jordan believes that it is here that the two strands of rape denial converge: police can readily accept that the majority of women are lying about rape because they do not believe that, in this day and age, rape at the hands of someone the woman knows is so serious. Jordan wrote in *The Word of a Woman*, "The hidden issue may well be that police see little harm in most rapes. Statements such as 'she had no physical injuries' to describe someone violated by unwanted sexual intercourse confirms such suspicions. This view allows police to define many rapes as 'false complaints' and underplay the effect on the victims."

Belief in false rape claims goes beyond police departments. For example, the British government, concerned about what it saw as the pressing issue of false rape claims, signaled its intention in June 2010 to grant anonymity to rape-trial defendants up to the point of charging. The ensuing controversy led to the legislation's withdrawal a few months later. Opponents of the legislation questioned whether rape complainants were less credible or reliable than victims of other violent crimes. Others declared that the change would reduce rape convictions and allow rapists to go free, because publicity about the defendant often brings forward witnesses and information about prior rapes committed by the accused.

The actual rate of false rape claims—2 to 8 percent—moves us beyond the "all or nothing" debate and into a more nuanced position. Because there are a number of false rape claims, each rape allegation needs a thorough investigation, lest innocent men and women be falsely accused or predatory rapists allowed to remain free to harm others. All sides have much to gain from embracing the facts of how prevalent false rape claims are.

## The Media's Role in False Rape Claims

For some years now, members of the media have been the allies of rape deniers. Reporters must present the facts of a case or trial in an unbiased manner, which they think they are doing when they try to present both sides of the story. However, constructing a story around a "he said, she said" narrative, without reference to other facts or issues, forces the conclusion that one of the two involved has to be lying. Because defense counsel will then convince the jury that it cannot find the accused guilty beyond a reasonable doubt, an acquittal becomes probable. Media critic Lynn S. Chancer wrote in her book *High-Profile Crimes* that in presenting two sides to every story, media coverage echoes the structural organization of the law. However, she argued that in principle, "Nothing prevents journalists from covering stories in more complex ways."

But the media have taken hold of the issue of false rape claims, a tendency apparent before the Duke lacrosse case but one that has only accelerated since then. Jan Jordan wrote:

> In the way in which they have seized upon and constructed the "new issue" of false rape complaints, the media have provided a central strand to backlash arguments of the last decade. . . . Media reporting of what are believed to be false rape allegations has become a fashionable area of inquiry and speculation in recent years. The coverage given to rape reports which are believed to be false is extensive, and

articles centered around the theme of women lying appear to be positioned with greater prominence and emphasis than stories covering rape charges that end in conviction.

Two noted researchers who reviewed media articles about false rape allegations between 1995 and 1999, even before the Duke case, found that "false rape has become the new issue of concern, following on from (and sharing the discursive characteristics of) the feminist movement's assertion of rape as a serious and widespread social problem." They believed that the newly discovered "social problem" was a worrying distraction from rape prevention in contemporary society.

The media has most frequently helped shape the perception that women lie about rape in its coverage of cases involving celebrity athletes. One sports talk-show radio host immediately reacted to a 2003 rape accusation against basketball star Kobe Bryant in what has become a typical response: "When you first hear that some woman has accused Kobe of sexual assault, your first thought is obviously that this must be some gold-digger or some woman who tried to 'entrap' an NBA star. After all, we know Kobe, and this is totally out of character for him. These women are out there, and it's a dangerous world for these guys."

Indeed, when researchers reviewed 156 articles about the Kobe Bryant rape accusation from seventy-six media sources, they found that 42 percent endorsed the idea that the young woman was lying about being raped. Still unclear from this study is whether those journalists perceived false rape claims to be a problem or whether their approach was employed to sensationalize the story or to present a balanced view.

We don't know what happened in Kobe Bryant's hotel room on the night in question, but focusing solely on Bryant's credibility and that of his accuser precludes a more complex analysis. For example, most news stories published very little about the physical evidence in the case. What easy narrative encompasses the young woman's vaginal lacerations, genital trauma inconsistent with consensual sex, and the blood on Bryant's shirt?

After a Harrah's Lake Tahoe hotel employee accused Pittsburgh Steelers star quarterback Ben Roethlisberger of rape in a civil suit in July 2009, for several days the ESPN sports network instructed its staff not to cover the story (except in the Pittsburgh market), thus keeping the rape complaint hidden from the public. The speculation was that ESPN was protecting the network's self-interest in maintaining media access to the star quarterback. Soon the Associated Press weighed in. Its article quoted legal experts who explained that, although the woman accusing Roethlisberger had no proof and a financial motive, she could win the case even if Roethlisberger was innocent. These opinions generated antagonism toward the young woman and sympathy for the sports icon.

Deborah L. Rhode, a professor at Stanford Law School who specializes in sex and the law, said there was no evidence; there were also no witnesses. The woman accusing Roethlisberger had a history of depression and some "obvious financial motives—none of which makes her a very appealing complainant." But, Rhode pointed out, "That said, it may well have happened. There are certainly more than enough examples of factual settings like this where celebrity athletes feel entitled. But that is not going to win a case."

When a Georgia prosecutor began investigating Roethlisberger after a rape complaint from another individual some months later, sports journalists continued to blame the young woman. *Bleacher Report* columnist Todd Kaufmann wrote, "But if you're Ben Roethlisberger, how do you put yourself in a situation where this kind of thing might happen to you again? Whether he assaulted the girl is irrelevant in my thinking at this point. What matters is why he put himself in this situation . . . again. Ben, you have to know that as an NFL quarterback that people are going to try to take advantage of you." One *Ms.* magazine columnist could not resist writing, "Yes, Ben, why *did* you put yourself in that situation? How could you leave yourself so vulnerable? Going to a bar, you were *asking* to be accused of sexual assault!"

"Apologists drink from a potent cocktail of hero-worship, almost military levels of team solidarity, and old-fashioned 'boys will be boys' gender essentialism," wrote cultural critic Jaclyn Friedman. The media reflect and perpetuate these sentiments in celebrity rape cases—to the detriment of all women who are raped.

And the media cannot resist determining for its readers—often without access to the evidence—the veracity of women who make rape claims against celebrities. In a discussion of a rape complaint against former vice president Al Gore in 2010, for example, *Salon* felt the need to publish an opinion piece pointing out three grounds on which to be skeptical about the woman's claims. However, the author of the piece did not investigate any of the facts. One of the reasons was not even evidence based: "We have seen plenty of cases of baseless (if vivid) sexual allegations against celebrities before."

Sports celebrities are not the only ones to provoke media attacks on women who report having been raped. Much ink has been spilled about whether or not author Arthur Koestler was a rapist, with several leading intellectuals unable to accept the allegation. A recent biographer demonstrated Koestler's interest in forced sex; there is no doubt that he subscribed to the belief that a little aggression added spice to sex, and he was not averse to saying so. The book mentioned Jill Craigie, now deceased, who reported to at least two people that Koestler had raped her in 1952. Yet, in his review of the biography, Jeremy Treglown felt it necessary to disbelieve Craigie, labeling her "unreliable" but not providing any proof for his assertion. Koestler's biographer, as well as historian Tony Judt, proceeded to defend Koestler's behavior as somehow being more acceptable at that earlier time.

## Building on a Cultural History of Rape Denial

Allegations of false rape claims are just a recent manifestation of an eternal problem: for thousands of years, men have feared women's rape accusations and presented them as false. As researcher Jan Jordan has written, "Beliefs in women's inherent deceitfulness appear to have existed almost as long as women themselves have trodden the earth, and show little sign of abating." Thus the work of false-rape-claims activists grows in rich cultural soil; the attitudes they help cultivate have blocked the effectiveness of legislation and case law enacted between 1975 and 1990 to overcome bias in rape prosecutions. The discovery of acquaintance rape and increases in the number of women reporting rapes during this period may well have reinvigorated the more recent campaign against false rape claims. And, in turn, this campaign has negated anticipated effects of rape-law-reform efforts.

From the Biblical account of the Fall, which presents Eve as the seducer and deceiver of Adam, to the Old Testament tale of Potiphar's wife, we see early and powerful depictions of women lying about rape. In the Potiphar story, the beautiful Egyptian wife of Potiphar is angry at Joseph, a Hebrew slave, for rejecting her sexual advances. She pulls off Joseph's loin cloth and, displaying it, tells her husband Joseph has tried to rape her.

Harper Lee's perennially popular 1960 novel, *To Kill a Mockingbird*, updates the tale, demonstrating the longevity of these influential symbolic stories. In the book, a black man, Tom Robinson, is accused of raping a young white woman, and attorney Atticus Finch defends him. Robinson claims that the accuser and her father are lying; the woman was making sexual advances toward the accused and her father caught her in the act and brutally beat her. Lee makes certain that readers believe in Robinson's innocence, buttressed by his useless injured left arm and the young woman's injuries, which are inconsistent with his disability. Despite the best efforts of Atticus Finch, Robinson is convicted and later killed while escaping from prison. It is a shame that the author makes a strong case for the horrific injustice blacks faced in the South by employing the device of a false rape claim; the storyline perpetuates the perception of false rape claims as being normative among women, even those who are already victims of violence.

Stories from Greek mythology also convey the theme of women's sexual falsity. Cassandra, whose name means "she who entangles men," refuses Apollo's sexual advances. He had already given her the gift of prophesy, so in revenge the god made sure that no one would believe Cassandra, symbolizing a patriarchal refusal to trust the words of women.

These strong cultural attitudes are difficult to challenge, based as they are on a seemingly timeless and absolute truth. Throughout his life, anthropologist Claude Lévi-Strauss sought to understand why myths operate so powerfully in all cultures, even when we are not aware that they are influencing us. "For it to become a myth, some kind of secret alchemy must enable the social group to assimilate the story because it answers the group's intellectual and moral needs," he said. Although the myth refers to events in the past, the lesson appears to be timeless, which also explains the present and the future. Accepting Lévi-Strauss's conclusions about myth puts into focus the strength of beliefs that deny rape prevalence, blaming it on women's lies or exaggerations. Today's rape denial is but a recent iteration of a long history, enshrined in powerful myth.

There is nothing as chilling, however, as the contribution Sigmund Freud made to belief in false rape claims. Patient "Anna O" experienced hallucinations, loss of consciousness, and disturbances of vision, hearing, and speech. In cases of women like these, Freud came to believe that their fathers had sexually abused them. But Freud's professional colleagues were unreceptive to his findings. Ultimately he abandoned his theory of childhood seduction for several reasons, the most important of which may have been his lack of success in curing his patients. In a letter, he explained to a friend and colleague that in each of these cases the father of the patient would have had to have sexually abused his patient. Freud could not embrace the premise, "whereas surely such widespread perversions against children are not very probable." Like countless others before and after him, Freud could not accept the fact that so many fathers could abuse their children. When faced with the reality of childhood sexual assault, he backed off, developing a whole new theory to account for the women's symptoms of distress.

One aspect of early law may have heavily contributed to fears of false rape claims. Provisions found in early English law—as well as Jewish, Hebrew, Roman, and medieval canon law—required an unmarried woman who said she was raped to marry her rapist. As a result, there was always suspicion that one motive for women to lie was to induce the accused man to wed them and thus to "marry upward." The law created a special set of safeguards for the defendant against false rape claims, making rape accusations difficult to prove in court. These included the doctrine of resistance, which required the woman to demonstrate she tried to fight off the attack but was overpowered. It was usually expressed as "earnest resistance" or resistance "to the utmost." One legal scholar has pointed out that in the twentieth century, courts intensified their insistence on "utmost resistance" and, lacking it, found implicit consent. This ruling spelled doom for young women like Riley and Tracy, who tried to comply in order to get the assault over with and to avoid severe injury or death. Another requirement was a prompt report, or fresh complaint, assuming that a delayed complaint was likely to be falsified. The third major rule barred conviction based solely on the complainant's testimony, requiring corroboration by independent witnesses or physical evidence. Still another practice was the incorporation of a warning, initiated from Lord Hale in the seventeenth century in England, that the jury must examine the accuser's testimony with special care because a rape charge was "easily made and once made, difficult to defend against, even if the person accused is innocent." During the last twenty-five years, law-reform efforts have eliminated all of these earlier requirements.

Holocaust historian Deborah Lipstadt has persuasively demonstrated that although it had early information about the Nazi concentration camps, the US media dismissed it as unbelievable propaganda. In her book on the topic, Lipstadt wrote, "Throughout the period of the Third Reich this pattern repeated itself: reliable sources told at least a portion of what was happening, and those far from the scene and unfamiliar with Nazism discounted the news as exaggerated or dismissed it as not quite possible." Although interest in strict neutrality and staying out of European affairs were factors in the press's indifference, Lipstadt found it difficult to fully understand.

After World War II, various ideologies, including anti-Semitism and anti-Zionism, caused (and still cause) certain individuals and groups to deny established facts of the Holocaust. The Holocaust was, and remains, a unique horrific crime and an unsurpassed evil. However, Holocaust denial resembles rape denial in its repudiation of recognized fact and its indifference, in the name of ideology, to the suffering of victims. For this reason, responses to rape denial should mirror strategies for dealing with Holocaust denial. Psychologist Patrizia Romito commented in her book on the current acceptability of rape denial, noting that "whereas pro-Nazi denial and anti-Semitism have been opposed and punished by society in their turn (in many European countries denying the Holocaust is against the law, for example), no punishment by society exists for those who trivialize male violence against women and children."

## False-Rape-Claims Assertions in Action

We rarely are privy to discussion in the jury room, but in 2000, researcher Judy Shepherd was chosen to sit on a jury in a rape trial in Alaska. She has described how the jury was able to ignore strong factual evidence, including a DNA analysis, to acquit the defendant based on strong cultural beliefs about false rape claims. The facts were as follows: A sixty-six-year-old Alaskan native consumed some alcoholic beverages with her friends and relatives while her husband was out of town on a fishing trip. She said she then returned home and went to bed. At 5:00 AM, she heard a knock on her door. Thinking it was her brother, who was due to come over for coffee, she opened it. She found a fifty-five-year-old man, someone from the small town whom she knew. She said that he then proceeded to rape her. DNA evidence introduced at trial showed that the likelihood of a similar DNA profile to the accused's would be in the range of three thousand to one. An internal examination of the woman showed severe vaginal bruising. Mistaken identity was the defendant's defense.

Although Shepherd found the woman credible and the DNA evidence unassailable—especially in light of the mistaken identity defense—to her astonishment, the jury deadlocked. Five voted to convict (three women and two men), and seven voted for acquittal (one woman and six men). She was surprised at the attitudes of jurors who minimized the seriousness of the crime or blamed or disbelieved the woman. Statements made during the jury deliberations included:

"She had sex with someone else and said it was him to cover it up."

"She claimed rape so her husband wouldn't get mad."

"She was drunk."

"How could she recognize who it was?"

"They were all soused; it just depends which drunk you want to believe."

"They all cover up for one another."

"We could ruin a guy's life."

"If there is a reasonable doubt, we are required to give a verdict of not guilty."

"I think he's guilty, but I don't feel comfortable passing a guilty verdict and knowing he's going to prison."

Shepherd also found the treatment of the woman to be astounding. Defense counsel grilled her about her alcohol consumption and whether she had sex with anyone at the party. Full-color pictures of her genital area taken during the colposcope examination were passed around to the jurors and displayed on two television screens with the caption, "Genital Area of [name of woman]." Shepherd concluded, "If a 66-year-old grandmother is treated this way and suspected of lying to cover up sexual escapades, one wonders what would be included in the court proceedings and jury deliberations of a date rape trial of a young woman."

The deadlocked jury mandated a retrial. A new jury, consisting of seven men and seven women, found the defendant guilty of rape. The second time around, jurors said they found the DNA evidence conclusive because of the defense's assertion of mistaken identity. In both trials, however, some jurors stated there would not have been a case if the defense had used consensual sex as a defense, and they wondered why the accused had not argued it. Concluded Shepherd:

> This case demonstrated that DNA evidence, culpascope [*sic*] pictures of bruising consistent with sexual assault, and the victim's identification of the assailant can all be readily disregarded by jurors who believe common rape myths that blame the victim and minimize the seriousness of the crime. . . . Members of both juries stated that in this case, a defense argument of consensual sex would have been readily believed.

David Lisak points to the psychology of those who disbelieve rape claims:

Vulnerability scares us, very deeply. To feel your body being forcibly penetrated by another human being is an experience of such utter, terrifying vulnerability and helplessness that most people recoil from the thought. To overcome that resistance, to actually identify with the experience and the person who suffers it, is an act of profound empathy, and considerable courage. Most people, frankly, are not up to the challenge; certainly not without a lot of support. . . .

This is the fertile ground in which the issue of false reports has taken root. When a room full of people feels the urgent need to shun and discard a rape victim, nothing makes it easier than adopting the belief that she made the whole thing up.

By misstating or ignoring existing research on false rape claims, rape deniers play into hundreds of years of belief in women's lying about rape, calling upon deep psychological responses to allegations of atrocity.

# [ 7 ]

# Defending Strauss-Kahn

Reactions to Dominique Strauss-Kahn's arrest illustrate how current beliefs about false rape claims can make rape prosecutions problematic. A clutch of apologists for the defendant—many of whom, as in the Julian Assange matter, argued the accusations were politically motivated—found a media ready to air their grievances. Strauss-Kahn's defenders were outraged that most of the American media embraced the veracity of the sensational indictment prior to trial and that they congratulated the prosecutor's office in choosing to believe a hotel housekeeper rather than an important and affluent international political figure. Without the advantage of having any facts on the matter, they took it upon themselves to attack Nafissatou Diallo before the trial. And the condemnation was vituperative.

French philosopher Bernard-Henri Lévy, a friend of Strauss-Kahn of twenty years' standing, said the housekeeper was lying because it was not the practice of most grand New York hotels to send in a lone maid to clean a suite. He also bitterly assailed the young French woman who had come forward with an additional rape complaint: "I hold it against all those who complacently accept the account of this other young woman, this one French, who pretends to have been the victim of the same kind of attempted rape, who has shut up for eight years but, sensing the golden opportunity, whips out her old dossier and comes to flog it on television."

Jean Daniel, editor of the weekly *Le Nouvel Observateur*, demanded to know why "the supposed victim was treated as worthy and beyond suspicion?" Lawyer Ben Stein asserted, without proof, that economists and heads of international economic entities have never been convicted of violent sex crimes.

Stein then went on to raise doubts about Diallo's account: "What do we know about the complainant besides that she is a hotel maid? . . . On the other hand, I have had hotel maids that were complete lunatics, stealing airline tickets from me, stealing money from me, throwing away important papers, stealing medications from me. How do we know that this woman's word was good enough to put Mr. Strauss-Kahn straight into a horrific jail?"

Notably, Strauss-Kahn's prominent defenders utterly failed to give even lip service to any concerns for rape victims, minimizing the seriousness of the incident as they were alleging false rape claims. Journalist Jean-François Kahn opined that the affair was just a matter of lifting a maid's skirt. Jack Lang, a former government minister, commented, "It's not like anybody died." Both later apologized for their insensitivity.

Economist Nouriel Roubini, joined by many others in France of the left persuasion, publicly speculated that the whole affair was a setup by political enemies, one intended to knock out Strauss-Kahn as a socialist candidate for French president in 2012. Naomi Wolf, a key Julian Assange defender, also espoused the conspiracy theory, but she made perfectly clear that she believes that, in many cases, those reporting rape are simply lying.

"This does not mean that Strauss-Kahn is innocent or that he is guilty," wrote Wolf. "It means that policy outcomes can be advanced nowadays, in a surveillance society, by exploiting or manipulating sex-crime charges, whether real or inflated."

A few days after his arrest, some 57 percent of the French public said they believed Strauss-Kahn was the victim of a smear campaign. Even

Russian prime minister Vladimir Putin expressed doubts about the allegations, hinting at hidden political motives.

As time went by and the prosecutor's office did further investigation, the media also undertook its own inquiries. In July 2011, the *New York Post* published a story asserting that the Sofitel housekeeper was a prostituted woman. The paper revealed the accusation in typical tabloid style: "The stunning new info surfaced yesterday as the accuser was unmasked as a pathological liar and scam artist by prosecutors whose rape case has unraveled." The *Post* even reported her address and publicized the building in which she lived as housing for AIDS patients, which could have put her in physical danger.

In a post on the blog of the *American Prospect*, Robert Kuttner speculated that Strauss-Kahn thought the housekeeper was the prostituted woman du jour expected by the financier. Despite Diallo's protests, Kuttner theorized, Strauss-Kahn didn't believe she was not there to service him, which would explain his subsequent conduct and absolve him of the charge of sociopathic behavior.

And, as the New York City prosecutor was further investigating the case, Cathy Young weighed in to remind readers that many women lie about rape. In her *Weekly Standard* article, she misquoted the FBI unfounded rate for rape—nearly doubling it—and cited Eugene J. Kanin's study. Young made no reference to any contemporary social-science research on false rape claims.

At this stage, the Strauss-Kahn case illustrated all the components of rape denial. The comical-sounding defense—that important economists or political figures cannot be rapists—captured in a nutshell our contemporary inability to hold rapists accountable. When the accused does not fit our stereotypical picture of a man with a ski mask in the bushes, we are astonished that such evil can exist in the world and simply cannot take in the unfathomable news. Denial and conspiracy theories result. These reactions, however, are ones that ultimately undermine the integrity of the legal system and negatively affect the credibility of all individuals who report being raped.

Once the charges against Strauss-Kahn became public, the French media aired numerous examples of inappropriate, sexually aggressive behavior attributed to him. Several of these situations occurred in work settings, revealing that this propensity of his was an open secret. Tragically, however, his conduct was handled as a private matter, even as the financial expert was preparing to campaign for the French presidency.

The media's rush to judgment, before facts at trial became available, provoked a powerful defense of Strauss-Kahn by his friends. Their statements involved a virulent attack on his accuser. As columnist Kathleen Parker has noted, the end result was simply a tragedy that set back efforts to deter rapists: "Women already struggle enough to find the courage to report rape and then to be believed. Good men struggle to prove their innocence when falsely accused. . . . At least we might postpone a verdict until after the trial."

# Blaming Tracy

Following Justin's assault, Tracy took shower after shower after shower, even though the water reaggravated the pain. She visited the student health center the next morning, where by chance she already had an appointment. She also knew a hospital emergency-room visit wouldn't be covered without a referral. Tracy had no idea that her state's law required hospitals to provide free postrape examinations and care, the costs for which the state reimbursed.

At the student health center, the primary nurse practitioner had an extreme reaction when Tracy gave her account. In Tracy's eyes, she became almost hysterical and on the verge of crying. Tracy's attorney, Celeste Hamilton, described how "[the nurse's] very emotional response felt very wrong to Tracy . . . particularly since Tracy was still processing and not comfortable with putting certain terms on it. I get the sense that part of what happened was that Tracy further shut down, which I think somehow ended up making the nurse feel like she shouldn't be treating it as a sexual assault."

A visual examination ensued, but the nurse made no attempt to do a digital (finger) rectal exam or complete a rape kit. She looked at Tracy's anus and marked down "no visible tears." However, given the bleeding, there was no possibility whatsoever that there wasn't tearing on the inside. Tracy was given stool softeners, Tylenol for the pain, and HIV medication.

Later, a representative from the university hospital's risk-management department told Hamilton that the nurse claimed she begged Tracy to go to the emergency room and get a rape kit done. Tracy was very clear that this did not happen. Instead, it was a failure of procedure that would prove problematic when Tracy attempted to have charges brought against Justin.

Hamilton wasn't sure whether or not the nurse practitioner distrusted Tracy's account. But clearly poor training, no training, or feeling overwhelmed by her own emotional response hampered her in her efforts to help Tracy. If the nurse did accept Tracy's account as true, that belief was not acted on appropriately.

Tracy's two friends were at war with one another about whether she should report the rape to the police. One was furious; she was "all about me going to the cops. She's angry, she's pissed off. She has been from the beginning," said Tracy. Her other friend, who had been a rape-victim volunteer, knew full well that the police reaction could be unsupportive and believed the decision whether to report was best left to Tracy. Tracy herself was worried about retaliation from Justin, who, after all, lived nearby.

Several days later, when the shock had worn off a bit, Tracy walked over to the campus police station. Unfortunately the secretary at the station snapped at her: "What are you doing here? Who do you have a meeting with? There is nothing scheduled." Tracy began to physically shake. Little did she know that her ordeal was just beginning.

Once she gave her account to the campus police while in their office, they summoned two city police officers. The campus police sat in on the interview. A campus rape advocate also appeared, but she had to leave halfway through. Tracy knew she wasn't making a good impression.

> I was just giving way too much detail. It allowed them
> to look at me as someone crazy. It would have been bet-
> ter had I had some sort of advocate who had been there
> to hear the entire story first and she and I had worked
> on boiling it down to something to report to the police,
> because that would have made a huge difference, and a
> huge difference when I talked to the detectives. But no

one told me. Otherwise they are going to write you off. I gave way more detail and emotion. I cried. They are not going to take you seriously if you do that, and that's what I realized.

They wanted to know why it had taken so long for her to report the rape. Tracy told them she didn't have a very good reason for that. She learned that police detectives would contact her for a follow-up interview. One of the college officers, a woman, wished her good luck. The other university officer essentially told her she was wasting her time.

Several days later, two male police detectives turned up at Tracy's co-op house. Because of the lack of privacy there, Tracy didn't want them to come inside, so they interviewed her for fifteen minutes in the squad car.

I was in the backseat of a car with two men I didn't know. They were in the front seat, which was very weird. I felt like I was in trouble for something. They were rude. They wanted to know why I didn't run screaming naked from the house. "First of all," they said, "that's a really dangerous neighborhood." It's two blocks away from where I live. "You're lucky that's all that happened." "That's what you get for going." "What's a smart girl like you doing in that neighborhood?" "Well, you are lucky his friends didn't come after you when you were screaming." I couldn't do anything right. Then the final thing they said to me was, "Well, you seem to be doing OK now, and now you know better for next time."

Tracy found the detectives' insistence on the need for serious injury distressing.

It was a big deal to the detectives that I didn't have broken ribs. If I didn't have broken ribs, did that mean I wasn't violently raped? All I had was bleeding. There was tearing, but they didn't bother to look for it. If you are on a date, is he going to use force? He already has you in his apartment. He doesn't have to throw you over the shoulders to get you there. I started to cry because my case wasn't valid enough for the state. Here this horrible thing happened, but it still wasn't horrible enough.

They would talk to Justin and get back to her, the detectives told Tracy. Upset about the encounter, she told the college rape advocate about it, which resulted in an interview with another set of city detectives. This time, the university sent an unmarked car and driver to transport Tracy and the rape advocate to the police station's conference room. Two detectives interviewed her there, one male and one female. The female officer told Tracy the first set of detectives didn't meet with Justin but just talked with him over the telephone. Tracy learned that he was now at the police station to be interrogated as well. Again, Tracy said she had difficulty telling what had occurred.

I gave way too much detail. She was the first person to say, "When the prosecutor comes, don't give that much detail. Just give him the story. He's going to ask you some questions; keep your answers simple. You do a good job, you're believable." It was the first advice that anyone had given me. I was so busy trying to make myself look less stupid.

The detective told Tracy that as Justin was being interviewed, he cried. He claimed the encounter was consensual. His roommates stated they did not hear anything that night. When the prosecutor arrived, he took Tracy alone to a small room, asked a few perfunctory questions, and left. Tracy immediately got the sense that things were going nowhere. Failure to take a rape kit and the lack of a detailed medical report—the absence of documented evidence of physical injury—made it difficult to proceed with a charge, the prosecutor later told her.

He said, "We can't do this to you. It won't be fair to you; we don't want to put you through that. It's very hard to do without evidence of physical damage."

And the detectives told her they thought they had scared the young man off and that Tracy should alert them if any further contact occurred.

Although a prosecution wasn't going to be forthcoming, Tracy did feel that the detectives had believed her: "I was delighted that people had listened to me."

In Tracy's case, it might have been blame or indifference operating as much as disbelief. It is likely that the first set of police believed her but weren't going to do anything because they felt it was her fault for going into a bad neighborhood. And, according to Tracy's attorney, Celeste Hamilton, "Even when the state's attorney said he wasn't going to take the case, he didn't say, 'We don't believe you.' He said, 'We don't have the evidence.' It wasn't so much about not being believed—it was about not having that belief acted on appropriately."

Hamilton suggested that "women mostly get a response that says, 'I believe you. You are telling the truth about what happened. But we are not going to do anything about it.' Then, when the women say, 'What are you talking about? If you believe me, why are you not doing anything about it?' then there tends to be a backtracking, and the people who are justifying not doing anything will then start to use terms like 'credibility.'"

For Hamilton, the problem was the lack of reaction to a rape like Tracy's, and she viewed the law enforcement response as contrary to legislative intent: "'Oh really, you were raped. Well, get over it.' Yet we act like rape is such a horrible thing. We have these laws on the books, draconian in their cruelty."

Tracy was still confused and suffering when she heard about a talk on campus given by an attorney named Celeste Hamilton, who was discussing civil remedies for holding rapists accountable. "Even if the criminal-justice system didn't want to take the case, it turned out you could bring a civil lawsuit for damages." Tracy talked with Hamilton, who told her she had a very good case. Hamilton's legal strategy was to obtain a stay-away order pursuant to state law and then file a lawsuit, seeking a summary judgment based on the evidence at the restraining-order hearing.

For Tracy, the hearing was an ordeal. Justin, represented by an attorney, glared at her throughout. Tracy felt that "someone was going to sit in judgment on me." Although she knew it probably wasn't going to happen, she worried about being lectured for her bad behavior. She felt she was being stared at by other people in the courtroom. Her parents came to town for the second session, and although she wanted them there to support her, she also didn't want them to worry. Hearing the details of her rape, she knew, was hurting them, and she didn't want to do that to them.

On cross-examination, Justin's attorney asked a great many questions, trying to imply a great many things. But Tracy countered by saying,

> I couldn't get out of that hallway because he took up all the room. I couldn't get out of that bed because he pulled me back. His upper body strength was simply much more than mine.

Justin testified that the encounter was consensual and that Tracy had had a good time. Other witnesses appeared: Justin's roommates, a police detective, Tracy's co-op mate. When the latter was pressed on cross-examination to say that Tracy was a party girl, he was incredulous, testifying, "She rarely goes out."

To Tracy's relief, the judge ruled immediately, issuing a two-year order of protection, or a stay-away order.

> The best part of the order of protection is that in it he specifically says that the reason was for forced sex, and he spelled it out. I was so grateful for that. I feel really good. Someone listened to the whole story, listened to his crappy version too, and they believed me.

Justin asked for a rehearing, but the judge denied it, telling him that he had believed Tracy and not him. When he claimed, "She's just upset because I asked her what her HIV status was," the judge replied, "Don't you think it's a little more than her just being angry at you for that?" Again, Tracy found the judge's response affirming.

After Hamilton filed a civil lawsuit on Tracy's behalf for damages against the young man, who was now represented by a different attorney, he agreed to settle the case with a substantial cash award. Tracy also sued the university. She alleged damages for its failure to collect medical evidence of the assault and for its violation of standards of medical care, which caused Tracy severe emotional pain because it prevented any chance of criminal charges based on the incident. In her lawsuit, Tracy maintained that the university health center should have taken the rape kit or immediately referred her to the nearby hospital emergency room for that purpose.

University officials fought the action, claiming that Tracy had been offered a rape kit (although this was not documented in the medical records). Furthermore, they argued that even with a rape kit, it was not certain that a prosecution would have gone forward.

For Hamilton, the university's failure of care caused an amount of trauma comparable to the rape: "What is frequently more devastating than discovering that individual humans are capable of criminal cruelty is discovering the systems that are in place . . . do not function."

Tracy agreed.

> I look back on it and I don't think about the guy who raped me that much in terms of what's wrong with the world. Things will always be wrong with certain individuals. It is the fact that the center didn't do anything.

Hamilton did believe the young man is "terrified" and may have changed his practices. Thus the civil lawsuit may have disrupted his activities and prevented harm to other women and girls. But the battle against the university continued. "We're not interested in money," explained the attorney. "We want an admission of neglect and negligence and some new policies and procedures to ensure this doesn't happen again."

Ultimately the university did revise the student manual to specify that postassault care is to be provided in the hospital emergency room and not in the student care center. The care must also be covered by the state and not charged either to the student or to insurance.

Tracy's lawsuit was dismissed in 2009. The judge ruled that the failure of the state to prosecute the case could not be directly traced to the lack of a rape kit and the university's actions.

# [8]

# Denial's Effects

## *Dangerous Indifference*

Rather than providing the same kind of ready sympathy, support, and services afforded other victims of violent crime, too many of our institutions—including police, church, educators, and media—often treat rape victims with indifference, disbelief, and punishment. Such treatment directly impacts the ways in which rape cases are viewed, processed, and charged. Tracy, for example, was met with indifference from law-enforcement officials, and the national statistics on the ratio of rape reporting to arrests tell a similar story.

There are grounds to believe that rape reporting has risen over time, which leads to speculation that the backlash against women who report rape is a result of this increase. From 1995 to 1996, researchers participating in the National Violence Against Women Survey (NVAW) obtained information about rapes occurring throughout the surveyed women's lives and asked whether they had been reported. After polling eight thousand females, they found that a rape occurring in the modern reform era (1990–1996) was significantly more likely to be reported than one that transpired before 1975, and the size of the difference was relatively significant.

The NVAW analysis, however, suggested that reporting rates have remained essentially unchanged since 1990. Data from the two Kilpatrick research studies confirmed this finding. His research in the 1990s found that 16 percent of all rapes were reported to law enforcement; in 2007, the rate remained merely identical. Likewise, the Department of Justice's National Crime Victimization Survey (NCVS) also found that half (49 percent) of all violent victimizations (rape, robbery, domestic violence, and aggravated assault) were reported to police in 2011 but that this percentage has remained relatively stable over the past ten years. According to the NCVS, rape reporting lags behind that of other violent crimes. In 2011, for example, 27 percent of the rapes were reported to law enforcement, although almost 52 percent of burglaries and 67 percent of aggravated assaults were reported.

However, the low number of rape cases uncovered by researchers in the NCVS makes this 27 percent reporting figure less than reliable. Respondents willing to disclose rape to Department of Justice surveyors may be disclosing only the most violent cases, which they would have been more likely to report to law enforcement. Other research studies find a range between 5 and 20 percent, as discussed in chapter 5.

Thus, although there has been a rise in rape reporting since 1974, no significant increases have occurred since the mid-1990s. This fact contradicts advocates of false rape claims who allege that more women are coming forward to report rape.

Despite increased rape reporting since the 1970s, the gap between the number of forcible rapes that are reported and the rate of those that result in arrest widened from 1971 to 2006. This trend differs markedly from other violent crimes. The ratio of reports to arrest for forcible rape was in the 50 percent range in the 1970s and has decreased steadily to 26.5 percent in 2006, the lowest rate of any recorded in the Uniform Crime Reports between 1971 and 2006. This pattern was not seen for other forms of violent crime during that time, where rates have held fairly steady.

Individual state ratios may well be different. In the state of Illinois in 1999, for example, the arrest rate for rape was 17 percent; an individual who reported rape had about a one-in-six chance of seeing an arrest. By 2007, the arrest rate in Illinois had declined to 11 percent, well below the national average. These data, too, contradict assertions that out-of-control prosecutors are pursuing rape charges at increasing rates.

The declining number of rape charges during this period can be explained when we look at how authoritative bodies in society respond to women who claim they've been raped. Today, women reporting rape are often met with three different responses: indifference, disbelief, or outright punishment.

## Indifference

### Police Indifference

Social-science research has not yet been able to explain the reasons for the precipitous decline in cases charged. Yet the statistics jibe with anecdotal evidence proffered by rape advocates and by young women, such as those whose experiences are described in this volume, who speak of police indifference to their cases of acquaintance rape.

Apathy about rape reached new heights in a case involving a Chicago-area gynecologist. Seven different patients accused the doctor of inappropriate sexual conduct (three of the seven accusations were of nonconsensual sexual penetration; one involved a pregnant woman in his care). Despite complaints to police and to the state's Department of Financial and Professional Regulation, not one official did anything to stop the doctor for seven years. When the state finally investigated in 2007, its actions led only to a nine-month suspension of the doctor's license. The state's attorney's office could not explain to the local newspaper why it did not prosecute any of the cases. As a result, the doctor was allowed to continue practicing—and sexually attacking women. Although an examination of one of the women turned up semen in 2002, law-enforcement officials did not secure a DNA sample from the doctor until the *Chicago Tribune* ran a story about the women's experiences in 2010. The DNA sample was a match.

In 2004, when sixteen-year-old Erin Justice reported that her new stepfather, Laurence Lovejoy, had raped her in their suburban Chicago apartment while Erin's mother was at work, he denied the allegation outright. Because police and prosecutors were awaiting the results of DNA tests from the county crime lab, Lovejoy wasn't immediately charged with rape. Although a DNA test takes only forty-eight hours to complete, backlogs and a lack of priority for rape cases delayed the result. The Illinois child protection agency knew of the matter, but it never made an investigation.

Three weeks later, Justice's body was found in a bathtub filled with bloody water. Authorities said she was beaten, her throat and wrists were slit, and she was drowned in the bathtub. When the DNA was finally tested, it linked Lovejoy to both the rape and the homicide, and he was ultimately convicted and sentenced to life in prison without parole.

In 2009, CBS News documented extensive backlogs in DNA testing of rape kits around the United States. It found at least twenty thousand kits lying untested in Detroit, Houston, San Antonio, and Albuquerque, with other major cities claiming they had no idea how many were untested. Five thousand cases of the Los Angeles County Sheriff's Department remained untested from an earlier larger backlog of untested rape kits. Backlogs result from a lack of funds for DNA testing in government crime labs—a problem that can easily be solved with federal and state dollars—and the failure to give priority to DNA testing in open or uncharged rape cases and other violent crimes.

Even worse than the national backlog was a fact uncovered by a 2009 investigation by Megan Twohey of the *Chicago Tribune*, who found that most of the thirteen suburban Chicago law-enforcement agencies reviewed didn't require that every rape kit be sent for DNA testing. The suburban departments said that they did not send kits to the lab if a prosecutor decided not to press charges, if the accused acknowledged the sex but claimed it was consensual, and if the woman who said she was raped didn't want to proceed with a charge or was not found to be credible. Over one hundred rape kits in these sampled suburban police agencies were stored untested at the time of her article. Some units believed they could not upload the DNA into the national database unless charges had been filed, an interpretation the FBI called erroneous.

In a survey of two thousand state and local law enforcement agencies in 2009, the National Institute of Justice found that from 2002 to 2007 they failed to send DNA evidence to labs in 18 percent of unsolved rapes. Forty-four percent of the responding police departments stated one of the reasons they did not send evidence to the lab was because a suspect had not been identified. This response betrayed ignorance of the now well-established Combined DNA Index System, a national DNA database that can help identify a perpetrator.

For example, when the Cook County Sheriff's officers took over the Ford Heights, Illinois, police department in 2008, they found seven rape kits covered in mold, sitting in an unplugged refrigerator. The luckily uncontaminated evidence linked a convicted felon, just about to be released, to a 2006 rape of a thirteen-year-old girl. According to the girl, the rape involved forced drinking of a date rape drug and violence. Although the suspect claimed he had been a Good Samaritan who rescued the teen when he saw her staggering down the street, a second DNA sample linked him again to the young girl. After charging him with criminal sexual assault, authorities began investigating whether he was tied to other unsolved rapes.

Processing of two hundred untested rape kits in Harvey, Illinois, linked a former Cook County Sheriff's correctional officer to a rape of a ten-year-old girl in her home. Authorities also charged a total of fourteen people based on evidence obtained from the rape kits.

"If you've got stacks of physical evidence of a crime, and you're not doing everything you can with the evidence, then you must be making a decision that this isn't a serious crime," commented Polly Poskin of the Illinois Coalition Against Sexual Assault.

*New York Times* columnist Nicholas Kristof expressed his outrage at the DNA testing backlogs: "It's what we might expect in Afghanistan, not in the United States."

A law passed in Illinois in September 2010, the Sexual Assault Evidence Submission Act, requires law-enforcement officers to submit DNA rape kits to the state lab for testing within ten business days of receiving the kit from the hospital. It also directs the lab to test the kit within six months and mandates an inventory of all untested DNA kits. By February 2011, the Illinois crime lab had identified more than four thousand cases of unexamined sex crime evidence statewide.

Police indifference to testing rape kits is unfathomable when you consider just how traumatic it is for a woman to undergo a rape kit. The process takes several hours. During the procedure, the examiner combs and plucks fibers and hair from all parts of her body, including her pubic hair. Swabs are used to collect DNA samples inside her mouth, vagina, and anal areas. Fingernail scrapings and cuttings are also collected, and a Wood's lamp is used to detect semen stains on the area in front of the anus and inner thighs. For many, this thorough examination, coming as it does just after a traumatic event, is a further invasion of their privacy and difficult to endure.

Julie, a twenty-five-year-old Illinois woman, described her four-hour rape-kit ordeal at a 2010 news conference: "After undressing in front of strangers, I was poked, prodded, scraped, swabbed, combed and photographed. I wouldn't wish it on anyone." Several months later, Julie learned the kit had not been and would not be sent for testing. Her case had been dropped, although she hoped evidence in the kit would corroborate her account.

Other police practices demonstrate indifference to catching and prosecuting rapists. Departments that manipulate rape statistics for political purposes endanger women and girls. In 2010, a New York Police detective revealed that the downgrading of crimes allowed a man to commit six rapes before he was finally caught. The initial rapes, carried out over a two-month period, went unnoticed by detectives because patrol supervisors had improperly labeled them as misdemeanors. This mishandling prevented detectives from spotting patterns of rape. Explained the detective, "What they do is continue to hide these complaint reports, and what happens is no one is alerted that they have a serious crime pattern in these areas."

Baffling is the indifference that still greets allegations of childhood sexual assault. There were nine allegations of rape against Ian Huntley in

Cambridgeshire, England, between 1995 and 1999. None were brought to court because the prosecutor was not hopeful of obtaining a conviction. But somehow a background check did not reveal any information that prevented Huntley from being appointed a caretaker at a local school. Two ten-year-old schoolgirls were found raped and murdered in 2002, and Huntley was eventually found guilty. A year later, the chief constable of the criticized police force resigned following allegations that, while inebriated, he sexually harassed a female official at a police conference.

## Church Indifference

Was it indifference or something else that caused the Illinois Department of Children and Family Services in 2005 to fail to notify Catholic officials that the agency had found credible evidence that a local priest had abused a child? These self-styled "mistakes" enabled the priest to remain at the parish, teaching algebra and coaching boys' basketball for five months after the accusation. He was removed only after a second boy came forward with fresh allegations.

Nothing could be more poignant than the specter of the deaf boys who tried for numerous years to get the attention of the Catholic Church and law-enforcement officials with their accusations against Reverend Lawrence C. Murphy, now accused of molesting at least two hundred young men at a Wisconsin boarding school for the deaf where he worked. Nobody, it seemed, was ready to believe it. Finally, in the mid-1990s, the Milwaukee Archbishop concluded that the priest needed to be removed. However, investigators reported that the archbishop experienced pressure from his superiors to halt defrocking proceedings because Father Murphy had reportedly shown good conduct since the accusations and could be limited in his duties. Thus was the healing of the priest given greater consideration over the healing of those who had been abused. Father Murphy died, still a priest, in 1998.

In a 2010 pastoral letter to the Catholics in Ireland, Pope Benedict XVI apologized for the church's "well-intentioned but misguided tendency to avoid penal approaches" in favor of therapy for pedophile priests. Its choices left them in close contact with youth, which led to multiple instances of sexual abuse over the years. He also admitted to "a misplaced concern for the reputation of the Church and the avoidance of scandal."

What stood out in the Pope's remarks, which made little reference to the suffering of the children, was a lack of understanding of the serious effects of rape. He allowed institutional concerns to trump the needs of the persons entrusted to their care. Has our culture's current trivialization of acquaintance rape enabled this avoidance of scandal to dominate the church's priorities?

### Educators' Indifference

The Catholic Church is certainly not the only institution to demonstrate indifference to rape allegations. Educational organizations also sometimes seem oblivious to the harms of acquaintance rape. Gabrielle Smart's 2009 experience is one example. A high school sophomore, Smart said she was with her on-and-off boyfriend when he held her down so that another student could rape her. After the boys said she had consented to the sex, police released them from custody. For most of the semester, they remained in their Chicago public school, launching vicious verbal attacks against Smart in person and through Facebook, e-mail, and telephone calls. They even threatened to kill her. When the school did not respond in a prompt manner to this harassment, Smart herself left the school. The boys were eventually expelled, but the dismissal did not occur until months later.

In fall 2010, parents complained that a school bus driver under investigation in Chicago for the rape of a special education student was still driving the vehicle a year later when a second episode was reported. Luckily, that time around, no completed assault occurred. The mother of the first teen commented, "It's like no one cared. And after all that happened, he was still out there driving a bus."

Even after holding institutional hearings, many schools nationwide fail to suspend young men who are found to have committed acts of rape. In 2010, the Center for Public Integrity published a study of 130 colleges and universities receiving federal funds to combat sexual violence. It found that the schools permanently suspended only 10 to 25 percent of those the university found responsible for rapes between

2003 and 2008. Suspension after an administrative hearing finds guilt is important, because many women greatly fear retaliation. If the student is not suspended, the woman herself is forced to drop out. Oblivious to these concerns, some college administrators stressed that not sanctioning the young men reflected the mission of higher education, which was to "teach students rather than punish them." They made statements like this despite a lack of evidence that a college campus can rehabilitate a predatory rapist.

Although not all do so, college administrations have every incentive to cover up and bury rape allegations they believe will cause the reputation of their institution to suffer. That some continue to let this agenda trump concerns for the health and safety of students raises questions about the basic humanity of these particular college officials. However, it may be likely that the officials' reactions are the end effect of rape denial, which has convinced them that acquaintance rape is not rape but just "bad sex."

### "Rape," Not "Sex": When Language Harms

Indifference, too, is exemplified by careless or euphemistic language. In 2009, as film director Roman Polanski fought extradition to the United States to face sentencing on charges of rape, the *New York Times* and CNN both reported he awaited sentencing for "having sex with a thirteen-year-old." Their choice of words made the incident out to be a consensual act with someone underage.

Lack of precision over language and, indeed, misrepresentation of the act in question betray a fundamental lack of understanding of rape—or an indifference to it. As columnist Katha Pollitt wrote:

> What happened was not some gray, vague he said/she said Katie-Roiphe-style "bad sex." A 43-year-old man got a 13-year-old girl alone, got her drunk, gave her a quaalude, and after checking the date of her period, anally raped her, twice, while she protested. . . . He was allowed to plead guilty to a lesser charge, like many accused rapists, to spare the victim the trauma of a trial and media hoopla. But that doesn't mean we should all pretend that what happened was some free-spirited Bohemian mix-up. The victim took years to recover.

Researchers have criticized lawyers and judges who use phrases, in writing their opinions and decisions, such as "had intercourse" or "the accused started to caress the victim." These expressions characterize rape as sex rather than sexual assaults, concealing the attacker's violence and need for power and control and the victim's fear, disgust, and pain.

For example, one judgment said, "He compelled her to perform fellatio upon him." Although force is acknowledged, the phrase still makes the victim the actor, performing a sexual act. A more accurate description would be, "He forced his penis into her mouth and compelled her by threats to suck on it."

When reading about rape charges against star quarterback Ben Roethlisberger, we learned that he "had sex with" a young woman, who, in reality, charged him with forcible rape. Another sportswriter referred only to "that drunken night in Milledgeville."

Amazingly, journalists reporting on the Penn State child-abuse cases reported that a graduate assistant testified "he saw Mr. Sandusky having anal sex with the boy." Yet the boy, age ten, had no ability to consent, which makes the act not anal sex but rape.

Another example of indifference to the seriousness of rape is the current popularity of rape jokes, which minimize and normalize rape. When comedian George Carlin died in 2009, journalist Adrian Nicole LeBlanc wrote an appreciation in a major newspaper praising Carlin for his assault on political correctness: "Self-righteousness needed to be punctured, and no one was immune; feminists who couldn't find the humor in rape . . ." But, as one rape victim wrote, "If females are making rape jokes [or approving of them] then it sends a message to men that, look, women can laugh about it, so it can't be *that* bad."

In October 2010, Delta Kappa Epsilon obviously thought it was a stitch to have its pledges at Yale University march blindfolded on Old Campus, which is home to most of the university's freshmen women. The pledges shouted chants such as "No means yes," "Yes means anal," and "Fucking sluts." An editorial in the *Yale Daily News* admitted the chanting was "idiotic and offensive" and "crossed the line," but it challenged the Yale Women's Center's depiction of the act as misogynistic. Instead, the author characterized the episode as merely an attempt at humor: "The provocateurs knew their audience's sensibilities and how to offend them for a childish laugh." Finding humor in mocking women's views of rape reveals deep fears young men have about women's sexual liberation and being charged with rape.

Sixteen Yale students and recent graduates then filed a complaint with the US Department of Education's Office of Civil Rights. They accused the university of violating Title IX of the federal gender-equity law by failing to take strong-enough steps to eliminate a hostile sexual environment on campus. The complaint recited a list of acts against women over a seven-year period. Some students dismissed the fraternity chants as inappropriate but did not think they encouraged acceptance of acquaintance rape on campus. Others said they believed the university must respond more punitively than it has in the past to deter such behavior there. Seven months after the episode, the university suspended the fraternity for a period of five years. A similar result occurred at the University of Vermont: the fraternity Sigma Phi Epsilon received a suspension after it circulated a survey asking members to name their preferred rape victims.

It took two months, 186,000 signatures on a petition to Mark Zuckerberg, and a Twitter campaign to get Facebook to remove "Rape Humor Pages" and others celebrating sexual violence against women. Initially, Facebook dismissed efforts to remove the pages, likening the rape humor to harmless "bar jokes."

The heavy hand of rape deniers can be seen in this flippant attitude toward the issue, which rests on characterizing the act as "bad sex." It is difficult otherwise to make sense of these examples of heartless indifference. Surely they are the result of ignorance of what acquaintance rape is, how and why it transpires, and its effects. Professor Patrizia Romito has written:

> Some months ago one of my students came to thank me: he had discovered during my lectures that rape was a cruel act that may leave the victim devastated. Until that time, like his friends, he had thought it was nothing serious, only rather ardent sex, in short. What meaning should we give to this fact? Must we despair that a man,

who was 20 years old in 2004, had never heard it said that rape is violence and violence is devastating, or be happy because, when he was told, he thought about it, understood and started changing his way of thinking and it is hoped also his way of behaving?

## Disbelief

Disbelief of women who report rape rests on two foundations: (1) assertions that the majority of rape claims are false, and (2) minimization of rape as "bad sex." Often the two are intertwined. Melanie Ross's case is a particularly sad example. After a brief relationship, Ross broke up with a college classmate, Daniel Day, the son of Georgia state representative Burke Day, whose family founded the Days Inn hotel chain. She ended their relationship because during one instance of sexual intercourse, he was hurting her but failed to stop when she asked him to. A month later, she said, Day raped her at a party. Ross brought a lawsuit for damages for sexual assault against him.

Saying that the judge hearing Ross's case was unsympathetic is an understatement. In 2008, he ruled that since Ross and Day previously had a sexual relationship, Ross should have known her claims were "frivolous . . . there was no reasonable belief that a court would accept Plaintiff's claims." He also required her to list all her past sexual partners; he then ruled against her because she wasn't a virgin. For this reason, the judge levied court costs and attorney's fees in the amount of $150,000 to be paid by Ross. Day's attorney claimed that Ross's lawsuit was an effort to extort money from Day's family.

If you disbelieve women's rape claims, then you certainly won't investigate the crime, and the accused gets off the hook. At George Washington University in 2007, a young woman said that at an off-campus house party, she was given a date rape drug that rendered her semiconscious. While she was in that state, one of the party hosts took her to a room and anally penetrated her. When she sought medical assistance at the university hospital for the rape, the hospital staff thought that her vomiting and drifting in and out of consciousness meant she was intoxicated. For this reason, they did not do a blood test or take a rape kit and simply sent her home. A second hospital also refused a rape kit because the first emergency room and the police had determined it was not necessary.

"A sexual assault kit is for police to recover evidence," said Sergeant Ronald Reid. "So if we don't have reason to believe a crime happened we wouldn't administer a rape kit."

These actions prevented the young woman from ever being able to prove she had ingested a date rape drug, and documentation and preservation of evidence of the rape was made impossible.

Despite repeated calls and complaints about violence at the house of convicted rapist Anthony Sowell in a low-income Cleveland neighborhood, nothing was ever done because the reports were coming from a woman in prostitution, Gladys Wade, whom the prosecutor deemed "not credible." Instead, police decided to believe Sowell's claim that he had been robbed and assaulted by Wade, even though she had run to the police bleeding and screaming for help. By the time they finally took some action about a year later, in 2009, police officers found six decomposed bodies in Sowell's house. After Wade saw news reports of the corpses being carried out of the house, she said she began to feel guilty that her complaint hadn't stopped him: "All those women that might be alive if these people had only believed me."

And after a jury found Emiliano Escobar guilty of raping an eighteen-year-old in Texas, judge Kevin Fine, who had to sentence Escobar, reportedly became hung up on several parts of the young woman's testimony. He questioned whether she was really raped, since he found it "odd" that she was on top of Escobar during the assault. According to those in the courtroom, he grilled her in a harsh manner, telling her, "I know these are tough questions and I don't like to have to ask them. It's just, you understand, that most rapes take place with the man on top so he has complete control of the female." Eventually the judge sentenced Escobar to twenty-five years in prison and apologized for the manner in which he went about his interrogation of the victim.

In 2010, Cuyahoga County Juvenile Court judge Alison Nelson Floyd ordered three teenage girls to take a lie-detector test after the conviction and before the sentencing of their rapists. The teenage boys who were found guilty were also ordered to undergo polygraph examinations as part of the presentencing assessment. To add insult to injury, court administrators would not pay for the required tests, causing all those ordered to undergo them to be financially responsible. That same year, at least three other teen girls were ordered to submit to the exam.

What message does this send about disbelief of those who report rape? The assistant county prosecutor in the Cuyahoga County case believed the court was trying to reinvestigate the case after the trial in a way that harassed and intimidated the rape victims. One of the girls' mothers stated that the perpetrators could interpret the polygraph requirement to mean that the judge did not believe her daughter: "It felt like the blame was back on her and she was being victimized, by not only him, but by the system as well."

Writer Jessica Valenti agreed. "By making these young women submit to polygraphs, the judge is sending a very clear message: I don't trust you, the system doesn't trust you, and you won't find justice here."

The polygraph test is known to be unreliable when administered to individuals in crisis. Requiring a polygraph test conveys disbelief of the account. This can increase stress levels, causing a complainant to fail the test. And an unsuccessful exam can result in prosecutors filing charges for making a false report. Recantations, before or after the test, are often an understandable result of the pressure, but they further convince investigators that rape charges are false. These factors caused Congress to conclude in 2005 that polygraph tests are simply inappropriate to use in rape cases. As a result, the jurisdictions requiring them lost federal funding.

## Punishment

These days, bringing criminal charges and harsh penalties against women for making false rape claims is more and more common. For example, a seventeen-year-old was charged with and convicted of filing a false rape report in Oregon. Many inconsistencies in the accounts of the three men and the young girl existed, said the judge, but he ruled the young men to be more credible. He explained that he relied on the testimony of a police detective and the girl's friends. They had said that she did not act traumatized in the days after the incident, although her companions had urged her to go to the police in the first place.

An eighteen-year-old Washington State woman reported being raped at the hands of an armed man, who tied her up and took photographs after raping her for four hours. Police officials not only disbelieved her account but also charged her with making a false report and fined her five hundred dollars. When investigators eventually caught up with an area rapist, they found photographs of the young woman's ordeal on his camera. The memory card had more than a hundred pictures of his victims.

Perhaps the most heartless example involves a young woman who reported being raped and robbed at gunpoint at the gas station–convenience store where she worked. The police officer suspected she had fabricated the account to hide her own theft of the money. Prosecutors charged her with falsely reporting a rape, and she spent five days in jail before she was able to post bail. Before her trial, a man confessed to the attack on her and others in the area that had occurred earlier. Later, it was revealed that at the time the police officer submitted the criminal complaint against her, the detective received another case in which a young woman reported being attacked by someone of the same general description. The woman said this attacker held her at gunpoint while he fondled her breasts and forced her to perform oral sex on him. Not only did the attack take place less than two miles from the gas station and at the same time of night as the earlier episode, but a similar weapon was also used. Despite these facts, the officer declined to consider the attacks linked in any way and proceeded with charging the first woman. He filed the criminal complaint against her on the same day that he learned from the state police that DNA analysis linked the attack to other rapes in the state.

Although a Welsh woman retracted allegations that her husband had raped her six times, authorities knew she had been abused for ten years and was undoubtedly a victim of rape as well as coerced prostitution. The woman said her husband and sister-in-law had pressured her to withdraw the charges. Yet authorities proceeded to charge her with the crime of perverting the course of justice by retracting *truthful* allegations. The judge ordered her to serve eight months in prison, separating her from her children. At the time of sentencing in November 2010, the judge lectured her that she had wasted a "substantial amount of time and money for police and prosecutors." After she had served eighteen days of her sentence, the Lord Chief Justice of England and Wales released her, criticizing the decision to prosecute the abused woman and ruling that the judiciary had a "duty of compassion" for a woman who had already been victimized. Later, however, the Court of Appeal refused her motion to expunge the criminal conviction and clear her criminal record.

A case along these same lines involves a twenty-year-old who said she was fondled by a police officer after she called him to her home during a domestic violence incident in Chicago. When she attempted to file a complaint against the officer, two internal affairs officials tried to dissuade her from filing the charges. She then used her BlackBerry to record the investigators and preserve the evidence of their malfeasance. Prosecutors charged her with a felony—taping a conversation without consent of the parties—which could have given her fifteen years in prison. Meanwhile, her complaint against the police officer languished.

Then, in August 2011, a jury took less than an hour to acquit the defendant of the eavesdropping counts. They relied on an exception in the statute that allows citizens to obtain evidence through a surreptitious recording if they have a reasonable suspicion that a crime may be committed. One juror said jury members believed the defendant should never have been prosecuted. According to testimony at the trial, the two internal affairs officers were never investigated, and one was even promoted to lieutenant.

Instances of inappropriate punishment of those who make rape complaints appear frequently. After a twenty-one-year-old woman reported in 2007 that a stranger raped her, police found a warrant out for her. She had committed auto theft during her teen years and owed $4,500 in unpaid restitution for the crime. Immediately after her rape report, police handcuffed her, arrested her, and sent her to jail, where allegedly she was unable to obtain the needed second dose of the morning-after pill. And just after a woman announced that Halliburton/KBR coworkers in Baghdad in 2006 had gang-raped her, the company put her under guard in a shipping container for twenty-four hours without food or water. They warned her that she would be out of a job if she left Iraq for medical treatment. Eventually she was able to convince a sympathetic guard to loan her a cell phone so she could call her father in Texas, who was able to organize her rescue from the incarceration.

In 2007, the University of Portland threatened a student with charges of underage drinking after she reported a rape. A university official sent a notice to the student that read, "Based upon my findings in my investigation, I am unable to determine if a sexual assault occurred. I have reason to believe that intercourse occurred, but both parties admit to drinking and therefore, consent—or lack of consent—is difficult to determine. Given these facts, there are possible violations for which you could be charged."

The ensuing uproar forced a rethink, and the college revised the school handbook a year later. To remove barriers to rape reporting, the university declared it would not pursue potential policy violations by those who come forward. In this particular case, the change was critical. The college could have invoked a violation of Catholic teaching, including sex outside of marriage, which could have led to expulsion from the community.

After a fifteen-year-old girl in southeast Wisconsin was gang-raped by some young men who got her intoxicated, she was left to lie in a hospital bed with vomit in her hair for eight hours. Meanwhile, the police wrote her a ticket for underage drinking.

In another case, in 2009 outside Edinburgh, Scotland, a woman named Ann Robertson broke down and fled the witness stand in tears, unable to complete her testimony against the defendant, an accused rapist. In response, judge Roger Craik said, "Well maybe a night in the cells will calm you down." At his direction, Robertson was arrested, taken to the police lockup, and left there overnight. Later Robertson filed a formal complaint against the judge, who, she said, treated her more like a criminal than a victim. Eventually Scotland's most senior judge issued an unprecedented reprimand, finding Craik's actions "unjustified and disproportionate." Tragically, Robertson, who suffered from epilepsy, was found dead in her home a few months later. According to her sister-in-law, she was perhaps a victim of the stress she suffered during the trial and her incarceration.

Not only do we punish those who report being raped, but we also attack the messengers, the people who assist these women. One might have thought the two girls who intervened and rescued a drunk young woman who was being publicly raped at a De Anza College baseball players' party were heroines, but some on the campus seemed not to agree. The young women suffered harassment; they were threatened by people who came up to them saying, "Stop your lying. Shut your f—king mouth." They considered the intimidation serious enough to report it to law enforcement.

In 2009, *New York Times* columnist Nicholas D. Kristof described a tour of a brothel in Cambodia where young women, abducted from Vietnam, were subjected to electric shocks by brothel owners. But skeptical readers could not accept that the conditions could be abusive. They accused Kristof, in his zeal to advance a feminist agenda, of either being played for a fool or outright lying. And when, in 2003, German writer Hans Magnus Enzensberger reissued the diary of a deceased woman who had experienced rapes at the hands of Soviet soldiers as they conquered Berlin in April 1945, one writer blamed him for publishing an outright fraudulent account. He charged the woman with lying, and he depicted Enzensberger as grossly negligent in his reprinting of a work that could not be authenticated. These allegations were repeated in a number of German newspapers. This sad episode illustrates the attempts that will be made to silence rape victims—even one who has passed away.

# Punishing Megan

Megan's experiences after being raped by a basketball player ran the gamut from encountering indifference and disbelief to receiving punishment.

Megan soon found out that three other college students had reported similar run-ins with this particular young man, suggesting that he engaged in repeat predatory behavior as identified by researcher David Lisak. In one reported case, a friend held a woman down while the young man sexually penetrated her; in the second, another woman said she was subjected to an attempted penetration; and in the third, yet another explained she was groped but managed to get away.

As in Tracy's case, Megan's college health service did not take a rape kit or even direct her to a hospital emergency room. Her eventual medical examination did note injuries consistent with force. Megan's father, an attorney, went with her to meet with police detectives and the prosecutor. But Megan didn't hear from the prosecutor until the day of the grand jury presentation seven months later.

Megan felt that the college administration was unsupportive, especially the female deans. They kept telling her, "It's water under the bridge," or "You need to get over it." During a Take Back the Night event, which Megan attended with her roommate and two friends from down the hall, their rooms were broken into and the sheets of her friends were slit.

Megan found this frightening, because she didn't realize the basketball player knew where she lived or who her friends were. Campus security was indifferent, claiming the sheets may have spontaneously torn during the Take Back the Night event. When Megan said she thought she knew who might have done it, the head of security accused her of slander.

Fearing their rooms would be broken into, other friends turned on her, and the young woman with whom she was planning to room the next year abandoned her. All that summer, Megan had sleep problems and experienced other symptoms of posttraumatic stress disorder. When she returned to campus, she could not fall asleep. Her friends continued to express resentment that fraternity members were treating them poorly because of her accusations.

> It was clear that the community was shunning me. Toward
> the end, I really had nobody. It was really hard. I decided
> to transfer. I just had to. I wasn't going to make it there.

At the time of the grand jury hearing, taunts against Megan's friends had stepped up. That week, a typed note was slipped under their door that read, "You'll lose." Although they were informed, security continued to studiously ignore the problem.

Then, at the hearing, the prosecutor informed Megan and her father that none of the other three complainants had bothered to show up. He also told Megan he was going to give the accused a voice-stress-analysis test, and if he passed, the prosecutor was going to "find it hard to try for an indictment." He ended up failing the test, and later Megan learned that, after all, the three other girls attended the grand jury hearing and testified about being assaulted. But the prosecutor did not secure an indictment— not surprising given his prior statements.

Megan proceeded with an administrative hearing at the school before a panel of teachers. She asked to have her father sit with her but was told by an angry dean of students that he was not allowed in. However, the accused had a dean sit by his side. That painful hearing, filled with hostile questions, caused Megan to question and blame herself even more. She thought, What if I hadn't gone to the party? What if I hadn't gone upstairs with him? What if I wasn't so socially awkward? What if I wasn't so stupid and naive? None of these things would have happened.

Armed with a copy of Megan's medical report, the young man speculated that Megan was making up the charge because she was on steroids (which she took for asthma). Despite the difficult hearing, Megan did manage to get the basketball player expelled from the college.

> I was shaken from having endured questioning for hours—some by him—but it was a victory. I felt good, until I found out that he was just going to enroll in another university. The reasons for his expulsion were apparently confidential.

Megan put all her hopes on the civil suit she had brought against the college, which had failed to take action even though it knew about the other rape reports.

> The fact that the school knew about the assailant but did nothing, and then let him enroll in another school was too much for me—I had to do something. Plus, we could see on the school's website the statistics that they are required to provide about crime were complete lies. They listed no assault, although they knew of at least half a dozen that had been reported to the school in the past year. The civil suit gave me something else to believe in. The year before, I had pinned all of my hopes on the criminal case, which went nowhere. Now, I had one more shot.

After filing, Megan transferred to another university.

> I hadn't wanted to leave. I chose the college, I did nothing wrong. . . . But I was isolated, and I couldn't sleep. The place was toxic for me.

Yet the nightmare simply would not end. A student journalist came to Megan, wanting to interview her about the case for an article he was writing in the school newspaper. She told him that she couldn't talk with him about the matter because of the pending lawsuit. The student went and interviewed the defendant and wrote a story about the accusation, and he printed Megan's full name. In the article, the defendant called Megan a "dirty whore" who just felt bad about what had happened. Not one person commented on the newspaper website about this one-sided presentation of the case. Megan's last friend stopped talking to her around this time.

> I felt powerless. I couldn't respond to the articles, but I felt like there was no way anyone who read them could possibly believe my side—my side was never being told. I wanted to show other victims that they needed to come forward to prevent other assaults, and that the school would have to act appropriately. Instead, my name was completely smeared, and the only message I was sending was that the school controls what information is presented, and if a victim makes a fuss, this is what happens.

The deposition she made in her civil lawsuit was anguishing.

> I understand the lawyers are only doing their job, but as a victim it was extremely painful and again got me to the lowest levels I could be at. Asking questions like, "Are you saying all this to get attention?" Somehow they went through family history that I didn't know. I didn't know that my great-grandfather had killed himself, and they brought this up. Aren't I just deranged and it runs in the family? They found counseling records from my parents who went to a couple of counseling sessions regarding me in high school because I had an eating disorder that was hard for them. I got to hear my parents saying they felt like I just did things for attention. It was really painful, because my parents were very supportive, but I started to question that support. I was really isolated.

Once Megan had transferred to her new school, her lawyers contacted her and let her know they didn't believe it made sense to continue. The suit would not be successful.

I had nothing more to pin my hopes on. Justice had completely failed me. The good news: I was in a new place, with new people. No one knew anything about me, and I could start anew. But I didn't feel like starting, and I didn't feel new. I felt tired and used, and the most I could do was just go through the motions and pretend that it never happened—pretend that I was someone I no longer could be.

To make matters even more stressful, once her lawsuit was dismissed the basketball player filed a pro se lawsuit against Megan and the school, claiming she had assaulted *him* and the college had improperly dismissed him. That legal action, which he lost, took about a year to resolve.

Later Megan went online and found eight college newspaper stories about her case, all in a four-month period, which she had never seen since she had left the campus. Full coverage of the male student's lawsuit and his allegations against her were given without her own account. In one of the articles, Megan was startled that several times the director of counseling services minimized rape at the college by describing it as "misconduct" and proclaiming that this "misconduct" was less prevalent and severe than at other schools.

Megan's experience shows how, in a rape case, indifference can develop into disbelief, then punishment. In the beginning people believed her, Megan said, but did not want to do anything about it. By the time of the newspaper report, however, incredulity had set in, followed by ostracism. To this day, years later, Megan feels bewildered: "How could I make all this up because I felt bad about what I did, when it happened to be a guy who had also assaulted three other people?"

The most painful aspect was the aftermath. It was what the community did to me that still keeps me awake at night and is still hard to get over. The rape is bad enough. Victims, after dealing with that, shouldn't have to go through a whole slew of self-doubt and loathing, all based on the way people—not the perpetrator, other people— treat them. If you know people this has happened to, let

them know you are there for them. If you see something
that you know is patently wrong, say something about it.
Your silence sends a huge message.

Two rape allegations on the campus of Notre Dame University have
elements similar to Megan's account. One case, however, ended in sui-
cide, a result that Megan thankfully avoided.

On September 1, 2010, Elizabeth Seeberg, age nineteen, reported
to Notre Dame campus police a sexual attack by a Notre Dame football player the day before. She obtained hospital treatment, DNA testing,
and, later, counseling. The next day, a friend of the football player sent a
threatening text message to Seeberg. He told her, "Messing with Notre
Dame football is a bad idea." On September 10, Seeberg died of an over-
dose of a drug prescribed to her for depression and anxiety.

Although all the facts were not immediately available, newspapers
reported that campus police did not interview the accused until September 15, fourteen days after Seeberg's report and five days after her death.
Nor did the campus police report the matter to the St. Joseph County
prosecutor's office. The football player was allowed to continue playing.

In the second case, also involving a nineteen-year-old, the rape
occurred in the morning hours of September 4, 2010, in a Notre Dame
dorm room. Later that day, the young woman, who had blood seeping
through her denim shorts, underwent DNA testing in the hospital. In
her statement given to campus police, she said she had been "very intoxicated" and could not remember what happened, but she was a virgin
and would never have consented to sexual intercourse. Two friends, she
said, were witnesses to the blood. She never heard back from campus
police, who assigned the case to a detective on September 8—more than
seventy-two hours after her report.

The girl's parents flew to South Bend, Indiana, to meet with the
detective on September 10, who told them that police were waiting
for their daughter to contact them again. Detectives did not attempt to
interview the accused until September 15, four days after her parents'
visit and ten days after the report. Campus police did not question the
young women's friends until five weeks after the rape. Several months

later, the local prosecutor let the young woman know he would not file criminal charges. In cases like this one, outside experts question the tardiness of the investigations, which can compromise evidence. Defense attorneys explain that delay only gives accused individuals time to get their stories straight.

At that very time, Notre Dame was under investigation by the US Department of Education for covering up two rape accusations against another student. In December 2010, the department announced the settlement of the case. It reportedly addressed problems identified at Notre Dame in the investigation of sexual assault cases.

In a 2011 investigation, the *Chicago Tribune* surveyed six Midwestern universities and found that since 2005, the schools had received reports of 171 sex crimes on campus. Of these, only twelve led to arrests. The University of Illinois at Chicago noted that the problem was getting the local prosecutor to charge a rape case that occurred on the college campus. In response, the prosecutor's office stated to the newspaper that filing charges is problematic: there is often a relationship between the individuals, the use of alcohol might be involved, and there are typically no witnesses to the incident.

One episode involving a Marquette University athlete illustrates how colleges, like prosecutors, fail to take these college rape charges seriously. Administrators admitted they broke state law by not reporting a rape to the police; indeed, they had failed to inform police in a number of other instances involving school athletes. In one case, the students had had a sexual relationship in the past, but the athlete had broken it off with the young woman. Later, she accepted an invitation to the athlete's campus apartment, and they began to have consensual sex. However, according to the young woman, she asked him to stop when he began making disparaging comments to her, but he held her down. Eventually the student went to the hospital with vaginal abrasions and injuries on her face, hip, foot, knee, and both thighs.

University administrators commented that the earlier sexual relationship prevented them from seeing this attack as a rape. They told the young woman that police wouldn't want to investigate her case and that the university's internal discipline process would likely cause her more harm than good. The student asserted that the dean of students discouraged her from pursuing charges and asked her if she had thought about praying about the situation. She has since transferred to another school.

Despite the fact that physical evidence pointed to an assault, the Marquette athlete was never held accountable for his actions. The indifference of college authorities resulted in the case's never being reported to local police, and the young woman was discouraged from approaching officers herself.

As a result of university indifference around the country, in April 2011 the US Department of Education delivered new regulatory guidance for colleges and universities responding to student complaints of campus sexual assault. Grievance procedures must be prompt, and institutions must take proper interim steps to protect complainants, such as moving either them or the accused to a new class or a different residence hall or prohibiting the accused student from attending class for a period of time. In adjudicating complaints, the school must use a preponderance of the evidence standard rather than the "clear and convincing" rubric, a higher standard of proof.

The Department of Education said that colleges and universities reported almost three thousand forcible sex offenses on campuses in 2009. Despite this statistic, at the time the guidelines were published, Heather Mac Donald resurfaced in the nation's newspapers, via a *National Review* online column syndicated in many a local newspaper, to deny that number and the problem:

> Biden has just announced more college red tape on the laughable ground that schools ignore sexual violence. In fact, virtually every campus has a robust sexual-violence bureaucracy which sits idle, waiting for the shell-shocked casualties of rape to crawl through their doors. These victims never come—because they don't exist. But pressure from the feds will undoubtedly give those lonely college rape counselors further clout to push for increased funding, even as schools cut their German and Latin programs for lack of money.

Indeed, the new federal requirements ignited a backlash. Some of the usual commentators, like Cathy Young, and new ones, like romance novelist Sandy Hingston and Peter Berkowitz in the *Wall Street Journal*, all wrote that the new rules will limit adolescent sexual exploration, create a male presumption of guilt, and work to convince the women they have been sexually assaulted instead of just having had bad sex. Berkowitz in particular, a fellow at Stanford University's Hoover Institution, minimized rape as just bad sex, despite the existence of traumatic experiences like Riley's, Tracy's, and Megan's. He poetically asked, "Where are the professors of literature who will patiently point out that, particularly where erotic desire is involved, intentions can be obscure, passions conflicting, the heart murky and the soul divided?"

When, in December 2010, prosecutor Roger Canaff wrote about these cases on his blog, ten to twelve women responded with their own similar accounts of college rapes. Explained Canaff, "I was inundated with heartfelt, heartbreaking accounts from women who were sexually attacked in a similar manner to Ms. Seeberg, and who either never reported or found it to be a completely worthless effort. I was deeply impacted by what I heard. I guess it's the accounts themselves that are getting to me, because they are the human face on the numbers. The numbers I know. These accounts are shocking."

One woman, for example, said three Notre Dame football players had raped her. She had two individuals who told her they had witnessed the rape but refused to come forward because they didn't want to get in trouble for being in the wrong place at the wrong time. The players were over six feet tall and more than 220 pounds each, and to prevent injury she did not fight. They wore condoms.

In 2006, Megan Wright, a freshman at Dominican College in New York, reported she was gang-raped in a dorm room. The hospital examination showed severe bruising and lacerations. Wright's parents, in a lawsuit they later brought, said that the school never conducted an investigation. Wright left the college because she said she feared her attackers, who were still on campus. She later suffocated herself with a plastic bag.

Megan finds these cases unbearably sad. "Society doesn't believe the woman until she takes a step to harm herself," she says. "No one questions now that Seeberg was raped, now that she's killed herself."

The lack of community support is the overriding theme of these accounts. Megan considers this more distressing than the rapes themselves.

# [9]

# Freeing Strauss-Kahn

Not surprisingly, the woman who accused Dominique Strauss-Kahn fared no better than Megan. On August 22, 2011, New York City prosecutors filed a motion to dismiss the indictment of Strauss-Kahn, informing the court that two criminal elements in the case—force and lack of consent—would rest solely on the testimony of the complaining witness at trial. Although physical evidence established a hurried sexual encounter, it could not independently prove Diallo's rape claim. But, the prosecutors stated, information gathered during the postindictment phase found evidence on other matters that fatally undermined the housekeeper's reliability. In an unusual twenty-five-page motion, the prosecutors proceeded to detail falsehoods in Diallo's earlier asylum application. They found links to individuals involved in criminal activities, including drug dealing and money laundering. These ties led them to believe that they could not reasonably rely on her account in a court of law, where a jury would have to be persuaded beyond a reasonable doubt that the complainant was credible. Most crucially, the housekeeper twice told prosecutors she had been gang-raped by soldiers in Guinea. When she finally admitted that the account was fabricated, she said she had made up the attack to ensure the success of her asylum application (although the application made no mention of any gang rape). Once the court dismissed the case, Strauss-Kahn left for France.

What followed, it is fair to say, was a total reversal: based on the prosecutor's motion, much of the media then rushed to a judgment that the housekeeper's rape account was untrue. Just before the prosecutor was to make his decision, Diallo's attorney arranged for his client to give an interview to *Newsweek* magazine. The publication then ran a cover story with the lurid headline THE DSK MAID SPEAKS: SHE SAID ONE OF THE WORLD'S MOST POWERFUL MEN TRIED TO RAPE HER—THEN FOUND HERSELF ACCUSED. In the lengthy article, the reporters let the reader know when they did not believe her accounts, especially when she talked about events in West Africa ("There were moments when her tears seemed forced"), although they do admit that her rape narrative "was vivid and compelling." But, in the end, the attempt at damage control by Diallo and her attorney resulted in the usual "he said, she said" exercise that undoubtedly made clear to rape victims everywhere—including Megan, Tracy, and Riley—that they would be put on trial themselves if they made a rape claim.

Why did prosecutors file such a detailed motion to dismiss that was so damning of the accuser? The practice is hardly common for them, and it went far beyond legal necessity. Obviously the intent was to placate a potentially disapproving public. But, in the words of one former prosecutor, this exercise was undertaken at the expense "of a seemingly disposable human being" and "chock full of affirmation for DSK picking this particular woman as his target."

As the dust cleared, some journalists applauded the prosecutor's decision as right and proper, even as they admitted that they found Strauss-Kahn's account simply implausible. As Stuart Taylor wrote, "The notion that Diallo would willingly perform oral sex on a complete stranger, in the space of less than eight minutes, strains credulity." He speculated that Strauss-Kahn undertook an aggressive attempt at seduction, and the woman, on the spur of the moment, consented, because she feared making a wealthy hotel guest angry.

However, Taylor should have realized that, in his scenario, such "consent" could have been held to be coerced under law. Similar confusion might have also affected Strauss-Kahn himself, who admitted on French television to "an error" and a "moral failure" he would regret his whole life—but not to a criminal act. Meanwhile, French authorities declined to prosecute Strauss-Kahn for the episode involving a French reporter who claimed he attempted to rape her in 2003; they said the statute of limitations had elapsed.

In late December 2011, the *New York Review of Books* saw fit to print an article about the case by investigative journalist Edward Jay Epstein. The piece was obviously based on materials provided by Strauss-Kahn's attorneys and intended to present readers with facts that would support a conspiracy theory. Although the story asked a few questions about a missing cell phone, it was unable to shed any light on what happened within those fateful eight minutes. Still, it led to a new round of news stories, which breathlessly informed readers that new doubts have been cast on the events at the Sofitel. Journalist Christopher Dickey wrote that Epstein's article read "as if it were dictated by" Strauss-Kahn's lawyers. He agreed with Stuart Taylor—that it would be unlikely that the "heavyset," "scarred" housekeeper was a willing "seductress"—and described a scenario very like Tracy's:

> Indeed, she says she was terrified of losing her job as he attacked her like a madman, and she was especially worried that if she hurt him that would be the end of her employment. She says she didn't know who this crazy, gray-haired, stark-naked man was, but she knew he was in one of the hotel's most expensive suites. As an illiterate immigrant, she would have had nowhere to turn if he denounced her to management. In the end, wrestled to the ground in the hallway, by her account, she decided to let DSK get off so she could just get out of there.

Because of its internal contradictions, the result in this case would prove deeply dissatisfying. If Strauss-Kahn's account didn't seem credible, then why couldn't charges be brought? The intense scrutiny of the housekeeper in this case also left many with grave misgivings. The fact that in 2012 a French prosecutor began an investigation into whether Strauss-Kahn had raped a woman in a Washington, DC, hotel in 2010 intensified concern about this case's outcome.

Ironically, however, the Strauss-Kahn case may have pushed us forward. Perhaps the public began to understand that a much-accomplished public servant, reportedly happily married, could also have a propensity for aggressively forcing himself on women. For until we are able to hold this thought, we simply have to believe that all accusers of celebrities are lying.

Tracy's attorney, Celeste Hamilton, reminds us that the public has to understand that it is not just only horrible monsters who commit rape. "Jerry Sandusky, Julian Assange, Dominique Strauss-Kahn, Kobe Bryant, Bill Clinton, Al Gore. All these men have demonstrated exceptional talent, skill, and intelligence in their respective fields," Hamilton pointed out. "All these men have also demonstrated, whether through lengthy marriages or publicly reported consensual sexual encounters, that they are capable of being charming, of earning trust and affection, of achieving consent."

Individuals who are raped, she said, are doubly victimized. First, a person they trusted, one with whom they were willing to be alone, was capable of denying their sexual integrity, exhibiting hostility and domination, and inflicting humiliation. Then, when they report the rape, they are subjected to further enmity and shaming.

But, ultimately, the recent unprecedented pileup of celebrity cases may convince the public to revise its views about acquaintance rape and hence its ideas about the veracity of those who report rape.

# Believing Riley

U nlike Tracy's, Megan's, and Diallo's legal travails, Riley's experience
with law enforcement demonstrates a world without rape denial. Happily she was the beneficiary of a forensic medical examination, a thorough
police investigation, and representation from a prosecutor willing to risk
defeat. But would that all be enough for Luke to be held accountable?

Riley had inadvertently done a good job of preserving the physical evidence. Luckily she had been so distraught that she hadn't gotten around
to taking a shower, and later a good friend advised her to stay away from
bathing. A friend took her to the hospital emergency room. Later Luke's
attorney berated Riley during the trial for telling her friend about the
attack, who then supposedly had to convince her she had been raped. At
the hospital, a rape-victim advocate and a specially trained sexual assault
nurse examiner helped Riley complete a rape kit, which included a black-
light examination for semen and collection of DNA evidence. The nurse
found and diagrammed vaginal lacerations from the struggle and administered antibiotics to prevent sexually transmitted disease. That the hospital
took her account seriously had a big impact on Riley as she thought about
whether she would tell the police.

> I wondered about what would happen if the police
> doubted me. I learned that if my friend and the nurse

and rape-victim advocate believed me, then hopefully the police would too. Those things made me more sure of myself before going to the police.

Riley made the decision to talk to the police about the rape.

I wanted what happened to be accounted for. I wanted to get all the details down officially and straightened out because I felt so wronged, and so abused, that it was hard for me to process anything until I finally came forward. I used that fury to help me go after him—as he went after me. But unlike him, I was seeking justice, prevention for other rapes, and he was seeking prey.

By reporting the attack to law enforcement, a rape victim takes an irrevocable step: she has decided not to deny but to confront the horror of what occurred.

Going to the police actually solidifies what happened. It forces you to admit every dreaded detail, face every gory fact, and accept what happens. This is the hardest part of all. It confirms we are now a victim, a statistic, no longer living as if it didn't happen or trying to make it go away. At first, we try to resist that something this awful has happened to us. So it's easy if you don't report it to isolate yourself and never have to face it.

Riley's account elicited a positive response. Once she named Luke, the police detective became animated. Like Megan, Riley had been assaulted by a serial predator.

She says, "We have been waiting for someone to come forward for a long time now. Because we know of other women he has attacked, but they have refused to prosecute."

When the DNA evidence came back with a match, Riley spoke with the prosecuting attorney, Vivian King. She made the decision to cooperate with the prosecution.

When I talked with Vivian, she told me what the process would be like and how hard it would be. One thing we talked about was that this is not going to be any harder than it was then, it might be just as bad, but it's not going to be any harder. I have already survived, and it's not about me anymore—it's about the women. If someone doesn't try to put a stop to it, he is going to continue, and he needs to be stopped.

And so I thought, I'm not going to let him get away with it. I don't want revenge, I want him to be away from the public, and I want women to be protected. I want to be protected too. If I could save one woman from suffering this and enduring this . . . that is the best thing to combat the issue. That is what motivated me.

In addition to Riley, five separate women in the county had reported rapes at the hands of Luke. Former assistant county attorney Vivian King explained, "[These women] didn't want to proceed; they didn't want anyone to know. You could tell from the progression, when you placed the files chronologically, you could tell how he had gotten better in every single sex abuse. At first, he was very rough, leaving injuries, not suave, and progressively, with each and every case, he got slicker, smarter. He knew how to apply force without leaving an injury and without applying physical pressure. I knew that if he was not convicted, the next time he raped that we were not going to be able to prosecute him. I knew that. Because of that, I placed a lot of effort into the case, because I felt responsible. If he did not get convicted, we were going to have a massive serial rapist and not do anything about it."

So Luke was charged with three felony counts of rape—two oral and one vaginal. King told Riley she was sure the jury wouldn't convict on all three counts. Juries, she said, often like to compromise.

According to King, prosecuting acquaintance rape cases is difficult. First, the public simply doesn't want to believe that something like that can happen in their town. "When somebody comes up and says I was the victim of sexual abuse," said King, "the first reaction of the listener is,

'That's not possible.' And even more so, if there are no injuries, if there was a relationship between the rapist and the victim, if they knew each other, if there was no weapon involved, if it was in the victim's home. If you don't fight tooth and nail and be on the verge of death, it is simply unbelievable. Compare that with someone who goes to the police and says someone she met in a bar broke into her house to steal something. Under no circumstances would anyone question a victim who makes that type of report. They would take it as truth and simply go with it. But somebody breaking into your house is the equivalent of somebody breaking into your body."

Then, said King, the public "confuses the ability of a person to avoid something and equates it with the person then being responsible for its happening. A woman who has gone back to this man's apartment and is raped, the public, the community will say, well, she should have known better. You put yourself in a situation where that could happen, and for that reason, this is really your fault. If you had not gone there, it would never have happened. I would explain to the jury, keep responsibility where it lies, don't mistake the possibility of avoiding something with being responsible for it."

Did King think she would get a conviction in this case? Ethically, as a prosecutor, she could not indict someone or charge a case if she did not believe she could prove the elements. Juries, however, can be unpredictable in cases dealing with sex.

"There were many cases that I felt I had a slam-dunk case, and I would go to trial and the jury would acquit the defendant. Again there were other cases—I know I have the evidence, whether the jury believes it or not is a completely different story, and I felt it was worth a chance. But I know there are problems, they are probably not going to convict the defendant—and then the jury would come back with a conviction."

The prosecutor did have one ace up her sleeve: Luke had changed his account. "He had gotten smart, but not smart enough." In a videotaped interview with a police detective, he said he had no physical contact whatsoever with Riley.

King described the tape. "He sat there very relaxed. He's sitting back, legs are crossed, chit-chatting with the officer. He's not concerned. He denies nineteen separate times that he had any contact that was physical in nature with this young woman. No kissing, no touching. 'If I got a DNA sample, what you're telling me is that your DNA isn't going to be there?' 'That's what I'm telling you. You're not going to find it.' At first, he denied knowing her. Then he said, 'Oh, Riley,' like it was just coming back to him. It was so unbelievable. And it was fatal. It was fatal to his case."

Riley then had to wait many months for the trial. There was a no-contact order against Luke, whom she continued to run into on campus. As a matter of fact, he was arrested twice for violating the order when he talked with and mocked Riley.

Even after the indictment and before trial, Luke continued his aggressive activities. Several women reported to the police that Luke approached them, not taking no for an answer. He kept following the women and would not just walk away when rebuffed, but luckily nothing happened in the end. His behavior conformed to researcher David Lisak's profile of the serial rapist, who will not be deterred or persuaded not to rape. These men "tend to be serial offenders, and most of them commit a variety of different interpersonal offenses. They are accurately and appropriately labeled as predators."

King agreed. "A normal person would be scared off of this behavior by a prosecution. You are not dealing with a normal person. These people are wired differently."

The day of the trial finally arrived. About fifteen members of Riley's family attended as a support group, including her mother and father, her sisters, her brothers, her brother-in-law, her aunts, and her cousin. Some family friends also attended. They all wanted to demonstrate that they did not doubt Riley at all.

"We wanted to be there to support Riley and her family," explained her cousin Richard. "I am almost embarrassed to say that my reaction in part was, 'Riley, please don't build up your expectations that this man will be convicted and imprisoned, because it is my sense that this often doesn't happen.' Her mother and others in the family understood that. We didn't broadcast it very loudly to Riley. I was, to be honest, pleased that the prosecutor was taking it very seriously, as she did, and pushing it as hard as she did. We had no doubts about Riley's veracity, but we knew it was hard to get a conviction."

Richard noted the defendant Luke with interest. The young man was big and strong and looked broad shouldered, mobile, and fit—an athletic type of guy. He sat during the trial not making eye contact with Riley and her family.

Jury selection took up most of the first day. For the prosecuting attorney, jury selection was the most important part of a rape trial. King was looking for jurors who were going to give her a fair shot. She did not want them to come in with preconceived notions, such as the only person who can be raped is a "woman who is a virgin, walking down the street, and a guy in a mask and with a weapon jumps out of the bushes. She fights, and she has injuries, and there is DNA. She immediately reports it, and there is nothing about her background, and she wasn't drinking."

King said of screening potential jurors, "The biggest problem is that people will not be honest with you, they will not say exactly how they feel about it. I can't tell you how many times I would ask a juror over and over the same question, but asked differently, and eventually they would say, 'You know, if she's wearing provocative clothing, yes, of course I am going to think that she was looking for it. Yes, if she was saying no, but depending on how she was saying it, it was very possible that she was not saying no.' People are simply not honest about saying what they think in regards to the subject."

Luke did not take the stand. Now he maintained that the sexual intercourse was consensual, the common defense of a predatory rapist, according to King.

"This is the way the rapist wants it to come across: 'Oh, this was a complete misunderstanding. I thought she wanted to have sex with me and I'm really sorry, I was wrong.' That's how they want people to see it. It is usually well intentional, very well thought out."

During the trial, the prosecutor played the interrogation videotape. King was also able to introduce other evidence showing false statements made by the defendant, like those about just moving from California or his family's having a beach house in California. His credibility was thrown into doubt.

But the videotape was key. According to King, "Without the video-tape, we would have had a harder time. Going back to those preconceived notions, [jurors] will try and find every single reason possible to believe it did not happen. 'She has a motive to make it up, she is mistaken about it, maybe it was somebody else, or she has a mental condition that caused her to hallucinate.' They will find any reason to acquit a person."

And, indeed, destroying Riley's credibility was the goal of Luke's attorney. His cross-examination was contentious and difficult. Riley didn't break down, but Richard said she was close. She was asked about the underwear she had on, why she didn't use her cell phone to call for help, and the message she was sending by going over there in the first place. "All of it being that I was in the wrong," Riley said. Even the movie Riley selected, *Captain Corelli's Mandolin*, was questioned.

> It's a war movie about this general who attempts to have sex with this woman. She refuses his advances, but eventually she realizes she's in love with him and they get together. "You're sending this message by watching this movie, that despite refusing his advances you want him to continue to pursue you. Why do you think Luke thought that 'no' meant 'yes'?" We weren't even watching the whole movie. He was attacking me during it. It was ridiculous.

For Riley, the trial was deeply traumatic.

> If you are not believed, that is just humiliating. What are they thinking of me? You are under such scrutiny, you are slandered by the defendant's attorney. The point is to get you to try to second-guess yourself.

Although he did not take the stand, Luke did try to manipulate events during the trial. During one of the recesses, King said, he approached the female judge and started flirting with her, chatting her up, and seeking to establish a relationship with her. Rebuffing him, the judge told Luke his behavior was inappropriate. When court reconvened, she put a summary of the encounter and her response in the record.

Two crucial facts, however, were kept from the jury during the trial. Prior and recent complaints against Luke from other women were not admissible during the adjudication phase, so they could not be a factor in the jury's determining guilt or innocence in this particular case. The judge also ruled that King could not admit Riley's cystic fibrosis into evidence. To the prosecutor's disappointment, the court determined this fact was irrelevant and likely to be prejudicial to the defendant, in that the jury might feel pity for Riley.

King pointed out, "This is a person who has a breathing problem, who is not as strong as other people. She is the perfect prey. And we're not able to explain that to the jury. The jury doesn't get the full picture that is going on here."

Jury deliberations lasted about two hours, and the waiting was hard. For Riley, who had taken a tranquillizer, it was "like torture." In the end, the jury convicted Luke on all three counts. The defendant was extremely upset and had to be restrained by his lawyer. Everyone else in the courtroom seemed to be crying, Riley and Vivian King among them. Riley said, "When the verdict was read, we both shed tears of relief, joy, and sadness for all that had happened. It was very moving."

After the verdict was announced, a couple of the jurors approached Riley, her mother, and some of Riley's aunts. They said they were persuaded by the evidence, although, at one point in the deliberations, one of the other jurors mentioned Riley's thong underwear. The youngest member of the jury, who often looked like she was falling asleep during the trial, piped right up and said that made no difference at all, as it was something all young women wore and should not have bearing. The jurors thought this was a significant moment in their deliberations.

At the later sentencing hearing, Riley chose to make a statement, and she was up for several nights writing it.

> I just said I suffered the loss of choice that night that has stuck with me ever since. I was damaged and I am trying really hard to repair that. It felt really good to say my piece.

Here is a small excerpt from her statement:

> I know there are females out there that have been
> assaulted by Luke. I only hope that these guilty verdicts
> are a consolation to them and can help them to survive. I
> am a survivor along with them. I wake up every day and do
> not allow what has happened to destroy me. I am recov-
> ering through a healing process: by struggling through
> counseling, reading books on self improvement, and rely-
> ing on other people for support. Everyone here can now
> be more aware, gain courage, and fight this unacceptable
> violence. I do not want vengeance. As a survivor, I do not
> want anyone else to feel the way I have.

Luke was sentenced to ten years in prison, with the felony sentences
to be served concurrently, rather than consecutively as argued by the
prosecutor. This made him eligible for release five years later, in 2010, as
long as he completed a mandatory sexual-offender treatment program.
Upon discharge, his name would be placed on the sex-offender registry.
Although Luke did appeal his conviction with the assistance of the State
Appellate Defender Office, he was not successful in obtaining a new trial.

Will this conviction, imprisonment, and treatment deter a serial rapist
like Luke? The answer is not known, but at least the system hadn't failed
Riley. For her, the outcome was critical.

> For me, the trial ended up being a part of my healing pro-
> cess. It was my turn to finally not be forced by him, but to
> tell my story, regaining control. And let other people hear
> it and decide what they think.
>
> The journey was trying, but once you can put your
> head to that pillow at night with more ease, knowing your
> rapist is in jail and far from harming more victims, it makes
> it all worthwhile. It doesn't make it OK, but it makes you a
> hero. And after you go through the police and take a stand,
> your self-esteem and good feelings about yourself slowly
> come back to you, which is essential for you to survive.

# [ 10 ]

# A World Without Rape Denial

Riley, Tracy, and Megan have repeatedly explained that the young men who assaulted them did not appear much interested in sex. Instead, they wanted to exercise power over them and humiliate them by forcing the women to bring them to climax and through spewing semen over them. In another case, after a North Carolina man raped a woman, he used a box cutter to carve the word "mine" onto her stomach. Clearly rape is not always about a person getting carried away by passion; it is sometimes about an individual exercising his power and humiliating his victim by means of controlling her most private parts.

Writer Chloe Angyal said it best:

> When we forget that rape is about power, when we choose instead to imagine that it is about sex, we make a terrible mistake. It's a mistake that worms into every aspect of how we deal with the phenomenon of rape. It affects how we think about and talk about rape, perniciously affecting how we treat rape victims, how we prosecute rapists and how we try to prevent future rapes from occurring.

If we take these accounts seriously, we quickly realize how our responses to acquaintance rape are totally off the mark.

First, research is demonstrating the possibility that a small population of men perpetrate a great number of acquaintance rapes in a series of predatory attacks, and these might be prevalent on college campuses in particular. By regarding most college rapes as alcohol-fueled miscommunications, university administrations are failing to protect their students from attacks by predatory rapists. In Megan's and Riley's cases, the college had already received complaints against the same individual, but no steps had been taken to investigate their activities on campus.

In acquaintance rape cases, the accused often raises the defense that the episode was consensual. Without witnesses, proving consent wasn't given can be difficult. However, physical evidence of an attack is sometimes present. When it's combined with similar complaints against the same man, prosecutors and college administrators should have no difficulty in finding the accuser's account credible. Indeed, the failure to take into account available facts is mind-boggling for acquaintance rape victims and impedes their recovery.

Second, our society's responses to rape further the rapists' humiliation of victims. Think about Riley's being interrogated about wearing thong underwear, which also was a topic in the jury room. Or juror Judy Shepherd's description of how photos of the Alaska woman's genitals were beamed up on large television screens in the courtroom. Or Danielle's fiancé backing off after she told him she was raped. Or the young women who were forced to take lie-detector tests after their assailant had been convicted in court (or their imprisonment when they broke down on the witness stand). Or the young woman in the Missbrenner case whom a judge ordered to watch the video of herself in which she was intoxicated and being attacked. Or the basketball player who raped Megan but was allowed to condemn her as a whore in the school newspaper, with his allegations reprinted in articles for months.

Nor should we be content with humiliating individuals who are being investigated or charged with rape. It may be time to ask what is gained for a truth-seeking criminal-justice system by practices such as a "perp walk" before cameras or divulging the names of suspects who are currently being investigated.

Third, according to prosecutor Roger Canaff, institutions such as churches, schools and colleges, social organizations, and the military, among others, provide a steady source of victims for predators. By turning an indifferent or blind eye, officials at these institutions conceal what perpetrators are doing and protect them by allowing them to remain in the community. We have seen this pattern time and time again. These institutions, Canaff explained, have turned inward, displaying a distrust of outside civil and criminal processes that keep law-enforcement officials at bay. To eliminate rape in American society, our major institutions need to learn not to be afraid of transparency. Importantly, asserted Canaff, the power and mystique of institutions need to be reduced by their valuing individual human beings above institutional concerns.

I hope this work has shown that we have gone too far in one direction. We regard women who report acquaintance rape with indifference and disbelief, and we punish them. The result has empowered acquaintance rapists, making the world unsafe for many women and girls.

But we *are* capable of doing something to change the culture in which these issues are being considered. What would that changed culture look like? The approaches detailed below will go a long way toward making credibility decisions easier. They will encourage rape reporting and end humiliation of both rape perpetrators and victims.

## Hospitals

As Tracy's and Megan's stories demonstrate, medical providers and universities have a unique and important role to play in helping rape victims. Hospital emergency rooms and student health centers are often first responders to those reporting rape. We cannot eliminate rape unless medical personnel are prepared to complete a thorough forensic examination, including taking a rape kit and drawing blood for an investigation of date rape drugs, in each case. It is not their duty to determine whether the person is credible or to decide which persons receive rape kits and which do not.

## Colleges and Universities

By taking acquaintance rapes seriously and not viewing all incidences as alcohol-fueled miscommunications, colleges and universities, the sites of many predatory rapes, can greatly contribute to eliminating rape in America. Colleges need to encourage rape reporting, which, over time, will enable them to identify predators among their student bodies and take action against them. All student rape complaints should be promptly reported to police and prosecutors. Students, too, need training and encouragement to help identify, report on, or interfere with predators in social settings.

Some critics believe that colleges are ill equipped to handle rape cases because they cannot subpoena witnesses and lack the training and staff to undertake criminal investigations. However, administrative hearings are important because colleges have an obligation under federal law to maintain safe and equal learning environments for everyone. Properly trained and staffed college judicial boards can investigate and should permanently expel those found guilty. However, they need special training on rape, and policies and procedures for hearing rape cases need to be in place. In 2010, a group of college students stated that they believed that having the same individuals making decisions on cases of plagiarism or underage drinking and rape cases was insulting to those who have been raped.

## Police

We have seen the problems that develop when medical professionals improperly respond as investigators rather than as evidence preservers. Police detectives, however, do view themselves as investigators and control the accuser's pathway to the prosecutor. But, as evidenced in Tracy's and Megan's cases, police often respond to dominant cultural narratives, beliefs, and stereotypes that have resisted change and interfere with serious inquiry into the allegations. Some experts believe that police training should emphasize what an officer's job is: to collect evidence and leave veracity judgments to prosecutors, judges, and juries.

Police officers and detectives should be educated about current rape research on sexual predators and given the charge of identifying them. Because delay can put the accuser in danger, an investigation should begin immediately after a report of rape.

Certainly all rape kits should be routinely and promptly sent for testing and DNA matching. Even when police know the suspect, matching the DNA might provide linkage with other rapes and thus help to identify a sexual predator. In addition, only twenty-three states collect DNA from arrested felons, which lessens the chances of the DNA database finding a match in cold cases. To better identify and isolate predators, all states must send DNA evidence on arrested individuals to the Combined DNA Index System. State and local crime laboratories should give priority to rape cases because they often involve predators still on the loose, and legislators should be certain to provide adequate funding as well as oversight over the testing process.

## Prosecutors

Prosecutors should not learn the wrong lessons from the Duke lacrosse case. The prosecutor there committed unethical acts, surely not a typical occurrence. But they should not shrink from charging in difficult cases. When acquaintance rape allegations receive major publicity, there is some evidence to believe that prosecutors back off filing charges for fear of public criticism. Columnist Kathleen Parker, for example, believed that the failure to prosecute the accused in the De Anza College case was the unfortunate heritage of the actions of Mike Nifong, the Durham County, North Carolina, district attorney: "Instead, his abuse of the justice system, indicting three innocent men for his own political gain, may have set the stage for other guilty parties to walk free and at least one 17-year old girl, thus far, to be denied access to justice." Surely the shadow of the Duke case lay across the deliberations of the prosecutor in the rape allegations against quarterback Ben Roethlisberger. Because we do not have access to all the evidence, we will never know for sure. Prosecutors should work overtime to make certain that the Duke matter does not inappropriately restrain them in their duty of bringing criminals to justice.

This balance is difficult to strike. Kaethe Morris Hoffer, legal director of the Chicago Alliance Against Sexual Exploitation, has thought a great deal about the problem. She posited, "That the jury won't convict is not an acceptable, or legal, reason for a prosecutor to refrain from charging a perpetrator with rape. To do so is the same as saying to a black man who was almost killed by a posse and a hanging, 'We totally believe you, but in this community we could never get a conviction, so we are not going to prosecute the lynch mob.' Fundamentally, if a prosecutor believes a crime was committed, he or she must not allow social biases to prevent him or her from seeking justice. Prosecutors certainly ought to tell victims when they think a conviction would be unlikely—due to social biases that make people doubt what women report—but they should always be willing to put the offender on trial if the victim, understanding the difficulty of winning, nonetheless wants the rapist charged."

Morris Hoffer lamented that "the laws that clearly outlaw rape are not utilized by the state to hold perpetrators accountable. Whether this is because girls and women are not believed by individual prosecutors, or because the state knows they will not be believed by the public, is an open question. Regardless of the answer, the reality is that girls and women do not receive the protection of the laws to which they are entitled, which invites men who rape to engage in rape with impunity."

Civil lawsuits like Tracy's are another important method to hold acquaintance rapists accountable. With these types of suits, an individual reporting rape need not rely on the prosecutor but can bring the lawsuit on her own. All too often, however, the media and the public portray victims who bring lawsuits—especially against sports figures—as gold diggers who want to cash in. They disregard other motivations, such as wanting to protect other women from being raped by the same individual. Women reply that no amount of money can give them back their childhoods or their lives or make them whole. But if publicized, civil lawsuits are a way to protect others from harm from the same predator. Plaintiffs hope that other victims of the same perpetrator will come forward, helping police and prosecutors to identify predatory rapists and thus leading to prosecution.

Prosecutors in several sexual abuse cases involving children have used new weapons to counteract public indifference. In addition to bringing charges against the abuser, they have filed charges against church or school officials for failing to report the crime to authorities, which is a violation of state law. In October 2011, for example, the Jackson County prosecutor indicted Bishop Robert Finn of the Kansas City, Missouri, Diocese with a single misdemeanor count of failure to report child abuse after he learned that a priest in his diocese had a laptop computer containing hundreds of images of child pornography. In September 2012, a court found Bishop Finn guilty on one misdemeanor charge and sentenced him to two years of court-supervised probation.

And in November 2011, two top Penn State officials were charged with covering up allegations against former football defensive coordinator Jerry Sandusky, who was accused of sexually abusing a number of young boys. All had been participants in an organization for at-risk children he founded and brought to the campus. Both officials were indicted for failure to report the rape of a child and for lying to the grand jury about the incident. A year later, ex–Penn State president Graham B. Spanier was arraigned on similar charges.

## Media

It is impossible to overstate the role the media can play in eliminating rape denial. In addition to publicizing *accurate* data on rape prevalence and false rape claims, journalists need to seriously rethink the "he said, she said" format in coverage of rape accusations. This narrow formula reduces every case to the credibility of the individual reporting rape, which prejudices judges and juries. In cases involving public figures or events dramatic enough to make the national media, the women and girls who report being raped are treated to character assassination when reporters give space to the abusive comments of others. Journalist Rebecca Traister gave us this useful summary in a *New York Times Magazine* piece:

Logan was herself trashed as an attention monger and for dressing in a manner that invited assault. A young woman who pressed rape charges against two New York City police officers could not be believed, in part, because she was drunk. When an 11-year-old Texas girl was allegedly gang-raped by 19 men, the *New York Times* ran a story quoting neighbors saying that she habitually wore makeup and dressed in clothes more appropriate for a 20-year-old. The maid who accused Dominique Strauss-Kahn of rape has been discredited for being a liar, and the *New York Post* claimed she was a prostitute. The young French woman who is pressing charges of attempted rape against Strauss-Kahn—an event she has recounted in a novel—has been painted as an unreliable narrator, young, overdramatic and unstable.

Indeed, when the celebrity cases are all put together, the question arises: Could *all* of these girls and women be so flaky that they cannot be believed? Surely not. Yet in every one the media lead us to believe there is doubt. And the media coverage works to the advantage of rapists. Calls to a rape-crisis center in Boulder, Colorado, fell 33 percent during the Kobe Bryant prosecution, and experts noted an 87 percent drop in sexual-assault reports to the Colorado State University Police Department from 2002 to 2003.

But things might be changing for the better. In November 2011, four women, two of whom remained anonymous, raised allegations of improper sexual behavior of US presidential candidate Herman Cain. Cain responded that all four allegations were false (though he also stated that there might be others in the future, but they too would be untrue). Cain's improbable argument showed the "false claims" defense for what it is: an unbelievable proposition that a majority of women lie about sex. As columnist Kathleen Parker wrote, "In journalism, three is a trend. Four is a tipping point."

Still, Cain's attorney persisted in the all-too-typical approach of attacking and intimidating those who report sexual abuse. L. Lin Wood, a prominent Atlanta lawyer, publicly warned that any other women who might be considering coming forward with similar allegations "should think twice." At the same time, conservative-leaning columnists made public details about the women's personal and work lives. The *New York*

*Post* called Sharon Bialek a "gold digger" who "flirted like a tart" with Cain, while Rush Limbaugh provided details of her financial troubles.

We can argue that the media's investigation of the facts in rape cases holds prosecutors accountable and may prevent all matter of miscarriages of justice. But does the media have the duty to present the public with others' uninformed attacks on victims—to give space to attackers with agendas? And does the media need to rush to judgment? Presentation of true investigative reporting and presentation of facts—not inflammatory opinions—would do much to prevent the media from aiding and abetting those in society who do not believe that men commit rape.

Members of the media should also think twice about publicizing the totally overblown issue of false rape claims. As research has demonstrated, false rape claims are not a major problem. Avoiding euphemisms will also help educate the public about rape and its effects. Rape is not "having sex with a minor" or "nonconsensual sex"—these rubrics minimize the force and humiliation involved in rape. Rape is rape.

We should continue to keep confidential the names of those who report rape. The many accounts in this book demonstrate the dangers women face when their identities become known, including damage to their rooms, as in Megan's case, actual confrontations, death threats, and even repeat rapes. For example, the young woman who charged that Kobe Bryant had raped her in a hotel room received seventy profanity-laced death threats from three different individuals, all of whom were sentenced to prison. These experiences show the seriousness of a rape charge in our culture and do much to explain the origins of the many types of rape denial and the backlashes described in this work.

Removing anonymity would not in itself decrease the shame and stigma of being raped, as many allege. Treating rape as just another crime is not going to be effective because it is not just another crime. What is worth considering, however, is providing anonymity for those being investigated or charged with rape. Given the enormity of the crime, would it not be more just to keep the names of both parties confidential until after the case is charged? What aspect of the public interest is served by trying cases in the media?

On the other hand, rape-victim advocates argue that publicizing an investigation can allow other victims of the same perpetrator to come forward, convincing authorities to bring a criminal charge in the case. Although this might be true in some cases, a *reduction* in publicity might encourage more individuals to report the crime because they would be able to retain some semblance of privacy. This increase in reporting would provide prosecutors and communities with even more information about rapes in the community. And one can readily see that those who report rape are as humiliated and damaged as perpetrators by the ways these cases play out in public. Humiliating those accused of rape and trying them in the media also causes a backlash against victims, destroying their privacy and reputations.

## Rape Research

Rape-victim-advocate groups must develop strong responses to rape deniers that rest on accurate data. They should seize every opportunity to educate the media about true rape prevalence and false-rape-claims data and seek ways to inform the media and the public about what acquaintance rape is really like. As a result of the polarized debate of the last few years, the public needs to be reassured that data from rape-victim advocates rests on a firm research base.

Researchers produce studies that are sometimes incomprehensible to the general public. In rape research, however, given the effects of rape deniers over the years, they could pay particular attention to readability. Often, their reports are not disseminated to the media and the public. No one should publicly quote a rape-prevalence figure without having read the report on which it is based. Mistaken or misstated research should always be corrected after it appears. The incorrect one-in-four college-campus rape statistic should be banned, and the "rape epidemic" and "2 percent false rape claims" campaigns should be permanently retired.

## Alcohol

As a culture, we must sort out our ideas about the role of alcohol in acquaintance rape. Do we want to continue to exonerate those who sexually penetrate a young woman who has passed out or is too drunk to consent? Should Danielle's and Shae's acquaintances be called rapists?

For many members of the public, treating drunken encounters as rapes is unjustifiable. One *Spectator* commentator noted:

> If a drunken woman and a drunken man have sex, our legal system treats the man as a rapist. That's wrong—and patronizing. . . . Most regretted sexual encounters do not result from a sober, calculating lounge lizard spiking the drinks of innocents; most happen, instead, when a pair of idiots—courtesy of shyness, inexperience or habit—drink each other under the table and into bed.

The author argued that a man who has penetrated an inebriated or passed out woman is "stupid but not criminal." Many agree.

Now, however, consider the lyrics to a song by Irish pop singer Brian McFadden:

> I like you just the way you are, drunk and dancing at the bar,
> I like it, and I can't wait to take you home so I can do some damage
> I like you just the way you are, jump in the backseat of my car,
> 'Cos I like it, and I can't wait to take you home so I can take
> advantage

The lyrics are clear: if the girl or woman is drunk, her partner for the evening can take advantage. This perspective reclassifies the behavior from a crime to something more trivial.

What is our response to someone who imitates McFadden and "takes advantage"? Has the person proceeded with malice, with a desire to oppress or assault? Does it matter whether the woman is asleep or passed out or just inebriated? Is "taking advantage" less serious than forcible penetration?

In consideration of these questions, several points are important. First, in the cases of Riley, Tracy, and Megan, alcohol was not involved, and one could not reasonably argue that the accused men were confused or mistaken as opposed to malicious. Yet, in two out of the three cases, the prosecutors were still unwilling to entertain charges. We are in danger of allowing confused attitudes about alcohol to dictate our response to all acquaintance rape cases, even those that did not involve inebriation.

Second, to my mind, sexually penetrating a person asleep or otherwise unable to consent should not be tolerated (gang rapes are especially reprehensible). Most state rape laws recognize this. Some states have lessened penalties for "taking advantage" as opposed to forcible rape, but they have not resulted in more rape charges and convictions. I find convincing novelist Scott Turow's take on a gang rape in his novella *Limitations*:

> It was crime at its purest, in which empathy, that most fundamental aspect of human morality, evaporated and another being became a target for untamed fantasy. The sexual acts were committed in emphatic plunging motions of pure aggression, and the way the boys exposed themselves to one another before and after, amid much wild hooting, could only be labeled depraved—not in any puritanical sense but because George sensed that these young men were dominated by impulses they would ordinarily have rejected. But if the purpose of the criminal law is to state emphatically that some behavior is beyond toleration, then this case surely requires that declaration.

## Encouraging Reporting

In 2005, the Violence Against Woman Act made clear that a sexually assaulted individual need not cooperate with law enforcement in order to be provided with a free forensic medical exam. Some experts believe that to encourage women to file a complaint, law enforcement should offer anonymous reporting (which the act does not mandate) by giving the victim a case number and letting her know that she can proceed if and when she is ready. This practice would preserve evidence for future prosecutions but would leave the decision to prosecute for another day, when the person who has undergone the trauma has calmed down and is out of immediate crisis.

Anonymity may provide comfort to a rape victim who may not be ready to divulge her name or that of the perpetrator, perhaps for safety reasons. However, implementing this procedure requires police and prosecutors to reconsider the preconceived idea that an individual who is unwilling to immediately prosecute has not truly been raped.

In the past, rape-victim advocates have always honored women's decisions not to report rape. However, those who blame themselves and feel shame unwittingly contribute to rape denial in the long run. Indifferent or punishing responses endemic today toward those claiming rape—"If she doesn't think it was rape, then it isn't," for example—are undoubtedly keeping reporting at low levels, confirming rape deniers' assertions of low rape prevalence. At the same time that we respect their wishes to remain in the shadows, we can also urge rape victims not to feel shame or self-blame and encourage them to go to the police. The national Voices and Faces Project (www.voicesandfaces.org) provides a safe space for victims to "come out" and divest themselves of blame. Let's hope that precarious funding will not prevent the continuation of this valuable project in the future.

It is important for victims of date or acquaintance rape to understand that their accounts may be similar to those of Riley, Tracy, Danielle, Shae, and Megan. Rather than blame themselves, they should realize that they had the bad luck to meet a predator. The task is to work collectively to identify and stop acquaintance rapists in their tracks. By telling their experiences in this book, Riley and the others seek to be exemplars.

Every one of us has a role to play. We can correct friends who minimize acquaintance rape. We can complain to the appropriate authorities when we notice that a rape report in our college or workplace is being minimized or handled incorrectly. We can protest rape jokes. We can actively support a friend, acquaintance, or coworker who reports that she or he has been raped. We can write to newspaper editors when space is given to a rape denier but not to another view. We all need to work to overcome the current culture of rape denial.

But we must always keep in mind that blaming the victim is a natural psychological response. To accept that such evil exists creates a vulnerability that can make life impossible. As psychologist Patrizia Romito explained in her book *Deafening Silence*, "Attributing responsibility to the victim makes us feel less vulnerable: if they suffered violence because they made a mistake, we can keep our belief in a just world or at least a predictable one, and we may find security in the fact that, if we behave well, nothing bad will happen to us." Psychiatrist Judith Herman has also reminded us that "the ordinary response to atrocities is to banish them from consciousness."

Compounding the difficulty is that it is not possible to imagine what rape is like until it happens to you. Remember what Riley said: people can't understand rape, she explained, because the humiliation is unfathomable. She said, "[Rape] isn't normal. . . . He pushed you down and came all over you like you were an animal. People shouldn't understand that. I think it is humiliating because you went through something that so few people understand."

In a world without rape denial, the following real scenario would not have occurred: When a graduate assistant saw retired Penn State football coach Jerry Sandusky forcing fellatio on a young boy in the school's showers, he told head coach Joe Paterno, who in turn informed athletic director Tim Curley. The assistant was then summoned to a meeting with Curley and the vice president of the university, Gary Schultz, during which he says he described the rape in graphic detail.

Then: nothing. No one attempted to learn the identity of the child in the shower or to find out what had happened to him. Not one person informed law-enforcement or child-welfare authorities. Thus the abuser remained free to assault other young boys for another nine years. The three officials, as well as the college president, all knew about the allegations, but not one lifted a finger to take any action. Nobody did what basic human decency required them to do. Ultimately all, including Coach Paterno and the university's president, lost their jobs.

I'm sure not one of the men could envision their esteemed retired coach—noted for his charitable activities with young, needy boys—as a rapist. But that is just the point. As *New York Times* columnist Frank Bruni wrote, "The predator to watch out for is less likely to don a trench coat and lurk behind a bush than wear a clerical collar and stand near the altar or to hold a stopwatch and walk the sidelines."

Writer Albert Camus understood that, in the face of evil, ordinary people must just respond out of simple decency: "All I maintain is that on this earth there are pestilences and there are victims, and it's up to us, so far as possible, not to join forces with the pestilences." Camus knew full well how being controlled by absolute ideas or ideology creates an intolerable situation: "And for all who cannot live without dialogue and the friendship of other human beings, this silence is the end of the world."

In November 2008, the United Nations reported that a thirteen-year-old Somali girl was stoned to death by Islamist militants after being accused of adultery. She had been raped by three men while she was traveling on foot to visit her grandmother in the war-torn capital of Mogadishu. Following the assault, the UN said, the young woman sought protection from the authorities, who instead accused her of adultery and sentenced her to death. The girl was buried in the ground up to her neck. Fifty men then pelted her with rocks in a stadium in front of approximately one thousand spectators. Three times, officials pulled her out to see if she was dead.

This brutal execution of Asha Ibrahim Dhuhulow outraged Western sensibilities. The act illustrated the centuries-old practice of stigmatizing and punishing survivors of sexual violence. But although this is an extreme example, how different is it really from our usual response in the United States? We do not stone survivors, but in our indifferent or hostile response we symbolically stone them, consigning them if not to a real death then to a social or living death. As Megan said, "[I wish] he had just killed me. Then I wouldn't have to feel anymore. Then people would believe me."

◆

This book began with Cassandra Hernandez's account, and it will end with it. Recall that the nineteen-year-old US Air Force member reported she was raped by three men at a party. However, she was the one charged with indecent acts, and the men involved went free. Did not the air force's actions in Hernandez's case represent the same response as in Somalia? What could she think but that the air force believed the incident was her fault?

As in Holocaust denial, ideology has trumped established fact. We have responded to today's Holocaust deniers by properly labeling them as cranks. The facts are mounting up. The time has come for rape denial to become as unacceptable as Holocaust denial. If this book has accomplished anything, I hope it has shown that there are no legitimate disagreements about statistics on forcible rape and research on false rape claims. There is only truth. And we must all tell the truth. Denying rape makes society unsafe for women and allows predators to go free.

Rape is rape.

# Epilogue

In the spring of 2010, Riley learned that Luke had been released from prison and had registered, as required, in her state as a convicted sex offender. The event reactivated her trauma and made her fear for her safety.

> That made for an incredibly hard time for me, anticipating that and facing it, but I decided he didn't deserve to take anymore happiness from me, and I made it a good day. No more tears now. I did all I could.

At the end of 2010, Riley informed me that she had been hospitalized every two months and had her tenth sinus surgery just before the end of the year. She also made the decision to go off prescribed painkillers, because she believed they were negatively affecting her personality.

"Things are still hard," she explained, "with Luke being out of jail now and my cystic fibrosis progressing."

On January 1, 2011, Riley married a young man who has been steadily providing her with so much love and support. "I have been lucky enough to rise above and experience a love that overcomes the tragedy I experienced."

In November 2011, I found Riley again in the hospital for a complete "tune-up." Her cystic fibrosis was steadily worsening, and she was spending most of her days fighting to clear her breathing passages and battling the subsidiary effects of the disease. "I know I'm not going to get any better," she told me. But all these years later, Riley remained deeply affected by that one night of hideous fear, torture, humiliation, and pain—an evening that most people may simply not be able to imagine. Under the circumstances—coping with the effects of the rape, worrying about Luke's release, and fighting the ravages of cystic fibrosis—Riley's commitment to sharing her experiences with me, in the hopes of changing attitudes about acquaintance rape, was nothing short of heroic.

In an earlier draft of this book, the last chapter finished with an optimistic statement that, after the trial, Riley's feelings of alienation and disconnection had finally been replaced by a sense of reconnection. The manuscript had concluded with these four sentences:

> A bad thing had happened, yes, but it had been acknowledged. Justice prevailed. The world was no longer alien or absurd. In fact, it was shaping up to be a good place after all.

As was her right, Riley took issue with it. "Jody," Riley said, "this is a strong ending, which I like; I try to be positive." But this conclusion, she asserted, wasn't really accurate.

> To be able to see the good in the world is a miracle after seeing the other side of it. I do see the good. I don't feel hopeless. I don't want to give you that idea. But I am a victim. I am damaged. I see myself as damaged, and I don't know that I completely believe the world is a good place.

# Acknowledgments

This book could not have been written without the pioneering research and analysis of Kimberly Lonsway, Joanne Archambault, and David Lisak, who have shared their knowledge with me and generously directed me to further resources.

Kimyatta Gainey at the DePaul University College of Law Rinn Law Library enthusiastically procured books and articles for me from libraries throughout the country, and Hallie Diego in faculty services rescued me from many a computer snafu.

Susan Betz acquired this book for Chicago Review Press, and senior editor Lisa Reardon carefully read every word of the manuscript, making remarkably useful and detailed suggestions that have greatly improved the text and removed redundancies. Editor Kelly Wilson brilliantly undertook copyediting and production duties.

Friends and colleagues have gone beyond the line of duty. Kaethe Morris Hoffer and Claire Renzetti uncomplainingly read countless versions of this work over the last five years. Katie Feifer and Kim Lonsway also gave an early draft a detailed read. Alan Raphael has, simply put, always been there for me.

TK Logan at the University of Kentucky taught me how to read rape-prevalence studies and led me to the latest reputable research. Not only did she read the most drafts and eliminate all the errors, but she also remained enthusiastic about the book and encouraged me to press on when a publisher willing to take on a book about rape didn't readily appear on the horizon. For these reasons, *Rape Is Rape* is dedicated to her.

# Notes

## Introduction

*Then the air force offered immunity*   David Zucchino, "Air Force Charges Airman Who Accused Others of Rape," *Los Angeles Times*, August 12, 2007, http://articles.latimes.com/2007/aug/12/nation/na-rape12.

*Some media commentators*   Carol Lloyd, "She Raped Herself," *Salon*, August 9, 2007, http://www.salon.com/2007/08/09/rape_herself/.

*As Jessica Valenti noted*   Jessica Valenti, *The Purity Myth: How America's Obsession with Virginity Is Hurting Young Women* (Berkeley, CA: Seal Press, 2009), 155.

*Throughout the narrative*   Although these accounts all involve men sexually attacking women, acquaintance rape can and does involve men attacking men and women attacking women. Assaults involving transsexual individuals also occur. But research shows that the bulk of rapes are directed at women. For this reason, and in the interest of conciseness, this work identifies victims as women and perpetrators as men. And, since research does not find that rape varies among races or ethnicities, I do not believe these differences are germane to the basic issues in this book, and I do not dwell on them.

## Chapter 1: Accusing Dominique Strauss-Kahn

*On May 14, 2011, Nafissatou Diallo*   All the facts in this chapter are taken from the petition filed by the State of New York recommending dismissal of Indictment No. 0526/2011 on August 22, 2011. Because Ms. Diallo agreed to the use of her name in media interviews, I use it in this narrative.

*One French media analyst*   "L'affaire DSK: Le summum du bruit médiatique," *Radio France Internationale*, May 26, 2011, www.rfi.fr/france/20110526 -affaire-dsk-le-bruit-mediatique-chiffres.

*Subsequently, a young French reporter*   "The Downfall of DSK," *Economist*, May 21, 2011.

## Riley

*Riley is the relative*   This is her real name, but her last name is omitted to preserve her confidentiality. I first interviewed Riley on November 15, 2008, and have been in e-mail and telephone communication with her since that time. All quotes from Riley come verbatim from these interviews.

*Riley's cousin Richard*   Richard, in discussion with the author, November 20, 2008. Richard is a pseudonym to preserve Riley's confidentiality. All quotes from Richard come verbatim from this interview.

*"In some feminist circles"*   Wendy Kaminer, "Feminism's Identity Crisis," *Atlantic Monthly*, October 1993, 67.

*"Comparing real rape"*   Nicola Gavey, *Just Sex? The Cultural Scaffolding of Rape* (New York: Routledge, 2005), 68.

## Chapter 2: The Distortion of Rape Statistics: Who's Doing It and Why

*The seeds of today's backlash*   Susan Brownmiller, *Against Our Will: Men, Women, and Rape* (New York: Simon and Schuster, 1975), 15.

*She saw rape*   Brownmiller saw rape as a political crime that can be eradicated like lynching, but only if it was understood not as deviant behavior but as the logical result of sexism. Ibid., 254. Brownmiller is also quoted in an article in *Time* magazine to this effect ("Women's Liberation Revisited," *Time*, March 20, 1972, www.time.com/time/magazine /article/0,9171,942512,00.html).

*"All men are rapists"*   The statement is made by a suburban housewife after the rape of her daughter. The full quotation is: "Whatever they may be in public life, whatever their relations with men, in their relations

with women, all men are rapists and that's all they are" (Marilyn French, *The Women's Room* [New York: Summit Books, 1977; New York: Penguin, 2009], 427). According to the *Los Angeles Times*, the novel has sold twenty million copies (Elaine Woo, "Marilyn French Dies at 79; Author of Feminist Classic 'The Women's Room,'" *Los Angeles Times*, May 5, 2009, http://articles.latimes.com/2009/may/05/local /me-marilyn-french5).

*"Men in positions of power"*    Catharine A. MacKinnon, *Women's Lives, Men's Laws* (Cambridge, MA: Harvard University Press, 2005), 247.

*MacKinnon appeared to be*    For example, conservative activist Carrie L. Lukas has written that MacKinnon creates a definition of rape that is open-ended, "suggesting that there's essentially no time that a man can feel confident that a woman could not later decide to characterize their sexual interlude as rape" (Carrie L. Lukas, *The Politically Incorrect Guide to Women, Sex, and Feminism* [Washington, DC: Regnery Publishing, 2006], 71). Some feminists have also seen the disadvantages of viewing rape as part and parcel of normal heterosexual practice and have been cautious to avoid, in their discussions of rape, what might be seen as condemnations of heterosexual sex (Gavey, *Just Sex?*, 34–35, 232).

*"It is insulting to women"*    Ibid., 34.

*"No one's defending men"*    Kathleen Parker, *Save the Males: Why Men Matter, Why Women Should Care* (New York: Random House, 2008), 31.

*Although they do not deny*    Christina Hoff Sommers rejects the idea of patriarchy: "By the nineties, I argued, American women were among the freest and most liberated in the world. It was no longer *reasonable* to say that as a group women were far worse off than men. Yes, there were still inequities, but to speak of American society as a 'patriarchy' or to refer to American women as second class citizens was frankly absurd" (Christina Hoff Sommers, "What's Wrong and What's Right with Contemporary Feminism?," [lecture, Hamilton College, Clinton, NY, January 8, 2009], www.aei.org/files/2008/11/19/20090108_Contemporary Feminism.pdf). Criminal violence, not patriarchal misogyny, is the problem; there is, she says, a general crisis of violence against persons, not a gender-specific attack on women (Christina Hoff Sommers, *Who Stole Feminism? How Women Have Betrayed Women* [New York: Simon and Shuster, 1994], 223–24).

*For example, college Republicans*   Alison Go, "Bowling Green Antifeminist Bake Sale Draws Ire," *U.S. News & World Report*, April 16, 2008, http://www.usnews.com/education/blogs/paper-trail/2008/04/16/bowling-green-antifeminist-bake-sale-draws-ire.

*The presumption that men*   Sommers, *Who Stole Feminism?*, 21.

*Individual young women*   Lukas, *The Politically Incorrect Guide*, 60.

*We will help your daughter*   Sommers, *Who Stole Feminism?*, 91.

*The conservative Independent Women's Forum*   The Independent Women's Forum states it offers an alternative to organizations that exaggerate victimhood to support big-government programs. For a summary of these views, see Abby Scher, "Post-Palin Feminism," *Public Eye* 23, no. 4 (2008), www.publiceye.org/magazine/v23n4/post_palin_feminism.html. The group considers governor Sarah Palin to be a red-state feminist. See Kay S. Hymowitz, "Red-State Feminism," *City Journal*, September 8, 2008, http://www.city-journal.org/2008/eon0908kh.html; see also Ronnee Schreiber, *Righting Feminism: Conservative Women and American Politics* (New York: Oxford University Press, 2008).

*Over the past ten years*   Kate O'Beirne, *Women Who Make the World Worse and How Their Radical Feminist Assault Is Ruining Our Families, Military, Schools, and Sports* (New York: Sentinel, 2006), 19.

*But no-contact restraining orders*   RADAR, *Women Ask: "Has VAWA Lived Up to Its Promises?"* (Westfield, NJ: Respecting Accuracy in Domestic Abuse Reporting), http://www.mediaradar.org/docs/RADARflyer-Has-VAWA-Lived-Up-to-its-Promises.pdf, accessed April 13, 2010.

*In a social-science survey*   Mary P. Koss, Christine A. Gidycz, and Nadine Wisniewski, "The Scope of Rape: Incidence and Prevalence of Sexual Aggression and Victimization in a National Sample of Higher Education Students," *Journal of Consulting and Clinical Psychology* 55, no. 2 (1987): 168. Although the researchers asked a series of ten questions that included psychological coercion, they used only those queries dealing with force to obtain the rape rate. See Mary P. Koss, "Defending Date Rape," *Journal of Interpersonal Violence* 7, no. 1 (1992): 123.

*Although Koss made clear*   Koss, Gidycz, and Wisniewski, "The Scope of Rape," 168. The victimization rate of women during a six-month period during the previous year was 3.8 percent, or thirty-eight women per one thousand (ibid., 168).

*Koss's study did much*   Mary P. Koss and Sarah L. Cook, "Facing the Facts: Date and Acquaintance Rape Are Significant Problems for Women," in *Current Controversies on Family Violence*, eds. Richard J. Gelles and Donileen R. Loseke (Newbury Park, CA: Sage Publications, 1993), 104.

*Instead, she posed*   Koss, Gidycz, and Wisniewski, "The Scope of Rape," 167.

*Only penetrations through force*   Koss, "Defending Date Rape," 123.

*The definitions of sexual abuse*   Neil Gilbert, "The Phantom Epidemic of Sexual Assault," *Public Interest* 103 (1991): 59, 61.

*Koss went back*   Koss and Cook, "Facing the Facts," 106.

*One of the striking things*   Gavey, *Just Sex?*, 67.

*In an influential*   Katie Roiphe, "Date Rape's Other Victim," *New York Times Magazine*, June 13, 1993, www.nytimes.com/1993/06/13/magazine/date-rape-s-other-victim.html?pagewanted=1.

*She implied that*   Sommers, *Who Stole Feminism?*, 211–13.

*For Sommers, unaccountably*   Ibid., 215–16.

*The statistic made*   Ibid., 213.

*Thus the great majority*   Koss, "Defending Date Rape," 124.

*Critics err in the assumption*   Ibid., 125.

*In fact, in a 2011 article*   Sarah L. Cook, Christine A. Gidycz, Mary P. Koss, and Megan Murphy, "Emerging Issues in the Measurement of Rape Victimization," *Violence Against Women* 17, no. 2 (2011): 291–318.

*It covers sex after*   "When No Means No," *National Review*, June 10, 1991, 12–13.

*In 2004, for example*   FoxNews.com commentator Wendy McElroy, "Rape Scandal Turns Sympathy into Skepticism," FoxNews.com, April 21, 2004, www.foxnews.com/story/0,2933,117690,00.html.

*Carrie L. Lukas recycled*   Carrie L. Lukas, "One in Four? Rape Myths Do Injustice, Too," *National Review Online*, April 27, 2006, http://old.national review.com/lukas200604270647.asp; Carrie L. Lukas, "One in Four? Rape Myths Do Injustice, Too," Independent Women's Forum, April 27, 2006, http://www.iwf.org/news/2432517/One-in-Four-Rape-myths-do-injustice-too; Carrie L. Lukas, *The Politically Incorrect Guide*, 55–74.

*Correcting for the biases*   Lukas, "One in Four?"

*If the one-in-four statistic* Heather Mac Donald, "The Campus Rape Myth," *City Journal* 18, no. 1 (winter 2008), www.city-journal.org/2008/18_1 _campus_rape.html. See also Heather Mac Donald, "What Campus Rape Crisis?," *Los Angeles Times*, February 24, 2008, http://articles.latimes .com/2008/feb/24/opinion/op-mac_donald24.

*And in her 2008 book* Kathleen Parker, *Save the Males: Why Men Matter, Why Women Should Care* (New York: Random House, 2008), 20–35.

*The Mac Donald piece* Robert VerBruggen, "Mac Donald vs. Koss on the Prevalence of Campus Rape," *National Review Online*, March 5, 2008, www.nationalreview.com/phi-beta-cons/42712/mac-donald-vs -koss-prevalence-campus-rape. Conservative activist David Horowitz reprinted the Mac Donald article on his blog, frontpagemag.com. Other URLs at which the reprinted article can be found include www.save themales.ca/campus_rape_crisis_is_politica.html (October 15, 2009), and www.thetruthseeker.co.uk/oldsite/print.asp?ID=11480 (October 15, 2009).

*Mac Donald's critique* See "Take Back the Nonsense," *The Western Right* (blog), April 20, 2008, http://wmugop.blogspot.com/2008/04/take -back-nonsense.html; and "Rape Statistics Far Less Scary than Colum- nist Claims," *Cornell Daily Sun*, April 19, 2007, http://cornellsun.com /node/2309.

*Criticizing the CDC* Barry Deutsch ("Ampersand"), "Why Don't They Give Up on Attacking Koss Already?," *Alas, a Blog*, January 26, 2005, www.amptoons.com/blog/archives/2005-01/26/why-dont-they -give-up-on-attacking-koss-already.

*In one life* Barry Deutsch, "Response to Christina Hoff Sommers, Part 3: Truths and Lies," *Blog by Barry*, January 27, 2009, http:// barrydeutsch.wordpress.com/2009/01/27/response-to-christina-hoff -sommers-part-3-truths-and-lies/.

*"I truly believe that"* Valenti, *The Purity Myth*, 164.

*Valenti struggles, unsuccessfully* Ibid.

*But journalist Leslie H. Gelb* Leslie H. Gelb, *Power Rules: How Common Sense Can Rescue American Foreign Policy* (New York: HarperCollins, 2009), 294.

*"Your criticisms seem"* This quote comes from an August 12, 2009, blog response to "Myths or Facts in Feminist Scholarship? An Exchange Between Nancy K. D. Lemon and Christina Hoff Sommers," *Chronicle Review*, August 10, 2009, http://chronicle.com/article/Domestic -Violence-a/47940.

*Their challenges reveal little* Koss, "Defending Date Rape," 125.

*It is nothing more than* "Valedictorian of UC Berkeley Tells Graduating Class That Men Are Raping Women on Campus with Abandon," *False Rape Society* (blog), May 26, 2009, http://falserapesociety.blogspot .com/2009/05/valedictorian-of-uc-berkeley-tells.html.

*In the writings of male rape deniers* Ibid.

*"Feminism is not about"* These quotes were found in comments posted on *Angry Harry* on January 16, 2004 (www.angryharry.com/esMostRape AllegationsAreFalse.htm).

*"The campus date rape campaigns"* "Guide to Feminist Nonsense," *Angry Harry*, accessed June 15, 2009, http://www.angryharry.com/notefeminism forstudents2.htm?main.

*And like some women* These comments were posted at *Angry Harry* on August 14, 2004 (www.angryharry.com/esRapeBaloney.htm).

*Supposedly, President Brodhead* Stuart Taylor Jr. and KC Johnson, *Until Proven Innocent: Political Correctness and the Shameful Injustices of the Duke Lacrosse Rape Case* (New York: St. Martin's Press, 2007), 392.

*Rempt's crackdown gives off* Stuart Taylor Jr., "'Rape' and the Navy's P.C. Police," *Atlantic* magazine, April 10, 2007, http://www.theatlantic.com /magazine/archive/2007/04/rape-and-the-navys-pc-police/305857/.

*"Pete, I had no other choice"* Ibid.

*"It would be justice"* Stuart Taylor Jr., "An Outrageous Rush to Judgment," *Atlantic* magazine, May 2, 2006, www.theatlantic.com/magazine/archive /2006/04/an-outrageous-rush-to-judgment/4904. Christina Hoff Sommers cites another unfortunate example of political correctness involving rape:

> Recently several male students at Vassar were falsely accused of date rape. After their innocence was established, the assistant dean of students, Catherine Comins, said of their ordeal: "They have a lot of

pain, but it is not a pain that I would necessarily have spared them. I think it ideally initiates a process of self-exploration. 'How do I see women?' 'If I did not violate her, could I have?' 'Do I have the potential to do to her what they say I did?' These are good questions." Dean Comins clearly feels justified in trumping the common law principle "presumed innocent until proven guilty" by a new feminist principle, "guilty even if proven innocent." Indeed, she believes that the students are not really innocent after all. How so? Because, being male and being brought up in the patriarchal culture, they *could easily have done* what they were falsely accused of having done, even though they didn't *actually* do it. Where men are concerned, Comins quite sincerely believes in collective guilt (*Who Stole Feminism?*, 92).

*"Doubt probes the dark side"*   Karen D'Souza, "'Doubt' Certainly Raises Questions," *Mercury News*, November 5, 2006.

*"People's tendency to become"*   Elizabeth Kolbert, "The Things People Say: Rumors in an Age of Unreason," *New Yorker*, November 2, 2009, 112.

*"Serving, for many"*   Ibid., 112–13.

*For example, in 2008, they claimed*   Kathryn Joyce, "Men's Rights Groups Have Become Frighteningly Effective," *DoubleX* (blog), November 5, 2009, http://www.doublex.com/section/news-politics/mens-rights-groups-have-become-frighteningly-effective.

*Yes, Angry Harry*   Ibid.

*In any movement*   Ibid.

*These rejoinders illustrate*   Paul Elam, "John Jasper's Hate Campaign and What to Do About It," *A Voice for Men* (blog), February 9, 2011, http://www.avoiceformen.com/feminism/feminist-lies-feminism/josh-jaspers-hate-campaign-and-what-to-do-about-it/.

## Tracy

*I first heard of Tracy*   I interviewed Tracy between April 3, 2007, and May 10, 2007. All quotes from Tracy come verbatim from these interviews. Tracy is a pseudonym to preserve the woman's confidentiality.

## Chapter 3: The Feminist Attack: Acquaintance Rape as the Price for Women's Sexual Freedom

*But the paradox now*   Laura Kipnis, *The Female Thing: Dirt, Sex, Envy, Vulnerability* (New York: Pantheon Books, 2006), 131.

*We spent such a long time*   Jennifer Scanlon, *Bad Girls Go Everywhere: The Life of Helen Gurley Brown* (New York: Oxford University Press, 2009), 215.

*"Accept the adventure"*   Camille Paglia, *Sex, Art and American Culture: Essays* (New York: Vintage Books, 1992), 71.

*My sixties attitude is*   Ibid., 63.

*"Without struggle"*   Katie Roiphe, *The Morning After: Sex, Fear, and Feminism on Campus* (Boston: Little, Brown and Company, 1993), 80.

*People have asked me*   Ibid., 79.

*For Roiphe, young women*   Ibid., 75.

*If we assume that women*   Ibid., 53–4.

*In the heat of the moment*   Ibid., 42.

*"If a woman's 'judgment is impaired'"*   Ibid., 53–4.

*As Gilbert delves further*   Ibid., 54.

*"In our highly individualistic"*   Linda Martin Alcoff, "On Prejudging the Duke Lacrosse Team Scandal" (speech, the Institute for the Study of the Judiciary, Politics and the Media at Syracuse University, Syracuse, NY, September 2006), www.alcoff.com/content/dukelacrosse.html.

*Tkacik: What's going to happen?*   Lizz Winstead, "Jezebelism," *Huffington Post*, July 4, 2008, www.huffingtonpost.com/lizz-winstead/jezebelism _b_110903.html.

*Doing what feels good*   Linda Hirshman, "The Trouble with Jezebel," *DoubleX* (blog), May 12, 2009, www.doublex.com/section/news-politics/trouble -jezebel.

*Columnist Katha Pollitt*   Katha Pollitt, "Amber Waves of Blame," *Nation*, June 15, 2009, 10. Author Naomi Wolf also criticized the weakness of today's pro-sex, individualistic feminism as ahistorical and apolitical: "Feminism had to reinvent itself—there was no way to sustain the uber-seriousness and sometimes judgmental tone of the second wave. But feminists are in danger if we don't know our history, and a saucy tattoo and a condom do not a revolution make" (Naomi Wolf, "Who Won Feminism?," *Washington Post*, May 3, 2009).

*These days, feminism isn't*    Susannah Breslin, "Trigger Warnings Don't Work. Here's Why," *True/Slant* (blog), April 14, 2010, http://trueslant.com /susannahbreslin/2010/04/trigger-warnings-dont-work-heres-why.

*"So uncool and passé"*    Vanessa, "Susannah Breslin: Certifiable Asshole," *Feministing*, April 13, 2010, http://feministing.com/2010/04/13/susannah -breslin-certifiable-asshole.

*To reach this conclusion*    Kipnis, *The Female Thing*, 136.

*In the first-ever survey*    Allen J. Beck and Paige M. Harrison, *Sexual Victimization in State and Federal Prisons Reported by Inmates, 2007* (Washington, DC: US Department of Justice, Bureau of Justice Statistics, December 2007), http://bjs.ojp.usdoj.gov/content/pub/pdf/svsfpri07.pdf.

*And in its 2008–2009 survey*    The 2008–2009 survey revealed 48,300 victims of rape, compared with 89,000 cases reported to the Federal Bureau of Investigation (FBI) in 2008 and 203,830 cases in the 2008 Criminal Victimization Survey. In the 2008 research, 4.7 percent of women and 2.9 percent of males in prison were victims. The number of prison rapes is an undercount, because this research only captures the experiences of those in prisons and jails at the time of the research. Because individuals go in and out of prisons and jails, the raw number of rape victims each year will be greater than revealed in this snapshot research. However, female victims will continue to outnumber males. See Allen J. Beck and Paige M. Harrison, *Sexual Victimization in Prisons and Jails Reported by Inmates, 2008–9* (Washington, DC: US Department of Justice, Bureau of Justice Statistics, August 2010), 7, http://bjs.ojp.usdoj.gov/content/pub/pdf /svpjri0809.pdf; Federal Bureau of Investigation, *Crime in the United States 2008* (Washington, DC: Federal Bureau of Investigation, 2008), http:// www2.fbi.gov/ucr/cius2008/index.html; Michael R. Rand, *Criminal Victimization, 2008* (Washington, DC: US Department of Justice, Bureau of Justice Statistics, September 2009), 1, http://bjs.ojp.usdoj.gov/content /pub/pdf/cv08.pdf.

*Compare this number*    Federal Bureau of Investigation, *Crime in the United States, 2007* (Washington, DC: Federal Bureau of Investigation, 2007), http://www2.fbi.gov/ucr/cius2007/index.html.

*Or the 248,300* Michael Rand and Shannan Catalano, *Criminal Victimization, 2007* (Washington, DC: US Department of Justice, Bureau of Justice Statistics, December 2007), 1, http://bjs.ojp.usdoj.gov/content/pub/pdf/cv07.pdf.

*Kipnis viewed worries* Kipnis, *The Female Thing*, 131.

*"Emotionally disappointing"* Ibid.

*"Who wouldn't get confused"* Ibid.

*Another woman said* David Allen Green, "Why Assange Lost," *New Statesman*, February 28, 2011.

*Before falling asleep* Ibid.

*I may be a chauvinist* Karla Adam, "Julian Assange's Unauthorized Autobiography Released in London," *Washington Post*, September 22, 2011.

*In arguments against extradition* "Julian Assange Extradition Appeal Hearing—Tuesday 12 July 2011," *Guardian News Blog*, http://www.guardian.co.uk/media/2011/jul/12/julian-assange-extradition-live-coverage.

*After naming one* Alexander Cockburn, "Julian Assange: Wanted by the Empire, Dead or Alive," *CounterPunch*, December 3–5, 2010, http://www.counterpunch.org/2010/12/03/julian-assange-wanted-by-the-empire-dead-or-alive/.

*In a posting* Naomi Wolf, "Julian Assange Captured by World's Dating Police," *Huffington Post*, December 7, 2010, http://www.huffingtonpost.com/naomi-wolf/interpol-the-worlds-datin_b_793033.html.

*Belittling the accusations* Ibid.

*If one makes a serious* Naomi Wolf, "Julian Assange's Sex-Crime Accusers Deserve to Be Named," *Guardian*, January 5, 2011, http://www.guardian.co.uk/commentisfree/2011/jan/05/julian-assange-sex-crimes-anonymity.

*Feminist columnist Katha Pollitt* Katha Pollitt, "The Case of Julian Assange," *Nation*, January 10/17, 2011.

*Journalist Nir Rosen* Mark Whittington, "Nir Rosen Makes Light of Lara Logan Sexual Assault," *Yahoo! Voices*, February 16, 2011, http://voices.yahoo.com/nir-rosen-makes-light-lara-logan-sexual-assault-7871726.html.

*Subsequently Rosen expressed* Mary Elizabeth Williams, "What Not to Say about Lara Logan," *Salon*, February 15, 2011, http://www.salon.com/2011/02/15/lara_logan_rape_reaction/.

*His employer, New York University*   Ibid.

*"Let's get this straight"*   Alex Knepper, "Dealing with AU's Anti-sex Brigade," *Eagle*, March 28, 2010, www.theeagleonline.com/opinion/story/dealing -with-aus-anti-sex-brigade.

*Attitudes like his*   Jonelle Walker, letter to the editor, *Eagle*, March 29, 2010, www.theeagleonline.com/opinion/story/letters-to-the-editor-000.

## Chapter 4: The Conservative Attack: Acquaintance Rape as the Result of Women's Promiscuity

*"There isn't this date-rape epidemic"*   "The Future of Feminism: An Interview with Christina Hoff Sommers," by Scott London, *Scott London* (blog), accessed August 20, 2009, www.scottlondon.com/interviews/sommers .html.

*"The booze-filled hookup culture"*   Heather Mac Donald, "The Campus Rape Myth," *City Journal*, Winter 2008, www.city-journal.org/2008/18_1 _campus_rape.html.

*Some students are going*   Ibid.

*And these are just the ones*   Naomi Schaefer Riley, "Ladies, You Should Know Better: How Feminism Wages War on Common Sense," *Wall Street Journal*, April 14, 2006, http://www.ncdsv.org/images/LadiesYouShould KnowBetter.pdf.

*Once women sexually objectify*   Kathleen Parker, "'Save the Males': Ho Culture Lights Fuses, but Confuses," *New York Daily News*, June 30, 2008, www.nydailynews.com/lifestyle/2008/06/30/2008-06-30_save_the _males_ho_culture_lights_fuses_b.html.

*"Friedman derived that"*   Charlotte Allen, "The New Dating Game: Back to the New Paleolithic Age," *Weekly Standard*, February 15, 2010, www .weeklystandard.com/print/articles/new-dating-game.

*Under the purity myth*   Jessica Valenti, *The Purity Myth: How America's Obsession with Virginity Is Hurting Young Women* (Berkeley, CA: Seal Press, 2009), 157.

*"Earth to liberated women"*   Dan Rottenberg, "Male Sex Abuse and Female Naivete," *Broad Street Review*, June 6, 2011, http://www.broadstreetre view.com/index.php/main/article/male_sex_abuse_and_female_naivete.

*"If you want to be"*   Ibid.

*"They sexually assaulted her"*   Jessica Wakeman, "Male Editor Blames Lara Logan's Boobs for Her Assault, Extols 'Conquering an Unwilling Sex Partner,'" *The Frisky*, June 9, 2011, www.thefrisky.com/post/246-creepy -philly-editor-blames-lara-logan-for-her-assault-extols-conquer.

*None of the women and girls*   Laura Sessions Stepp, "A New Kind of Date Rape," *Cosmopolitan*, www.cosmopolitan.com/sex-love/tips-moves/new -kind-of-date-rape, accessed October 17, 2007. For a more in-depth treatment of hooking up and "gray rape," see Laura Sessions Stepp, *Unhooked: How Young Women Pursue Sex, Delay Love and Lose at Both* (New York: Penguin, 2007).

*"When things end up in bed"*   Ibid.

*Presumably conservatives should*   Wendy Shalit, *A Return to Modesty: Discovering the Lost Virtue* (New York: Free Press, 1999), 42.

*In pursuit of a unisexual society*   Ibid., 44.

*Unfortunately, if a man*   Wendy Shalit, *Girls Gone Mild: Young Women Reclaim Self-Respect and Find It's Not Bad to Be Good* (New York: Random House, 2007), 277.

*Some feminists believe*   See Jessica Valenti, "Speechifying: So-called Hook Up Culture and the Anti-feminists Who Love It," *Feministing*, February 20, 2009, http://feministing.com/2009/02/20/speechifying_so-called _hook_up/. For a summary of feminist views, see Stephanie Rosenbloom, "A Disconnect on Hooking Up," *New York Times*, March 1, 2007, http:// www.nytimes.com/2007/03/01/fashion/01hook.html?pagewanted=all.

*There is an expectation*   Americanchoicegirl, in a response posted February 20, 2009, at http://feministing.com/2009/02/20/speechifying_so-called _hook_up/.

*They fight to protect*   Suzanne Venker and Phyllis Schlafly, *The Flipside of Feminism: What Conservative Women Know—and Men Can't Say* (Washington, DC: WND Books, 2011), 152.

*"Inebriated women who end up"*   Ibid.

*The ensuing firestorm*   Alan Travis, "David Cameron Urged to Sack Kenneth Clarke over Rape Comments," *Guardian*, May 18, 2011.

*"Clarke's comments highlight"*   Jane Martinson, "Rape Is Rape, Ken Clarke," *Guardian*, May 18, 2011.

*Responsibility is still laid*   Carine M. Mardorossian, "Toward a New Feminist Theory of Rape," *Signs* 27 (2002): 753, 756.

*Another backlash against feminists*   Michelle L. Meloy and Susan L. Miller, *The Victimization of Women: Law, Policies, and Politics* (New York: Oxford University Press, 2011): 23–36.

*"Far more important"*   Charles J. Sykes, *A Nation of Victims: The Decay of the American Character* (New York: St. Martin's Press, 1992), 185.

*"Almost categorical dismissal"*   Meloy and Miller, *Victimization*, 26.

*Self-reflection will often*   Sharon Lamb, *The Trouble with Blame: Victims, Perpetrators, and Responsibility* (Cambridge, MA: Harvard University Press, 1996), 184.

*To me it's a man*   Rachel Coen, "The Stossel Treatment: Selective Editing and Other Unethical Tactics," *Fairness & Accuracy in Reporting*, March/April 2003, www.fair.org/index.php?page=1134. The *Providence-Journal Bulletin* reported that the orderly rally degenerated into a free-for-all after Stossel stepped out of his journalist role and that Stossel provoked one woman with a sexual innuendo.

*"Thrusts sex into"*   Jenna Johnson, "AU Date Rape Column Angers Students," *Washington Post*, March 29, 2010, http://voices.washingtonpost.com /campus-overload/2010/03/column_questions_date_rape_ang.html.

*I guess my question*   Amy Dickinson, Ask Amy, *Chicago Tribune*, November 27, 2009.

*"Take responsibility for the only thing"*   Amy Dickinson, Ask Amy, *Chicago Tribune*, December 8, 2009.

*In 2010, one-third*   BBC News, "Women Say Some Rape Victims Should Take Blame," February 15, 2010, http://news.bbc.co.uk/2/hi/8515592.stm.

*Wearing makeup and fashions*   James C. McKinley Jr., "Vicious Assault Shakes Texas Town," *New York Times*, March 9, 2011.

*A nationwide petition drive*   Shelby Knox, in e-mail communication with the author, March 11, 2011.

*Several days later*   Arthur S. Brisbane, "Gang Rape Story Lacked Balance," *Public Editor's Journal* (blog), *New York Times*, March 11, 2011, http://public editor.blogs.nytimes.com/2011/03/11/gang-rape-story-lacked-balance/.

*A community's concern*   Ibid. A subsequent story in the paper appeared several weeks later, but it strewed more confusion in its wake because of the lack of available information from law enforcement. It also intermixed statements about sexual assault with phrases like "engaged in sexual intercourse and oral sex with several of the men present" (James C. McKinley and Erica Goode, "3-Month Nightmare Emerges in Rape Inquiry," *New York Times*, March 28, 2011, http://www.nytimes.com/2011/03/29/us/29texas.html?pagewanted=all).

*"And her parents let"*  Jason Linkins, "In Wake of Texas Gang Rape, Florida Lawmaker Proposes School Dress Code Legislation," *Huffington Post*, March 16, 2011, http://www.huffingtonpost.com/2011/03/16/texas-gang-rape-aftermath-florida-law_n_836841.html.

*"It would appear"*  Joanne Ardovini-Brooker and Susan Caringella-MacDonald, "Media Attribution of Blame and Sympathy in Ten Rape Cases," *Justice Professional* 15 (2002): 16.

*It would have limited*  Sady Doyle, "John Boehner's Push to Redefine Rape," *Salon*, February 1, 2011. See also *No Taxpayer Funding for Abortion Act: Hearing on H.R. 3, Before the Subcommittee on the Judiciary, House of Representatives, 112th Cong., First Session (2011)*, http://judiciary.house.gov/hearings/printers/112th/112-9_64404.PDF.

*"If it's a legitimate rape"*  Editorial, "The Repugnant Code Behind Todd Akin's Words," *Washington Post*, August 20, 2012.

*Horrifyingly, Akin's contention*  Emily Bazelon, "Charmaine Yoest's Cheerful War on Abortion," *New York Times Magazine*, November 2, 2012.

*President Obama also responded*  Sam Stein, "Obama on Todd Akin: 'Rape Is Rape,'" *Huffington Post*, August 20, 2012.

*Although the number of pregnancies*  American Congress of Obstetricians and Gynecologists, "Statement on Rape and Pregnancy," news release, August 20, 2012, http://www.acog.org/About_ACOG/News_Room/News_Releases/2012/Statement_on_Rape_and_Pregnancy.

*For Bergelson, these situations*  Vera Bergelson, *Victims' Rights and Victims' Wrongs: Comparative Liability in Criminal Law* (Stanford, CA: Stanford University Press, 2009), 41–43.

*Bergelson put the crime*  Ibid., 101.

*"A rape victim is not"*  Ibid., 43.

*Voluntarily engaging in*  Vanessa Place, *The Guilt Project: Rape, Morality, and Law* (New York: Other Press, 2010).

*"Absent any real evidence"*   Ibid., 144.

*During a recent*   "Chicago Police Don't Give a Shit About Women," *Feministing*, April 30, 2010, http://community.feministing.com/2010/04 /chicago-police-dont-give-a-shi.html.

*And in January 2011*   Jessica Valenti, "SlutWalks and the Future of Feminism," *Washington Post*, June 3, 2011.

*The jurist commented*   Paul W. Valentine, "Maryland Judge Under Fire for Comments on Rape," *Washington Post*, May 9, 1993.

*One juror explained*   Lynn Hecht Schrafran, in e-mail communication with the author, July 27, 2010.

*Individuals with multiple vulnerabilities*   Betsy Stanko and Emma Williams, "Reviewing Rape and Rape Allegations in London," in *Rape: Challenging Contemporary Thinking*, eds. A. H. Horvath and Jennifer M. Brown (Portland, OR: Willan Publishing, 2009), 215.

*Rapists may very well*   Ibid., 219.

*The unfortunate reality*   Teresa P. Scalzo, *Prosecuting Alcohol-Facilitated Sexual Assault* (Alexandria, VA: American Prosecutors Research Institute, 2007), 20.

*"It is quite well-known"*   Joseph Shapiro, "Myths That Make It Hard to Stop Campus Rape," National Public Radio, March 4, 1010, http://www.npr .org/templates/story/story.php?storyId=124272157.

*Novelist Scott Turow wrote*   Scott Turow, *Limitations* (New York: Picador, 2006).

*When she awoke*   These facts, and the ensuing information about the case, are all contained in Christy Gutowski and Georgia Evdoxiadis, "'I Feel Great,'" *Daily Herald*, March 4, 2006.

*One juror commented*   John Bisognano, "Juror: Tape Key to Verdict," *Chicago Tribune*, March 9, 2006.

*"Good drugs are really"*   Ibid.

*The judge gave*   Dan Rozek, "Judge: Woman Need Not View Tape," *Chicago Sun-Times*, March 2, 2006.

*But the insensitivity*   Eric Zorn, "Why the 'Make Her Watch' People Are Wrong," *Chicago Tribune*, March 2, 2006.

*"I suffered more"*   Art Golab, "I Suffered More than Girl, Says Missbrenner," *Chicago Sun-Times*, March 9, 2006.

*"Herself too impaired"*   Zorn, "Why the 'Make Her Watch' People Are Wrong."

*Consider the case*   "The Case of Beckett Brennan: Katie Couric Reports on One Woman's Claim of an In-Campus Sexual Assault and How It Was Handled," *60 Minutes*, April 17, 2011, www.cbsnews.com/stories /2011/04/17/60minutes/main20054339.shtml.

*She did nothing*   Richard Huff, "Lara Logan: 'Life Is Not About Dwelling on the Bad,'" *New York Daily News*, January 22, 2012.

*This provides her with*   Steven Pinker, *The Better Angels of Our Nature: Why Violence Has Declined* (New York: Viking, 2011), 397.

*"Are suspected of"*   Deborah Tuerkheimer, "Slutwalking in the Shadow of the Law" (working paper, DePaul University College of Law, Chicago, 2012), http://papers.ssrn.com/sol3/papers.cfm?abstract_id=2009541.

## Danielle and Shae

*Danielle, from a small town*   The author interviewed Danielle on January 30, 2009. All quotes from Danielle come verbatim from these interviews. Danielle is a pseudonym to preserve her confidentiality.

*But Shae too*   The author interviewed Shae on January 29, 2009. All quotes from Shae come verbatim from these interviews. Shae is a pseudonym to preserve her confidentiality.

## Chapter 5: Is There a Rape "Epidemic"?

*Only 16 percent*   *Rape in America: A Report to the Nation* (Arlington, VA: National Victim Center and Crime Victims Research and Treatment Center, Medical University of South Carolina, 1992), 3, 6, http://www .musc.edu/ncvc/resources_prof/rape_in_america.pdf.

*Eighteen percent said*   Dean G. Kilpatrick et al., *Drug-Facilitated, Incapacitated, and Forcible Rape: A National Study* (Charleston, SC: Medical University of South Carolina, 2007), 27, 44, www.ncjrs.gov/pdffiles1 /nij/grants/219181.pdf. Note that, because of population increases, the absolute number of adult women in the United States estimated to have ever been forcibly raped will increase between 1991 and 2006. Surveyors asked six rape-screening questions, but the questions about alcohol and drugs were segregated from the forcible questions:

1. Has a man or boy ever made you have sex by using force or threatening to harm you or someone close to you? Just so there is no mistake, by having sex, we mean putting a penis in your vagina.

2. Has anyone, male or female, ever made you have oral sex by force or threatening to harm you? So there is no mistake, by oral sex, we mean that a man or boy put his penis in your mouth or someone penetrated your vagina or anus with their mouth or tongue.

3. Has anyone ever made you have anal sex by force or threatening to harm you? By anal sex, we mean putting their penis in your anus or rectum.

4. Has anyone ever put fingers or objects in our vagina or anus against your will by using force or threatening to harm you?

5. Has anyone ever had sex with you when you didn't want to after you drank so much alcohol that you were very high, drunk, or passed out? By having sex, we mean that a man or boy put his penis in your vagina, your anus, or your mouth.

6. Has anyone ever had sex with you when you didn't want to after they gave you, or you had taken enough drugs to make you very high, intoxicated, or passed out? By having sex we mean that a man or boy put his penis in your vagina, your anus, or your mouth (Ibid., 16).

*Furthermore, many people*   Ibid., 56.

*And the large majority*   Michele C. Black et al., *The National Intimate Partner and Sexual Violence Survey (NISVS): 2010 Summary Report* (Atlanta, GA: National Center for Injury Prevention and Control, Centers for Disease Control and Prevention), 18–19, http://www.cdc.gov/Violence Prevention/pdf/NISVS_Report2010-a.pdf.

*The CDC chose*   Roni Caryn Rabin, "Nearly 1 in 5 Women in U.S. Survey Say They Have Been Sexually Assaulted," *New York Times*, December 14, 2011.

*At the same time, she made*   Christina Hoff Sommers, "How the CDC Is Overstating Sexual Violence in the U.S.," *Washington Post*, January 27, 2012.

*Two other studies*   From 1995 to 1996, researchers interviewed a sample of 8,000 women about rape in the United States. They found that 14.8 percent reported a completed rape within their lifetimes. Rape was defined as "forced vaginal, oral, or anal penetration without the victim's consent" (Patricia Tjaden and Nancy Thoennes, *Extent, Nature, and Consequences of Rape Victimization: Findings from the National Violence Against Women Survey* [Washington, DC: US Department of Justice, 2006], 9, www .ncjrs.gov/pdffiles1/nij/210346.pdf). Between 2001 and 2003, researchers completed 4,877 random-digit-dial surveys, finding that 10.6 percent of the women (or 11.7 million) had experienced forced sex at some time in their lives. They also found that 2.1 percent of men were victims. Forced sex was defined as "any type of vaginal, oral, or anal penetration or intercourse in situations against your will" (Kathleen C. Basile et al., "Prevalence and Characteristics of Sexual Violence Victimization Among U.S. Adults, 2001–2003," *Violence and Victims* 22, [2007]: 441). For a summary and comparison of the various contemporary research studies, see Dean G. Kilpatrick and Kenneth J. Ruggiero, "Making Sense of Rape in America: Where Do the Numbers Come from and What Do They Mean?," (paper, National Online Resource Center on Violence Against Women, 2004), http://new.vawnet.org/Assoc_Files_VAWnet/MakingSenseofRape.pdf.

*Although four important*    See, for example, Roni Caryn Rabin, "Nearly 1 in 5 Women in U.S. Survey Say They Have been Sexually Assaulted," *New York Times*, December 14, 2011.

*"I don't think"*    Ibid.

*One CNN story*    Jessica Ravitz, "Rape Victims Offer Advice to Today's College Women," CNN, December 15, 2009, http://articles.cnn.com/2009 -12-15/living/sexual.assaults.college.campuses_1_rapes-students-today -sexual-assault?_s=PM:LIVING.

*"Studies estimate that"*    Piper Fogg, "Programs Proliferate, but 'It's Hard to Know' Whether They Work," *Chronicle of Higher Education*, November 29, 2009, http://chronicle.com/article/Rape-Prevention-Programs/49151.

*In interviews with two thousand*    Kilpatrick et al., *Drug-Facilitated, Incapacitated, and Forcible Rape*, 27–8. An earlier study found a slightly higher lifetime rape rate for college students; their finding was 13.1 percent ("Youth Risk Behavior Surveillance: National College Health Risk Behavior Survey—United States," *Morbidity and Mortality Weekly Report* 46 [1995], www.cdc.gov/mmwr/preview/mmwrhtml/00049859.htm).

*Only about 12 percent*    Ibid., 44.

*Researchers then estimated*    Bonnie S. Fisher, Francis T. Cullen, and Michael G. Turner, *The Sexual Victimization of College Women* (Washington, DC:

US Department of Justice, December 2000), 10, http://www.ncjrs.gov /pdffiles1/nij/182369.pdf.

*A startlingly small number* Ibid., 23.

*In 2007, a college study* Christopher P. Krebs et al., *The Campus Sexual Assault (CAS) Study* (Research Triangle Park, NC: RTI International, 2007), 5-2, www.ncjrs.gov/pdffiles1/nij/grants/221153.pdf.

*Research involving younger* Danice K. Eaton et al., "Youth Risk Behavior Surveillance—United States, 2009," *Surveillance Summaries* 59, 5 (2010): 6, http://www.cdc.gov/MMWR/preview/mmwrhtml/ss5905a1.htm.

*Important, however, is* Kilpatrick et al., *Drug-Facilitated, Incapacitated, and Forcible Rape*, 23.

*Eight percent, or 9,524,000* Black, *National Intimate Partner*, 22.

*In Kilpatrick's general population* Ibid., 30.

*An important study* Tjaden and Thoennes, *Extent, Nature, and Consequences*, 21.

*One study, for example* Raquel Kennedy Bergen, *Marital Rape: New Research and Directions* (Harrisburg, PA: National Online Resource Center on Violence Against Women, 2006), http://vawnet.org/assoc_files_vawnet /ar_maritalraperevised.pdf.

*Only forty-four young men* David Lisak and Paul M. Miller, "Repeat Rape and Multiple Offending Among Undetected Rapists," *Violence and Victims* 17 (2002): 78.

*By attacking women* Ibid., 81.

*Interestingly, most reported* Stephanie K. McWhorter et al., "Reports of Rape Reperpetration by Newly Enlisted Male Navy Personnel," *Violence and Victims* 24 (2009): 209–10, 213.

*New sample members* Michael Rand, "The National Crime Victimization Survey: 34 Years of Measuring Crime in the United States," *Statistical Journal of the United Nations* ECE 23 (2006): 291.

*After his introduction of this question* Ibid., 299.

*Rape researchers, however* Kilpatrick and Ruggiero, "Making Sense of Rape in America," 5.

*Prevalence estimates were* Bonnie S. Fisher, *Measuring Rape Against Women: The Significance of Survey Questions* (Washington, DC: US Department of Justice, 2004), 1–4, 10, www.ncjrs.gov/pdffiles1/nij/199705.pdf.

*Because of the small*   Jennifer L. Truman and Michael Rand, *Criminal Victimization, 2009* (Washington, DC: US Department of Justice, 2010), 11, http://bjs.ojp.usdoj.gov/content/pub/pdf/cv09.pdf. Jennifer L. Truman, *Criminal Victimization, 2010* (Washington, DC: US Department of Justice, 2011), 14, http://bjs.ojp.usdoj.gov/content/pub/pdf/cv10.pdf.

*To offset the smaller*   Michael R. Rand, *Criminal Victimization, 2007* (Washington, DC: US Department of Justice, 2008), 2, http://bjs.ojp.usdoj.gov /content/pub/pdf/cv07.pdf.

*For these reasons*   Truman, *Criminal Victimization, 2010,* 1.

*In his book* The Better Angels   Pinker, *The Better Angels,* 402.

*As for rape*   Jennifer L. Truman and Michael Planty, *Criminal Victimization, 2011* (Washington, DC: US Department of Justice, 2012), 8, http://bjs data.ojp.usdoj.gov/content/pub/pdf/cv11.pdf.

*Other research studies*   For example, in a sample of 3,000 women reported in 2007, only 18 percent had reported the forcible rape to law-enforcement officials (Kilpatrick et al., *Drug-Facilitated, Incapacitated, and Forcible Rape,* 43). In a sample of 8,000 women surveyed between 1995 and 1996, 19.1 percent said they had reported the rape (Tjaden and Thoennes, *Extent, Nature, and Consequences,* 33). Fewer than 5 percent of the 4,446 college women sampled who reported rape and attempted rape said they had told law-enforcement officials, although two-thirds said they did inform another person about the incident (Fisher, Cullen, and Turner, *The Sexual Victimization of College Women,* 23).

*Other explanations*   In research with a sample of 3,000 women, 63 percent of those subjected to forcible rape said they didn't want family or others to know, 76 percent feared reprisal, 52 percent believed there was a lack of proof, 44 percent feared bad treatment from the criminal-justice system, and 55 percent said they didn't know how to report (Kilpatrick et al., *Drug-Facilitated, Incapacitated, and Forcible Rape,* 48).

*These include assaults*   The Uniform Crime Reports define forcible rape as "the carnal knowledge of a female forcibly and against her will." Assaults and attempts to commit rape by force or threat of force are also included. However, statutory rape without force and other sex offenses are excluded (Kilpatrick and Ruggiero, "Making Sense of Rape in America," 4).

*In January 2012*   Charlie Savage, "U.S. to Expand Its Definition of Rape in Statistics," *New York Times,* January 7, 2012.

*Furthermore, an investigation*   Jeremy Kohler, "Philadelphia's Pain: Parents Blame Police Practice in Daughter's Killing," *St. Louis Post-Dispatch,* August 29, 2005.

*Another practice was*   Ibid. Similar practices were alleged in New Orleans (Laura Maggi, "NOPD Downgrading of Rape Reports Raises Questions," *Times Picayune,* July 11, 2009). For a survey of problems in other cities, see Mark Fazlollah, "City, National Rape Statistics Highly Suspect," *Women's eNews,* January 8, 2001, http://womensenews.org/story /rape/010108/city-national-rape-statistics-highly-suspect. In New York City, police officers had classified victims' rape complaints as criminal trespassing. As a result, a serial perpetrator was able to commit six rapes before he was captured (Graham Rayman, "NYPD Tapes 3: A Detective Comes Forward About Downgraded Sexual Assaults," *Village Voice,* June 8, 2010).

*Beginning in 2008*   Federal Bureau of Investigation, *Crime in the United States* (Washington, DC: Federal Bureau of Investigation, 2011), http:// www.fbi.gov/about-us/cjis/ucr/crime-in-the-u.s/2011/crime-in-the -u.s.-2011/tables/table-1. The figures reported are as follows:

| Year | Number of cases |
|------|-----------------|
| 2000 | 90,178 |
| 2001 | 90,863 |
| 2002 | 95,235 |
| 2003 | 93,883 |
| 2004 | 95,089 |
| 2005 | 94,347 |
| 2006 | 94,472 |
| 2007 | 92,160 |
| 2008 | 90,750 |
| 2009 | 89,241 |
| 2010 | 85,593 |
| 2011 | 83,425 |

*The Wikipedia entry*   "Rape Statistics," Wikipedia, last modified October 17, 2012, http://en.wikipedia.org/wiki/Rape_statistics.

*Inconsistent definitions*   Ibid.

*What one frequently finds*   Many websites repeat playwright Eve Ensler's statement that "one in three women on the planet will be raped or beaten in her lifetime" (http://www.guardian.co.uk/society/video/2012 /sep/25/rosario-dawson-1bn-rising-video). The origin for this statistic is unknown, but it is a global figure that also includes domestic violence. However, on some websites, the statistic gets mangled. For example, see the statement on the Women Organized Against Rape (WOAR) website: "[One] in [three] American women will be sexually abused during their lifetime" (http://www.woar.org/resources/sexual-assault-statistics.php).

*Thus, on college campuses*   A page on the Bates College website made the statement that one out of four women will be sexually assaulted on a college campus (http://abacus.bates.edu/admin/offices/scs/salt7.html, accessed April 20, 2010). See also the University at Buffalo's Wellness Education Services page asserting the one-in-four statistic (http://wellness .buffalo.edu/wes/rapesa.php) and the Skidmore College page that also states it (http://cms.skidmore.edu/health/education/sexual_Health/rape -and-sexual-assault.cfm). An article in the Massachusetts Institute of Technology newspaper reported that one in four women surveyed were victims of rape or attempted rape while on campus (Eliot Levine and Carol Waldmann, "Rape Has Become an Epidemic in the College Environment," *Tech Online Edition*, April 21, 1989, http://tech.mit.edu /V109/N19/levine.19o.html).

*In her graduation speech*   Emma Shaw Crane, "A Time to Rejoice, and a Time to Be Heartbroken," *Press Democrat*, May 24, 2009, http://www.press democrat.com/article/20090524/NEWS/905241040.

*One poster seen*   TK Logan, e-mail message to the author, October 16, 2012.

*One prominent feminist*   Barry Deutsch ("Ampersand"), "Rape Prevalence Statistics on Donohue," *Alas, a Blog*, February 6, 2003, http://www .amptoons.com/blog/2003/02/06/rape-prevalence-statistics-on-donohue/.

*A feminist website*   Ann Wright, "Is There an Army Cover Up of Rape and Murder of Women Soldiers?," *Common Dreams*, April 28, 2008, www .commondreams.org/archive/2008/04/28/8564.

*This statistic was then*　Chicago Foundation for Women, "News: Analysis," *Tuesday Blast*, May 27–June 2, 2008, www.cfw.org/Page.aspx?pid=916.

*In testimony before*　Rob Quinn, "Sex Assaults Against Women in Military 'Epidemic,'" *Newser*, August 1, 2008, www.newser.com/story/33913/sex -assaults-against-women-in-military-epidemic.html.

*Indeed, use of the term*　Responding to Governor Haley's 2012 veto of funding for rape-crisis centers, the South Carolina Coalition Against Domestic Violence and Sexual Assault wrote in a press release that rape "is also one of the most serious health epidemics facing South Carolinans" (www .sccadvasa.org/about/newsroom/232-press-statement-in-response-to -governor-haleys-veto-of-funding-for-rape-crisis-centers.html). In 2012, a Texas group, the Rape Crisis Center, promoted the film *The Invisible War*, which "catalogues the conditions that have protected perpetrators and allowed this epidemic to continue" (www.rapecrisis.com/events .php), while an American Association of University Women (AAUW) fact sheet called sexual assault "the silent epidemic" (www.aauw.org/act /laf/library/assault_stats.cfm).

*And a former president*　Lonnie Bristow, MD, as quoted in "Sexual Assault: The Silent, Violent Epidemic," Infoplease Database, 2007, www.info please.com/ipa/A0001537.html.

*An "epidemic" indicates*　"Epidemic," *Free Dictionary*, accessed August 23, 2010, http://medical-dictionary.thefreedictionary.com/epidemic.

*One can readily agree*　Christina Hoff Sommers, "What's Wrong and What's Right with Contemporary Feminism?"

*The blog concluded*　"Must-Read Op-ed Piece Exposes the Lie That Rape Is Rampant," *False Rape Society* (blog), April 20, 2009, http://falserapesociety .blogspot.com/2009/04/must-read-op-ed-piece-exposes-myth-that.html.

*A federal grant application*　Jennifer Epstein, "Overreporting Sexual Assaults," *Inside Higher Ed*, October 2, 2009, www.insidehighered.com /news/2009 /10/02/davis.

*Science journalist Michael Specter*　Michael Specter, *Denialism: How Irrational Thinking Hinders Scientific Progress, Harms the Planet, and Threatens Our Lives* (New York: Penguin, 2009), 21.

*Aptly, writer Barbara Ehrenreich*　Barbara Ehrenreich, *Bright-Sided: How the Relentless Promotion of Positive Thinking Has Undermined America* (New York: Henry Holt, 2009), 205.

## Megan

*Megan is a student*   The author interviewed Megan on February 1, 3, and 5, 2010. All quotes from Megan come verbatim from these interviews. Megan is a pseudonym to preserve her confidentiality.

## Chapter 6: The Truth About False Rape Claims

*"It's time to stop"*   Comments posted February 24, 2009, to "Woman Reports Rape on UC San Diego Campus," *San Diego Union-Tribune*, www3.signon sandiego.com/stories/2009/feb/24/1m24pubsafe00183-public-safety.

*By late afternoon*   Ibid.

*In a letter*   Christina Hoff Sommers, "Rape and Holocaust Denial," letter to the editor, *Women's Review of Books* 26 (January/February 2009): 2.

*For example, a woman*   Kimberly Lonsway, *Successfully Investigating Acquaintance Sexual Assault: A National Training Manual for Law Enforcement* (Beverly Hills, CA: National Center for Women and Policing, 2001), www .mincava.umn.edu/documents/acquaintsa/participant/allegations.pdf.

*According to the FBI's*   Ibid.

*At first blush*   Eugene J. Kanin, "False Rape Allegations," *Archives of Sexual Behavior* 23 (1994): 81–90.

*However, in this jurisdiction*   Ibid., 83.

*This practice has now*   Joanne Archambault and Kimberly Lonsway, *VAWA 2005 Restricts the Use of Polygraphs with Victims of Sexual Assault* (Addy, WA: End Violence Against Women International, 2006), www .ncdsv.org/images/VAWAPolygraphPromising%20Practices.pdf. Archambault, a retired sex-crimes investigator and now law-enforcement trainer, writes, "I also find that these interrogation tactics can sometimes create a 'false report' by intimidating victims into withdrawing their cooperation or even recanting their report."

*Kanin himself cautioned*   Kanin, "False Rape Allegations," 85.

*With the polygraphing*   Ibid., 90.

*In a sample of 109*   Ibid., 84.

*Nor does Kanin describe*   David Lisak, "False Allegations of Rape: A Critique of Kanin," *Sexual Assault Report* 11 (September/October 2007): 2.

*Polygraphing was not an issue*   Kanin, "False Rape Allegations," 90.

*For his actions*   This summary of the case is taken from Taylor and Johnson, *Until Proven Innocent*—primarily pages 16–102 and 317–31.

*After presenting the facts*   Ibid., 372.

*First was a statement*   Ibid., 374.

*A perusal of that*   Linda Fairstein, e-mail message to author, October 12, 2007.

*Finally, the authors*   Taylor and Johnson, *Until Proven Innocent*, 375.

*It is all part*   http://durhamwonderland.blogspot.com.

*A number of false rape*   RADAR website, www.mediaradar.org; the Center for Military Readiness, www.cmrlink.org.

*One is by freelancer*   Cathy Young, "Who Says Women Never Lie About Rape?," *Salon*, March 10, 1999, http://www.salon.com/1999/03/10/cov_10news/.

*"I would need"*   Wendy McElroy, "False Rape Accusations May Be More Common than Thought," FoxNews.com, May 2, 2006, http://www.foxnews.com/story/0,2933,194032,00.html.

*"In today's politically correct"*   Taylor and Johnson, *Until Proven Innocent*, 373.

*And another wrote*   "Judge Dismisses Rape Charges in Pawtucket Case," *False Rape Society* (blog), April 23, 2009, http://falserapesociety.blogspot.com/2009/04/judge-dismisses-rape-charges-in.html.

*Inflammatory reader responses*   Ibid.

*"I also agree with"*   Ibid.

*Perhaps the most strident*   "Rape Baloney," *Angry Harry* (blog), August 14, 2004, www.angryharry.com/esRapeBaloney.htm.

*The purpose of their*   Ibid.

*"And given that some"*   Ibid.

*Next, Harry added all*   Ibid.

*Concluding that the vast*   Ibid.

*But as journalist*   Charles Pierce, *Idiot America: How Stupidity Became a Virtue in the Land of the Free* (New York: Doubleday, 2009), 41.

*"When women accuse men"*   Jan Jordan, *The Word of a Woman: Police, Rape and Belief* (Basingstoke, UK: Palgrave Macmillan, 2004), 243.

*Because few organizations*   Barry Deutsch's blog, *Alas, a Blog,* has presented more recent and accurate material on false-rape-claims research. He stated that on the day he provided a critique of the Kanin study on his blog, he had 5,800 visitors. "The ongoing usefulness of a blog like *Alas* is that we can make information available to Google searchers. My post about Kanin is now the top Google search result for 'Eugene Kanin,' and in the top five for searches like 'Kanin false rape' and 'false rape reports'" (Barry Deutsch, e-mail message to author, May 4, 2009).

*O'Reilly was then able*   "O'Reilly Slams Group Who Convicted Duke Players Already," *O'Reilly Sucks* (blog), April 21, 2006, http://vps.thehotweb .net/~oreilly/viewtopic.php?p=14401&sid=d6f5e7766293b772751674 8086837ff3.

*"I was set up"*   Gail Dines, "CNN's 'Journalism' Is a Fool's Paradise," *Common Dreams,* January 19, 2007, http://www.commondreams.org/views07 /0119-21.htm.

*Later, she agreed that*   Rachel Smolkin, "Justice Delayed," *American Journalism Review,* August/September 2007, www.ajr.org/Article.asp?id=4379.

*However, one of her comments*   Wendy Murphy, interview by Tucker Carlson, *The Situation with Tucker Carlson,* MSNBC, June 5, 2006, http://www .msnbc.msn.com/id/13165471/ns/msnbc-the_ed_show/t/situation -tucker-carlson-june/#.UIB7KWeltiw.

*She wrote that when*   Brownmiller, *Against Our Will,* 387. Edward Greer spoke with Brownmiller and obtained a copy of the speech before the Association of the Bar of the City of New York, which mentioned the 2 percent figure. However, none of the speechwriters could remember precisely how they obtained the 2 percent figure (Edward Greer, "The Truth Behind Legal Dominance Feminism's 'Two Percent False Rape Claim' Figure," *Loyola of Los Angeles Law Review* 33 [2000]: 957).

*Yet, although it does not*   For example, feminist legal scholar Deborah Rhode quoted the 2 percent figure in a book, and in a review in *Atlantic Monthly,* Katha Pollitt wrote, "As Rhode says, the overwhelming consensus among researchers using government statistics is that only 2 percent of rape complaints are false—no more than for other crimes" (Katha Pollitt, "Feminism's Unfinished Business," *Atlantic Monthly,* November 1997, http://

www.theatlantic.com/past/docs/issues/97nov/pollitt.htm). Edward Greer located twenty-four law review articles proclaiming the 2 percent false-rape-claims figure (Greer, "The Truth Behind Legal Dominance," 949).

*Because the man continued*  Jeremy Kohler, "Philadelphia's Pain: Parents Blame Police Practice in Daughter's Killing," *St. Louis Post-Dispatch*, August 20, 2005.

*Of the 2,059 cases*  Kimberly A. Lonsway, Joanne Archambault, and David Lisak, "False Reports: Moving Beyond the Issue to Successfully Investigate and Prosecute Non-stranger Sexual Assault," *Voice 3* (2009): 2, www.ndaa.org/pdf/the_voice_vol_3_no_1_2009.pdf.

*They concluded that seven*  Ibid.

*A little more than*  Ibid.

*The final determination*  Ibid.

*After this investigation*  Ibid., 3.

*In 2000 and 2003*  Ibid.

*Interestingly, the police department*  David Lisak et al., "False Allegations of Sexual Assault: An Analysis of Ten Years of Reported Cases," *Violence Against Women*, 16 (2010): 1327–31.

*Even though half of*  Ibid., 1329.

*We know, however*  Joanne Belknap, "Rape Too Hard to Report and Too Easy to Discredit Victims," *Violence Against Women* 16 (2010): 1335–44.

*"A culture of suspicion"*  Liz Kelly, "The (In)credible Words of Women: False Allegations in European Rape Research," *Violence Against Women* 16 (2010): 1351.

*In addition to citing*  Kimberly Lonsway, "Trying to Move the Elephant in the Living Room: Responding to the Challenge of False Rape Reports," *Violence Against Women* 16 (2010): 1357.

*The FBI does make*  Federal Bureau of Investigation, *Uniform Crime Reporting Handbook* (Clarksburg, WV: Federal Bureau of Investigation, 2004), 77–78, www2.fbi.gov/ucr/handbook/ucrhandbook04.pdf. See also Lisak et al., "False Allegations of Sexual Assault."

*However, these scenarios*  Lonsway, Archambault, and Lisak, "False Reports," 5; Lisak et al., "False Allegations of Sexual Assault," 1319–21.

*Since the unfounded category*   An FBI analyst provided these data to the author on September 4, 2009, via e-mail. A 2011 report notes that from 2001 to 2009 the national average for municipal police agencies to categorize rape complaints as unfounded was 5.66 percent. The same study finds that the Chicago Police Department averages a rate of unfounded sexual-assault complaints of 17 percent for the same time period, more than three times the national average. This rate raises serious questions about whether the department is confusing "unfounded" with other factors (Tracy Siska, *Felony Sex Crime Case Processing: Report, Analysis, & Recommendations* [Chicago: Chicago Justice Project, 2011], http://www.chicagojustice.org/research/long-form-reports /felony-sex-crime-case-processing-report-analysis-recommendations /CJP_Felony_Sex_Crime_Case_Processing_Report_Analys.0.pdf).

*Compare the 2008*   Ibid.

*Cathy Young, in a July*   Cathy Young, "The Feminine Lie Mystique," *Weekly Standard*, July 29, 2011.

*And defense attorney*   Roy Black, "Why We Should Protect Those Accused of Rape," *Salon*, July 27, 2011, http://www.salon.com/2011/07/27 /dsk_kobe_assange_flatley/.

*As recorded by*   See "False Accusation of Rape," *Wikipedia*, last modified June 13, 2012, http://en.wikipedia.org/wiki/False_accusation_of_rape.

*Because the studies*   Lonsway, "Trying to Move the Elephant," 1358.

*"The hidden issue"*   Jordan, *The Word of a Woman*, 72.

*Others declared that*   Patrick Wintour, "Nick Clegg Signals Rethink over Rape Trial Anonymity," *Guardian*, June 10, 2010.

*"Nothing prevents journalists"*   Lynn S. Chancer, *High-Profile Crimes: When Legal Cases Become Social Causes* (Chicago: University of Chicago Press, 2005), 262.

*In the way in which they have seized*   Jordan, *The Word of a Woman*, 5. See also Jenny Kitzinger, "Rape in the Media," in *Rape: Challenging Contemporary Thinking*, eds. Miranda A. H. Horvath and Jennifer M. Brown (Portland, OR: Willan Publishing, 2009): 82.

*They believed that the newly discovered*   Nicola Gavey and Virginia Gow, "'Cry Wolf,' Cried the Wolf: Constructing the Issue of False Rape Allegations in New Zealand Media Texts," *Feminism Psychology* 11 (2001): 354. In 2010,

*Slate* covered the false-rape-claims problem: Emily Bazelon and Rachel Larimore, "How Often Do Women Falsely Cry Rape?," *Slate*, October 1, 2009, http://www.slate.com/articles/news_and_politics/jurisprudence/2009/10/how_often_do_women_falsely_cry_rape.html. BBC News also highlighted the effects of false rape claims on innocent men: Andrea Rose, "Forever Accused," BBC News, February 27, 2008, http://news.bbc.co.uk/2/hi/uk_news/magazine/7265307.stm. And the *New York Times* has published numerous articles on men convicted of rape but exonerated by DNA testing: Adam Liptak, "Study Suspects Thousands of False Convictions," *New York Times*, April 19, 2004; Adam Liptak, "DNA Exonerations Highlight Flaws in U.S. Justice System," *New York Times*, July 22, 2007.

*One sports talk-show radio host*    Kevin Jackson, "Who's the Victim Here?," *ESPN Page 2*, accessed June 4, 2009, http://espn.go.com/page2/s/jackson/030721.html.

*Still unclear from this study*    Renae Franiuk et al., "Prevalence and Effects of Rape Myths in Print Journalism," *Violence Against Women* 14 (2008): 293, 302.

*What easy narrative*    Jeff Benedict, "The Science of the Brief Encounter," *Sports Illustrated*, August 31, 2004, http://sportsillustrated.cnn.com/vault/article/magazine/MAG1106407/index.htm.

*The speculation was that ESPN*    Bob Raissman, "Journalism Basics Are News to ESPN While Covering Ben Roethlisberger Civil Suit," *New York Daily News*, July 24, 2009, www.nydailynews.com/sports/football/2009/07/24/2009-07-24_while_dealing_with_ben_rjournalism_basics_are_news_to_espn.html.

*But, Rhode pointed out*    Associated Press, "Legal Experts: Roethlisberger May Pay Even if Innocent," *USA Today*, July 26, 2009, www.usatoday.com/sports/football/nfl/steelers/2009-07-24-roethlisberger-analysis_N.htm.

*"But if you're Ben"*    Todd Kaufmann, "Is Ben Roethlisberger Guilty of More than Just Bad Judgment?" *Bleacher Report*, March 9, 2010, http://bleacherreport.com/articles/359794-is-ben-roethlisberger-guilty-of-more-than-just-bad-judgment.

*"Yes, Ben, why did you"*    Annie Shields, "Apologizing for Ben Roethlisberger," *Ms.* magazine, March 10, 2010, http://msmagazine.com/blog/blog/2010/03/10/apologizing-for-ben-roethlisberger.

*"Apologists drink from"*   Jaclyn Friedman, "Sports Misogyny and the Court of Public Opinion," *American Prospect*, July 27, 2009, www.prospect.org /cs/articles?article=sports_misogyny_and_the_court_of _public_opinion.

*"We have seen plenty"*   Steve Kornacki, "3 Reasons to Doubt the Al Gore Sex Assault Story," *Salon*, July 23, 2010.

*Koestler's biographer*   June Purvis, "Arthur Koestler and Women," letters to the editor, *Times Literary Supplement*, August 13, 2010, 6; Tony Judt, *Reappraisals: Reflections on the Forgotten Twentieth Century* (New York: Penguin, 2008), 34.

*"Beliefs in women's"*   Jordan, *The Word of a Woman*, 243.

*In the Potiphar story*   This Genesis tale is retold in many places, including Brownmiller, *Against Our Will*, 22.

*Despite the best efforts*   Harper Lee, *To Kill a Mockingbird* (New York: HarperPerennial, 2002). The book has sold nearly one million copies a year, and in the past five years, it has been the second bestselling backlist title in the United States (Julie Bosman, "A Classic Turns 50, and Parties Are Planned," *New York Times*, May 24, 2010).

*He had already given her*   Jordan, *The Word of a Woman*, 36.

*These strong cultural attitudes*   For a discussion of the role myth plays in cultural belief about women, see Elizabeth Fallaize, "Beauvoir and the Demystification of Woman," in *A History of Feminist Literary Criticism*, eds. Gill Plain and Susan Sellers (New York: Cambridge University Press, 2007), 89.

*"For it to become a myth"*   Didier Eribon, *Conversations with Claude Lévi-Strauss* (New York: Basic Books, 1963), 209.

*Although the myth refers*   Ibid.

*"Whereas surely such widespread"*   Han Israels and Morton Schatzman, "The Seduction Theory," *History of Psychiatry* 4 (1993): 48.

*As a result, there was always suspicion*   Keith Burgess-Jackson, "A History of Rape Law," in *A Most Detestable Crime: New Philosophical Essays on Rape*, ed. Keith Burgess-Jackson (New York: Oxford University Press, 1999), 16–18. See also Susan Caringella, *Addressing Rape Reform in Law and Practice* (New York: Columbia University Press, 2009).

*Still another practice was*   Ibid., 22–23.

*During the last twenty-five years*    Burgess-Jackson, "A History," 15–31.

*"Throughout the period"*    Deborah Lipstadt, *Beyond Belief: The American Press and the Coming of the Holocaust, 1933–1945* (New York: Free Press, 1986), 27.

*Although interest in strict*    Ibid.

*"Whereas pro-Nazi denial"*    Patrizia Romito, *Deafening Silence: Hidden Violence Against Women and Children* (Bristol, UK: Polity Press, 2008), 39.

*Mistaken identity was*    Judy Shepherd, "Reflections on a Rape Trial: The Role of Rape Myths and Jury Selection in the Outcome of a Trial," *Affilia* 17 (2002): 75–80.

*"I think he's guilty"*    Ibid., 83–84.

*"If a 66-year-old"*    Ibid., 88.

*This case demonstrated*    Ibid., 91–92.

*Vulnerability scares us*    David Lisak, "Behind the Torment of Rape Victims Lies A Dark Fear: Reply to the Commentaries," *Violence Against Women* 16 (2010): 1373.

## Chapter 7: Defending Strauss-Kahn

*"I hold it against"*    Bernard Henri-Lévy, "Bernard-Henri Lévy Defends Accused IMF Director," *Daily Beast*, May 16, 2011, http://www.thedaily beast.com/articles/2011/05/16/bernard-henri-lvy-the-dominique-strauss -kahn-i-know.html.

*"The supposed victim"*    David Rieff, "An Indefensible Defense: French Intellectuals' Despicable Response to Dominique Strauss-Kahn's Arrest," *New Republic*, May 18, 2011.

*"What do we know"*    Ibid.

*Journalist Jean-François Kahn*    "After DSK: What Did They Know?," *Economist*, May 26, 2011.

*"It's not like anybody"*    Ibid.

*Economist Nouriel Roubini*    Steve Clemons, "The Meaning of Strauss-Kahn," *Huffington Post*, May 16, 2011, http://www.huffingtonpost.com/steve -clemons/the-meaning-of-strauss-ka_b_862357.html.

*"This does not mean that Strauss-Kahn"*   Naomi Wolf, "A Tale of Two Rape Charges," *The Great Debate* (blog), Reuters, May 23, 2011, http://blogs.reuters.com/great-debate/2011/05/23/a-tale-of-two-rape-charges.

*A few days after*   "The Downfall of DSK," *Economist*, May 21, 2011.

*Even Russian prime minister*   Andrew Osborn, "Vladimir Putin Hints at Dominique Strauss-Kahn Conspiracy," *Telegraph*, May 29, 2011.

*The stunning new info*   Laura Italiano, "Maid Cleaning Up as Hooker," *New York Post*, July 2, 2011.

*The* Post *even reported*   Jennifer Bain and Bob Fredericks, "IMF Accuser in Apt. for HIV Vics," *New York Post*, May 18, 2011.

*In a post on the blog*   Robert Kuttner, "Applying Occam's Razor to Strauss-Kahn," *American Prospect*, June 30, 2011, http://blog.prospect.org/robert_kuttner/2011/06/applying-occams-razor-to-strau.html.

*And, as the New York City*   Cathy Young, "The Noble Lie, Feminist Style," *Weekly Standard*, August 1, 2011.

*"Women already struggle"*   Kathleen Parker, "Dominique Strauss-Kahn: Sex, Drugs and Then," *Washington Post*, July 1, 2011.

### Blaming Tracy

*"[The nurse's] very emotional"*   Celeste Hamilton, author interview, November 23, 2009. Celeste Hamilton is a pseudonym to protect Tracy's identity. All quotes from Hamilton are taken verbatim from this interview.

### Chapter 8: Denial's Effects: Dangerous Indifference

*After polling eight thousand*   Kimberly A. Lonsway and Joanne Archambault, "The 'Justice Gap' for Sexual Assault Cases: Future Directions for Research and Reform," *Violence Against Women* 18, no. 2 (2012): 147.

*His research in the 1990s*   *Rape in America: A Report to the Nation*, 6, http://academicdepartments.musc.edu/ncvc/resources_pprof/rape_inamerica.pdf; Kilpatrick et al., *Drug-Facilitated, Incapacitated, and Forcible Rape*, 27, 44.

*Half (49 percent) of all*   Jennifer L. Truman and Michael Planty, *Criminal Victimization, 2011* (Washington, DC: US Department of Justice, 2012), 8, http://bjsdata.ojp.usdoj.gov/content/pub/pdf/cv11.pdf. See also Eric P. Baumer, *Temporal Variation in the Likelihood of Police Notification by Victims of Rapes, 1973–2000* (report submitted to the US Department of Justice, 2004), 7, www.ncjrs.gov/pdffiles1/nij/grants/207497.pdf.

*27 percent of the rapes*   Ibid., 10.

*The ratio of reports to arrests*   Lonsway and Archambault, "The Justice Gap," 150.

*In the state of Illinois*   *"I Used to Think the Law Would Protect Me": Illinois's Failure to Test Rape Kits* (Washington, DC: Human Rights Watch, 2010), http://www.hrw.org/reports/2010/07/07/i-used-think-law-would-protect-me-0.

*The state's attorney's office*   Megan Twohey, "Women Charged Rape; Doctor Still Practiced," *Chicago Tribune*, April 30, 2010.

*The DNA sample was a match*   Megan Twohey, "Sex Charges Against Gynecologist," *Chicago Tribune*, August 5, 2010. A month after the *Tribune*'s story, the state's attorney's office charged the doctor with the 2002 rape.

*When the DNA was finally tested*   Christy Gutowski, "Could Erin Justice Have Been Saved?," *Daily Herald*, July 3, 2005; Art Barnum, "Naperville Man Gets Life in Prison," *Chicago Tribune*, March 16, 2011.

*Five thousand cases*   Armen Keteyian, "Exclusive: Rape in America: Justice Denied," CBS News, November 9, 2009, www.cbsnews.com/stories /2009/11/09/cbsnews_investigates/main5590118.shtml. Another news story puts the number of untested kits in Los Angeles at 13,000, 7,000 of them under the jurisdiction of the Los Angeles Police Department, and another 5,635 in the County Sheriff's Department (Amy Goodwin, "Rape Kits in Cold Storage," *Ms.* magazine, Winter 2009, www .msmagazine.com/winter2009/RapeBacklog.asp). A report from the US Department of Justice, describing a survey of more than 2,000 law enforcement agencies, found that in 18 percent of open, unsolved rape cases, forensic evidence had not been submitted to a crime lab (Editorial, "Respect for Rape Victims," *New York Times*, November 14, 2009).

*Backlogs result from*   In 2010, the federal government made 115 awards totaling $64 million to state and local governments to reduce DNA backlogs.

Illinois received $2.5 million (National Institute of Justice, "DNA Analysis Backlog Elimination Act of 2010, Report to Congress," January 25, 2011, www.nij.gov/topics/forensics/lab-operations/evidence-backlogs /dra-backlog-reduction-report-to-Congress-2010.pdf).

*Some units believed*   Megan Twohey, "Dozens of Rape Kits Not Submitted for Testing by Chicago Suburban Police Departments," *Chicago Tribune*, June 14, 2009.

*Forty-four percent*   Nancy Ritter, *The Road Ahead: Unanalyzed Evidence in Sexual Assault Cases* (Washington, DC: National Institute of Justice, 2011), www.nsvrc.org/publications/road-ahead-unanalyzed-evidence-sexual -assault-cases.

*After charging him*   CBS News, "Moldy Rape Kits Found in Illinois Police Department," March 19, 2010, www.cbsnews.com/stories/2010/03/19 /national/main6316143.shtml.

*Processing of two hundred*   Frank Main, "Cook Co. Corrections Officer Charged in 1997 Rape of 10-Year-Old Girl," *Chicago Sun-Times*, September 22, 2011.

*"If you've got stacks"*   Nicholas D. Kristof, "Is Rape Serious?," *New York Times*, April 30, 2009.

*"It's what we might expect"*   Ibid.

*A law passed in Illinois*   Sexual Assault Evidence Submission Act, Public Act 096-1011 (passed September 1, 2010).

*By February 2011*   Megan Twohey, "State Has Backlog of Rape Evidence," *Chicago Tribune*, February 18, 2011.

*Fingernail scrapings*   In an editorial, the *New York Times* called it "a huge insult to rape victims, who submit to a lengthy and intrusive process to have the DNA evidence harvested from their bodies" (Editorial, "Respect for Rape Victims," *New York Times*, November 13, 2009.) For information about the rape kit, see Diane K. Beebe, "Emergency Management of the Adult Female Rape Victim," American Academy of Experts in Traumatic Stress, www.aaets.org/article130.htm.

*"After undressing in front"*   Kari Lydersen, "Law Came Too Late for Some Rape Victims," *New York Times*, July 9, 2010.

*Her case had been dropped*   Ibid.

*"What they do is continue"*   Graham Rayman, "NYPD Tapes 3: A Detective Comes Forward About Downgraded Sexual Assaults," *Village Voice*, June 8, 2010.

*There were nine allegations*   "Evidence to the Bichard Inquiry Arising from the Soham Murders," March 25, 2004, http://www.womenagainstrape .net/SohamLetter2.htm.

*Two ten-year-old schoolgirls*   "Huntley Guilty of Soham Murders," BBC News, December 17, 2003, http://newsvote.bbc.co.uk/2/hi/uk_news /3312551.stm.

*A year later, the chief*   David Batty, "Cambridgeshire Police Chief Resigns," *Guardian*, June 1, 2005.

*These self-styled "mistakes"*   Ofelia Casillas and Manya A. Brachear, "DCFS Failed to Notify Archdiocese in Priest Abuse Case," *Chicago Tribune*, February 22, 2006. In the article, the Chicago Archdiocese also admitted to making such errors as failing to pursue an aggressive investigation.

*Thus was the healing*   Laurie Goodstein and David Callender, "For Half a Century, Deaf Boys Raised Alarm on Priest's Abuse," *New York Times*, March 27, 2010.

*"Well-intentioned but misguided"*   Pope Benedict XVI, "Pastoral Letter of the Holy Father Pope Benedict XVI to the Catholics of Ireland," March 19, 2010, www.vatican.va/holy_father/benedict_xvi/letters/2010/docu ments/hf_ben-xvi_let_20100319_church-ireland-en.html.

*When the school did not*   Megan Twohey, "School Districts Struggle to Deal with Dating Violence Among Students," *Chicago Tribune*, January 10, 2010.

*"It's like no one cared"*   Cynthia Dizikes and Matthew Walberg, "Parents Outraged That Sexual Assault Suspect Was Still Driving His School Bus," *Chicago Tribune*, August 30, 2010. Initially prosecutors declined to file charges, but they later charged the driver with intimidation after the student said he threatened to kill her for going to the police. After the second assault, prosecutors charged him with rape.

*It found that the schools*   Kristen Lombardi, "A Lack of Consequences for Sexual Assault," Center for Public Integrity, February 24, 2010, www .publicintegrity.org/investigations/campus_assault/articles/entry/1945.

*"Teach students rather than"*   Ibid.

*In 2009, as film director*   Matthew Saltmarsh, "Swiss Court Approves Bail for Polanski," *New York Times*, November 25, 2009. The author heard the CNN news announcer use this phrase in a news roundup on October 20, 2009.

*What happened was not*   Katha Pollitt, "What's with These Friends of a Rapist?," *Chicago Tribune*, October 2, 2009.

*A more accurate description*   Janet Bavelas and Linda Coates, "Is It Sex or Assault? Erotic Versus Violent Language in Sexual Assault Trial Judgments," *Journal of Social Distress and the Homeless* 10 (2001): 39.

*"That drunken night"*   Stephanie Gilmore, "Disappearing the Word 'Rape,' " *On the Issues*, February 9, 2011, www.ontheissuesmagazine.com/cafe2 /article/138.

*"He saw Mr. Sandusky"*   Arthur S. Brisbane, "Confusing Sex and Rape," *New York Times*, November 19, 2011.

*"Self-righteousness needed"*   Adrian Nicole Leblanc, "Hard Laughs," *New York Times*, December 28, 2008.

*"If females are making"*   Poppy Gallico, "Why Rape Jokes Aren't Funny," *Poppy Gallico*, August 3, 2009, http://poppygallico.com/me/why-rape-jokes -arent-funny (site discontinued).

*In October 2010*   Stephanie Reitz, "Yale Fraternity Under Fire for Alleged Misogyny," *Boston Globe*, October 19, 2010.

*"The provocateurs knew"*   "New's View: The Right Kind of Feminism," *Yale Daily News*, October 18, 2010.

*The complaint recited*   Lisa W. Foderaro, "At Yale, Sharper Look at Treatment of Women," *New York Times*, April 8, 2011.

*Some students dismissed*   Ibid.

*Seven months after*   Jason Kessler, "Yale Suspends Fraternity for Raunchy Chants," CNN, May 18, 2011, http://articles.cnn.com/2011-05-18/us /connecticut.yale.frat_1_dke-yale-students-fraternity-activities?_s=PM:US.

*A similar result occurred*   Mike Donoghue, Joel Baird, and Adam Silverman, "UVM Suspends Fraternity After Survey Asks Members Who They Want to Rape," *Burlington Free Press*, December 13, 2011.

*Initially, Facebook dismissed*   Vanessa, "Facebook Removes Rape 'Joke Pages,' " *Feministing*, November 7, 2011, http://feministing.com/2011/11/07 /facebook-removes-rape-joke-pages.

*Some months ago*　Patrizia Romito, *Deafening Silence: Hidden Violence Against Women and Children* (Bristol, UK: Polity Press, 2008), 165.

*For this reason*　Jessica Valenti, "Georgia Rape Case Dismissed Because of Victim's Sexual History?," *Feministing*, May 15, 2008, http://feministing .com/archives/009206.html.

*Day's attorney claimed*　Walter Putnam, "Woman Appeals Sex Assault Case to State Supreme Court," *Atlanta Journal-Constitution*, April 15, 2008, www .ajc.com/metro/content/metro/stories/2008/04/15/assault_0415.html.

*"A sexual assault kit"*　Aya Mueller, "GW Sued for Negligence, Malpractice," *GW Hatchet*, October 4, 2007, http://www.gwhatchet.com/2007/10/04 /gw-sued-for-negligence-malpractice/.

*"All those women"*　Rachel Dissell, "Cleveland Woman Says She Fought, Fled Anthony Sowell in 2008 Attack but Authorities Didn't Believe Her," *Cleveland Plain Dealer*, November 16, 2009, http://blog.cleveland.com /metro/2009/11/Cleveland_woman_says_police_fa.html.

*Eventually the judge*　Richard Connelly, "On Top? It's Not Rape, and Full-Service Journalism," *Houston Press*, August 20, 2009, http://www .houstonpress.com/2009-08-20/news/on-top-it-s-not-rape-and-full -service-journalism/.

*"It felt like the blame"*　Rachel Dissell, "Cuyahoga Juvenile Court Judge Ali-son Floyd Orders Sex Assault Victims to Take Polygraph Tests," *Cleveland Plain Dealer*, March 19, 2010.

*"By making these young"*　Jessica Valenti, "Ohio Judge Forces Rape Victims to Take Polygraph Tests," *Feministing*, March 22, 2010, www.feministing.com /archives/020445.html.

*These factors caused Congress*　Archambault and Lonsway, *VAWA 2005 Restricts the Use of Polygraphs*.

*They had said that*　James Joyner, "Oregon Teen Sentenced for False Rape Charge," *Outside the Beltway*, December 4, 2005, www.outsidethebeltway .com/archives/oregon_teen_sentenced_for_false_rape_charge.

*The memory card*　Ellen Tumposky, "Pictures in Accused Rapist's Camera Provide Chilling Evidence Against Him," ABC News, April 15, 2011, http://abcnews.go.com/US/pictures-accused-rapists-camera-clear -woman-false-rape/story?id=13382917#.UIA42meltiw.

*Before her trial*  Shannon P. Duffy, "3rd Circuit Revives Rape Victim's Civil Rights Case," Law.com, August 4, 2010, www.law.com/jsp/article .jsp?id=12024642230329rd_Circuit_Revives_Rape_Victims_Civil _Rights_Case.

*He filed the criminal complaint*  These facts are taken from Sara R. Reedy v. Frank S. Evanson, United States Court of Appeals for the Third Circuit, opinion August 2, 2010, 615 F. 3d 197. The young woman brought a civil case for damages against the police officer. Although it was dismissed by the district court, the federal Court of Appeals for the Third Circuit reinstated her action, ruling that "no reasonably competent officer could have concluded at the time of Reedy's arrest that there was probable cause for the arrest," remanding the case for trial on the merits.

*"Substantial amount of time"*  Helen Pidd, "Rape Case Woman to Appeal Against Jailing for Withdrawing Allegations," *Guardian*, November 8, 2010.

*"Duty of compassion"*  Helen Pidd, "Woman Jailed for Falsely Retracting Rape Claim Is Freed," *Guardian*, November 23, 2010.

*Later, however, the Court*  Amelia Hill, "Woman Fails to Quash Conviction for Falsely Retracting Rape Claim," *Guardian*, March 13, 2012.

*Meanwhile, her complaint against*  Don Terry, "Eavesdropping Laws Mean That Turning On an Audio Recorder Could Send You to Prison," *New York Times*, January 22, 2011.

*Then, in August 2011, a jury*  Jason Meisner and Ryan Haggerty, "Woman Who Recorded Cops Acquitted of Felony Eavesdropping Charges," *Chicago Tribune*, August 25, 2011. In May 2012, the Seventh Circuit Court of Appeals ruled the Illinois eavesdropping law unconstitutional (Ryan Haggerty, "Ban on Eavesdropping Enforcement," *Chicago Tribune*, May 9, 2012).

*Immediately after her rape report*  Valerie Kalfrin, "Rape Victim's Arrest Prompts New Policy," *Tampa Tribune*, January 31, 2007. After the incident, police chief Stephen Hogue revised the department policy that led to the woman's arrest.

*Eventually she was able*  Brian Ross, Maddy Sauer and Justin Rood, "Victim: Gang-Rape Cover-up by U.S., Halliburton/KBR," ABC News, December 10, 2007, http://abcnews.go.com/Blotter/story?id=3977702 &Page=1.

*"Based upon my findings"*  Jessica Valenti, "University of Portland Changes Rape Reporting Policy," *Feministing*, March 4, 2009, www.feministing.com/archives/014027.html.

*The college could have invoked*  Ibid.

*After a fifteen-year-old girl*  Bryan Polcyn, "Nearly a Thousand Rape Kits Sit Untested by Crime Labs," FOX6 News, http://fox6now.com/news/investigators/witi-100725-rape-kits,0,410663.story.

*At his direction*  "Judge Locked Up Rape Case Witness," BBC News, February 2, 2009, http://news.bbc.co.uk/2/hi/uk_news/scotland/tayside_and_central/7876649.stm.

*Later Robertson filed*  "Rape Witness in Cell Ordeal Anger," BBC News, February 23, 2009, http://news.bbc.co.uk/2/hi/uk_news_scotland_tayside_and_central_7906389.stm.

*Tragically, Robertson, who suffered*  Lorraine Davidson, "Sheriff Who Jailed 'Rape Victim' to Talk on Handling Witnesses: Fellow Judges Condemn Invitation to Seminar," *Times* (London), July 11, 2009.

*"Stop your lying"*  C. W. Nevius, "Alleged Rape Victim's Rescuers Threatened: Soccer Players Are Called Names After Intervening at Party," *San Francisco Chronicle*, June 3, 2007, http://articles.sfgate.com/2007-06-03/news/17250740_1_sexual-assault-team-soccer-players-girl.

*They accused Kristof*  Nicholas D. Kristof, "If This Isn't Slavery, What Is?," *New York Times*, January 4, 2009.

*He charged the woman*  Luke Harding, "Row over Naming of Rape Author," *Observer*, October 5, 2003.

*This sad episode*  Hans Magnus Enzensberger, e-mail message to author, December 10, 2005: "In the background of all this, is, I think, a lingering tendency to blame the rape victim—an attitude which is rooted in a long and disgraceful tradition."

## Punishing Megan

*The student went*  These articles will not be cited so as to preserve Megan's confidentiality.

*The football player was allowed*   Cormac Eklof, "Trouble Brewing at Notre Dame Several Weeks After Elizabeth Seeberg Tragedy," *From the Bleachers*, November 22, 2010.

*She never heard back*   Stacy St. Clair and Todd Lighty, "Family Criticizes Notre Dame in 2nd Sex Attack Case," *Chicago Tribune*, February 17, 2011.

*Defense attorneys explain*   Ibid.

*It reportedly addressed problems*   Kristen Lombardi, "Education Department Touts Settlement as 'Model' for Campus Sex Assault Policies," Center for Public Integrity, December 8, 2010, www.publicintegrity.org /articles/entry/2747.

*Of these, only twelve*   Todd Lighty, Stacy St. Clair, and Jodi S. Cohen, "Arrests, Convictions Rare in College Cases," *Chicago Tribune*, June 17, 2011.

*There is often a relationship*   Ibid.

*The student asserted*   Ryan Haggerty and Stacy St. Clair, "Marquette Failed on Attack Reports," *Chicago Tribune*, June 22, 2011.

*"Clear and convincing"*   Lauren Sieben, "Education Dept. Issues New Guidance for Sexual-Assault Investigations," *Chronicle of Higher Education*, April 4, 2011, http://www2.ed.gov/about/offices/list/ocr/letters /colleague-201104.html.

*The Department of Education said that*   Russlynn Ali, "Dear Colleague Letter," Department of Education, April 4, 2011, http://www2.ed.gov/about /offices/list/ocr/letters/colleague-201104.html.

*Biden has just announced*   Heather Mac Donald, "Don't Buy into Tale of Campus-Rape Crisis," *Chicago Sun-Times*, April 6, 2011.

*Some of the usual commentators*   Cathy Young, "The Politics of Campus Sexual Assault," *Real Clear Politics*, November 6, 2011, www.realclear politics.com/articles/2011/11/06/the_politics_of_campus_sexual _assault_111968.html; Sandy Hingston, "The New Rules of College Sex," *Philadelphia Magazine*, September 2011, www.phillymag.com/articles /the_new_rules_of_college_sex.

*"Where are the professors"*   Peter Berkowitz, "College Rape Accusations and the Presumption of Male Guilt," *Wall Street Journal*, August 20, 2011.

*"I was inundated"*   Roger Canaff, personal communication with the author, December 2, 2010.

*She later suffocated*    Jessica Valenti, "Colleges' Rape Secret," *Daily*, March 19, 2011, http://www.thedaily.com/page/2011/03/19/031911-opinions -column-campus-rape-valenti-1-2/.

## Chapter 9: Freeing Strauss-Kahn

*On August 22, 2011*    The People of the State of New York Against Dominique Strauss-Kahn, Recommendation for Dismissal, Indictment No. 02526/2011, August 22, 2011, www.talkleft.com/legal/dskmotiontodis miss.pdf.

*"Was vivid and compelling"*    Christopher Dickey and John Solomon, "The Maid's Tale," *Newsweek*, July 25, 2011.

*"Of a seemingly disposable"*    Roger Canaff, personal communication with the author, August 25, 2011.

*"The notion that Diallo"*    Stuart Taylor Jr., "Drop the DSK Charges," *Atlantic*, August 8, 2011, www.theatlantic.com/national/archive/2011/08/drop -the-dsk-charges/243262.

*Similar confusion might*    Steven Erlanger and Maia de la Baume, "Strauss-Kahn Concedes 'Error' in Sexual Encounter with Maid," *New York Times*, September 18, 2011.

*Meanwhile, French authorities*    "Strauss-Kahn Sex Assault Investigation Dropped," France 24, October 13, 2011, www.france24.com/en/2011 11013-french-prosecution-sex-assault-inquiry-banon-rape-attempt -france-justice. In May 2012, Dominique Strauss-Kahn filed a countersuit, claiming $1 million from the Sofitel housekeeper ("Dominique Strauss-Kahn Files $1M Countersuit Against New York Maid," *Guardian*, May 15, 2012).

*The piece was obviously*    Edward Jay Epstein, "What Really Happened to Strauss-Kahn?," *New York Review of Books*, December 22, 2011.

*Still, it led to a new*    See, for example, Paul Harris, "New Questions Raised over Dominique-Strauss Kahn Case," *Guardian*, November 26, 2011.

*Indeed, she says she was*    Christopher Dickey, "Why Dominique Strauss-Kahn Needs to Tell his Side of the Story," *Daily Beast*, November 28, 2011, www.thedailybeast.com/articles/2011/11/28/why-dominique-strauss -kahn-needs-to-tell-his-side-of-the-story.html.

*The fact that in 2012 a French*   Doreen Carvajal and Maia de la Baume, "Strauss-Kahn Faces Allegations of Sexually Assaulting Woman at a Hotel in Washington," *New York Times*, May 5, 2012.

*"Jerry Sandusky, Julian Assange"*   Celeste Hamilton, author interview, September 13, 2011.

### Believing Riley

*"[These women] didn't want"*   Vivian King, author interview, April 1, 2009. Vivian King is a pseudonym to preserve Riley's confidentiality. All quotes from Vivian King come verbatim from this interview.

*Tend to be serial offenders*   David Lisak, "Understanding the Predatory Nature of Sexual Violence" (paper, University of Massachusetts Boston, undated), http://www.middlebury.edu/media/view/240951/original/Predatory Nature.pdf.

*"We wanted to be there"*   Richard, author interview, November 20, 2008.

### Chapter 10: A World Without Rape Denial

*In another case*   Chloe Angyal, "Sex and Power, from North Carolina to Congo," *Huffington Post*, March 11, 2010, www.huffingtonpost.com /chloe-angyal/sex-and-power-from north_b_495296.html.

*When we forget that rape*   Ibid.

*Importantly, asserted Canaff*   These observations are taken from Roger Canaff's talk at DePaul University College of Law, February 8, 2012.

*Some critics believe that*   Kristen Lombardi, "A Lack of Consequences for Sexual Assault," Center for Public Integrity, February 24, 2010, www .publicintegrity.org/investigations/campus_assault/articles/entry/1945.

*Properly trained and staffed*   Jaclyn Friedman, "To Combat Rape on Campus, Schools Should Stop Keeping It Quiet," *Washington Post*, March 14, 2010.

*In 2010, a group of college*   Alyssa Colby, Caitlin Libby, and Ariel Perry, "Guest Post: How Does Your Private College Respond to Rape and Sexual Assault?," *Feministing*, May 12, 2010, www.feministing.com/archives /021177.html.

*But, as evidenced in Tracy's*   Jordan, *The Word of a Woman*, 247. Jordan writes that changing these prejudicial beliefs in practice is near to impossible because centuries of negative attitudes have resulted in the "crime of rape being one of the most concealed, minimized and misunderstood offences that we have on the statute books."

*Some experts believe*   Stephanie O'Keeffe, Jennifer M. Brown, and Evanthia Lyons, "Seeking Proof or Truth: Naturalistic Decision-Making by Police Officers When Considering Rape Allegations," in *Rape: Challenging Contemporary Thinking*, ed. Miranda A. H. Horvath and Jennifer Brown (Portland, OR: Willan Publishing, 2009), 252.

*In addition, only twenty-three*   Joanne Archambault, "A Little Bit of DNA History," *Sexual Assault Report* 14, no. 3 (2011): 35.

*"Instead, his abuse of the justice"*   Kathleen Parker, "Picking Up After Duke Debacle," *Orlando Sentinel*, June 20, 2007.

*"That the jury won't"*   Kaethe Morris Hoffer, interview with the author, April 16, 2010.

*Plaintiffs hope that*   Barbara Blaine, comments made at a public forum at DePaul College of Law, April 14, 2011.

*In October 2011*   Mitchell Landsberg, "Charge Against Catholic Bishop Unprecedented in Sex Abuse Scandal," *Los Angeles Times*, October 14, 2011.

*In September 2012*   John Eligon and Laurie Goodstein, "Kansas City Bishop Convicted of Shielding Pedophile Priest," *New York Times*, September 6, 2012.

*Both officials were indicted*   Eugene Robinson, "In Penn State's Scandal, Where Was the Leadership," *Washington Post*, November 7, 2011.

*A year later*   Steve Eder, "Former Penn State President Is Charged in Sandusky Case," *New York Times*, November 1, 2012, http://www.nytimes .com/2012/11/02/sports/ncaafootball/graham-b-spanier-former-penn -state-president-charged-in-sandusky-case.html?pagewanted=all&_r=0.

*Logan was herself*   Rebecca Traister, "Ladies, We Have a Problem: Sluts, Nuts, and the Clumsiness of Reappropriation," *New York Times Magazine*, July 24, 2011.

*Calls to a rape-crisis center*   Renae Franiuk, "The Impact of Rape Myths in Print Journalism," *Sexual Assault Report* 12, no. 2 (2009): 8.

*"In journalism, three"* Kathleen Parker, "Herman Cain Can't Park His 'Woman' Problem," *Seattle Times*, November 8, 2011.

*"Should think twice"* Jim Rutenberg, "Cain's Lawyer on Accusing: 'Think Twice,'" *New York Times*, November 9, 2011.

*Rush Limbaugh provided* Libby Copeland, "Cain's Accuser Must Be a Money-Grubbing Slut," *Slate*, November 7, 2011, www.slate.com/blogs/xx_factor/2011/11/07/rush-limbaugh_implies_sharon_bialek_is_well_a_hooker.html; Irin Carmon, "Right-Wing Smears of Herman Cain Accusers Karen Kraushaar and Sharon Bialek Are Disgusting and Offensive," *New York Daily News*, November 11, 2011.

*For example, the young* Associated Press, "Man Sentenced to 9 Months for Threatening Bryant Accuser, Prosecutor," June 27, 2005.

*If a drunken woman* Carol Sarler, "The Hangover from Hell," *Spectator*, February 5, 2010.

*"Stupid but not criminal"* Ibid.

*I like you just* Chloe, "Pop Star Brian McFadden Pens New Ode to Date Rape," *Feministing*, February 28, 2011, http://feministing.com/2011/02/28/pop-star-brian-mcfadden-pens-new-ode-to-date-rape/.

*It was a crime at its purest* Turow, *Limitations*, 37.

*This practice would preserve* Sabrina Garcia and Margaret Henderson, "Options for Reporting Sexual Violence: Developments over the Past Decade," *FBI Law Enforcement Bulletin*, May 2010.

*"Attributing responsibility to the victim"* Patrizia Romito, *Deafening Silence: Hidden Violence Against Women and Children* (Bristol, UK: Polity Press, 2008), 57.

*"The ordinary response"* Judith Lewis Herman, *Trauma and Recovery* (New York: BasicBooks, 1997), 1.

*Ultimately all, including Coach* Associated Press, "Penn State Scandal Timeline: Key Dates in the Jerry Sandusky Sex Abuse Case," *Huffington Post*, January 11, 2012, www.huffingtonpost.com/2011/11/09/penn-state-scandal-timeline-jerry-sandusky_n1084204.html.

*"The predator to watch out for"* Frank Bruni, "The Molester Next Door," *New York Times*, November 7, 2011.

*"All I maintain"*   Albert Camus, *Camus at Combat: Writing 1944–1947* (Princeton: Princeton University Press 2006), 259.

*Three times, officials*   "Islamists Stone Somali Woman to Death for Adultery," Reuters, October 28, 2008, http://www.reuters.com/article/2008/10/28 /us-somalia-stoning-idUSTRE49R47P20081028?sp=true.

*Did not the air force's*   See introduction. And how apt is her name, Cassandra, the figure from Greek mythology who spurned Apollo's advances but was doomed by him not be believed.

# Resources

## Support for Rape Victims

*The National Sexual Assault Hotline*

1-800-656-HOPE (4673)

www.rainn.org

The hotline links rape victims with nearby counseling and advocacy services and provides telephone counseling. If a victim does not wish to call, she or he can visit the website to communicate with personnel, read information for victims, and access listings of local services.

*The Voices and Faces Project*

www.voicesandfacesproject.org

This national effort provides a forum for rape victims to share their accounts.

## Information About Rape in the United States

Two other websites provide a variety of research reports on rape prevalence and false rape claims, as well as other information.

CounterQuo: www.counterquo.org

National Sexual Violence Resource Center: www.nsvrc.org

# Recommended Reading

## Rape Research Studies

### General Population Studies

Basile, Kathleen C., Jieru Chen, Michele C. Black, and Linda E. Saltzman. "Prevalence and Characteristics of Sexual Violence Victimization Among U.S. Adults, 2001–2003." *Violence and Victims* 22 (2007).

Black, Michele C., Kathleen C. Basile, Matthew J. Breiding, Sharon G. Smith, Mikel L. Walters, Melissa T. Merrick, Jieru Chen, and Mark R. Stevens. *The National Intimate Partner and Sexual Violence Survey (NISVS): 2010 Summary Report.* Atlanta, GA: National Center for Injury Prevention and Control, Centers for Disease Control and Prevention. http://www.cdc.gov/ViolencePrevention/pdf/NISVS_Report2010-a.pdf.

Kilpatrick, Dean G., Christine N. Edmunds, and Anne Seymour. *Rape in America: A Report to the Nation.* Arlington, VA: National Center for Victims of Crime and the Crime Victims Research and Treatment Center, 1992. www.musc.edu/ncvc/resources_prof/rape_in_america.pdf.

Kilpatrick, Dean G., Heidi S. Resnick, Kenneth J. Ruggiero, Lauren M. Conoscenti, Jenna McCauley. *Drug-Facilitated, Incapacitated, and Forcible Rape: A National Study.* Charleston, SC: Medical University of South Carolina, 2007. www.ncjrs.gov/pdffiles1/nij/grants/219181.pdf.

Tjaden, Patricia, and Nancy Thoennes. *Extent, Nature, and Consequences of Rape Victimization: Findings from the National Violence Against Women*

*Survey*. Washington, DC: US Department of Justice, 2006. www.ncjrs .gov/pdffiles1/nij/210346.pdf.

### Campus Studies

Eaton, Danice K., Laura Kann, Steve Kinchen, Shari Shanklin, James Ross, Joseph Hawkins, William A. Harris, Richard Lowry, Tim McManus, David Chyen, Connie Lim, Lisa Whittle, Nancy D. Brener, and Howell Wechsler. "Youth Risk Behavior Surveillance—United States, 2009." *Surveillance Summaries* 59, no. 5 (2010): 6. http://www.cdc.gov/MMWR /preview/mmwrhtml/ss5905a1.htm.

Fisher, Bonnie S., Francis T. Cullen, and Michael G. Turner. *The Sexual Victimization of College Women*. Washington, DC: US Department of Justice, December 2000. http://www.ncjrs.gov/pdffiles1/nij/182369.pdf.

Kilpatrick, Dean G., Heidi S. Resnick, Kenneth J. Ruggiero, Lauren M. Conoscenti, Jenna McCauley. *Drug-Facilitated, Incapacitated, and Forcible Rape: A National Study*. Charleston, SC: Medical University of South Carolina, 2007. www.ncjrs.gov/pdffiles1/nij/grants/219181.pdf.

Krebs, Christopher P., Christine H. Lindquist, Tara D. Warner, Bonnie S. Fisher, and Sandra L. Martin. *The Campus Sexual Assault (CAS) Study*. Research Triangle Park, NC: RTI International, 2007. www.ncjrs.gov/pdf files1/nij/grants/221153.pdf.

### Predatory Rapists

Lisak, David, and Paul M. Miller. "Repeat Rape and Multiple Offending Among Undetected Rapists." *Violence and Victims* 17 (2002): 73–84.

McWorther, Stephanie K., Valerie A. Stander, Lex L. Merrill, Cynthia J. Thomsen, and Joel S. Milner. "Reports of Rape Reperpetration by Newly Enlisted Male Navy Personnel." *Violence and Victims* 24 (2009): 204–18.

## Articles on Rape-Prevalence Research, False Rape Claims, and Criminal-Justice Responses

Fisher, Bonnie S. *Measuring Rape Against Women: The Significance of Survey Questions*. Washington, DC: US Department of Justice, 2004. www.ncjrs .gov/pdffiles1/nij/199705.pdf.

Kilpatrick, Dean, and Jenna McCauley. *Understanding National Rape Statistics*. Harrisburg, PA: VAWnet/National Resource Center on Domestic Violence, 2009. http://new.vawnet/org/Assoc_Files_VAWnet/AR_RapeStatistics.pdf.

Lisak, David, Lori Gardinier, Sarah Cope, and Ashley M. Cote. "False Allegations of Sexual Assault: An Analysis of Ten Years of Reported Cases." *Violence Against Women* 16, no. 12 (2010): 1318–34.

Lombardi, Kristen. "A Lack of Consequences for Sexual Assault." Center for Public Integrity, February 24, 2010. www.publicintegrity.org/investigations/campus_assault/articles/entry/1945.

Lonsway, Kimberly A., and Joanne Archambault. "'The Justice Gap' for Sexual Assault Cases: Future Directions for Research and Reform." *Violence Against Women* 18, no. 2 (2012): 145–68.

Lonsway, Kimberly A., Joanne Archambault, and David Lisak. "False Reports: Moving Beyond the Issue to Successfully Investigate and Prosecute Nonstranger Sexual Assault." *Voice* 3 (2009): 1–11.

National Institute of Justice. *2010 DNA Analysis Backlog Elimination Act of 2000: Report to Congress, January 25, 2011*. Washington, DC: US Department of Justice, 2011. www.nij.gov/topics/forensics/lab-operations/evidence-backlogs/dna-backlog-reduction-report-to-Congress-2010.pdf.

Scalzo, Teresa P. *Prosecuting Alcohol-Facilitated Sexual Assault*. Alexandria, VA: American Prosecutors Research Institute, 2007. http://vawnet.org/category/Documents.php?docid=1160.

## Books

Brownmiller, Susan. *Against Our Will: Men, Women, and Rape*. New York: Ballantine Books, 1993.

Estrich, Susan. *Real Rape*. Cambridge, MA: Harvard University Press, 1988.

Friedman, Jaclyn, and Jessica Valenti. *Yes Means Yes: Visions of Female Sexual Power and a World Without Rape*. Berkeley, CA: Seal Press, 2008.

Gavey, Nicola. *Just Sex? The Cultural Scaffolding of Rape*. New York: Routledge, 2005.

Jordan, Jan. *The Word of a Woman: Police, Rape and Belief*. Basingstoke, UK: Palgrave Macmillan, 2004.

Romito, Patrizia. *Deafening Silence: Hidden Violence Against Women and Children.* Bristol, UK: Polity Press, 2008.

Solomon, John. *DSK: The Scandal That Brought Down Dominique Strauss-Kahn.* New York: St. Martin's Press, 2012.

Valenti, Jessica. *The Purity Myth: How America's Obsession with Virginity Is Hurting Young Women.* Berkeley, CA: Seal Press, 2009.

# Index

16799

364.1532
R217

LINCOLN CHRISTIAN UNIVERSITY

127222

3 4711 00217 8293